Vision's Immanence

Vision's Immanence

Faulkner, Film, and the Popular Imagination

Peter Lurie

11/6/05 Chicago

To Uncle Mark —

To a constant friend and valued colleague: thank you. Fondly, Peter

The Johns Hopkins University Press
Baltimore and London

© 2004 The Johns Hopkins University Press
All rights reserved. Published 2004
Printed in the United States of America on acid-free paper
9 8 7 6 5 4 3 2 1

The Johns Hopkins University Press
2715 North Charles Street
Baltimore, Maryland 21218-4363
www.press.jhu.edu

Library of Congress Cataloging-in-Publication Data
Lurie, Peter, 1965–
Vision's immanence : Faulkner, film, and the popular imagination /
Peter Lurie.
    p.   cm.
Includes bibliographical references and index.
ISBN 0-8018-7929-9 (hardcover : acid-free paper)
1. Faulkner, William, 1897–1962—Film and video adaptations. 2. Popular
culture—United States—History—20th century. 3. Motion pictures—
United States—History and criticism. 4. American fiction—Film and video
adaptations. 5. Film adaptations. I. Title.
PS3511.A86Z884 2004
813'.52—dc22
2003023209
A catalog record for this book is available from the British Library.

In loving memory
of
Nancy Green Lurie

Contents

To anyone in the habit of thinking with his ears, the words "cultural criticism" (Kulturkritik) must have an offensive ring, not merely because, like "automobile," they are pieced together from Latin and Greek. The words recall a flagrant contradiction. The cultural critic is not happy with civilization, to which alone he owes his discontent. He speaks as if he represented either unadulterated nature or a higher historical stage. Yet he is necessarily of the same essence as that to which he feels superior.

— THEODOR ADORNO, "CULTURAL CRITICISM AND SOCIETY"

"So maybe you will enter the literary profession as so many Southern gentlemen and gentlewomen too are doing now and maybe some day you will remember this and write about it. You will be married then I expect and perhaps your wife will want a new gown or a new chair for the house and you can write this and submit it to the magazines."

— ROSA COLDFIELD IN *ABSALOM, ABSALOM!*

My task which I am trying to achieve is, by the power of the written word, to make you hear, to make you feel—it is, before all, to make you see!

— JOSEPH CONRAD, "PREFACE" TO *THE NIGGER OF THE "NARCISSUS"*

The visual is *essentially* pornographic.

— FREDERIC JAMESON, *SIGNATURES OF THE VISIBLE*

Acknowledgments

If Acknowledgments often possess a wistful tone, it is because with them an author looks back on a period of one's life while thanking those people whose help was essential during it. In this case that period was long and my efforts over it were sustained alike by family, teachers, students, and friends. To express my appreciation to them, and to note their contributions to this project in its various stages, it is also necessary then to describe beginnings as well as endings.

This work began as a dissertation under the direction of John Matthews, whose contribution and support extended far beyond the role of thesis advisor. His influence is evident on several levels of this book as well as in areas outside of Yoknapatawpha and academe. For that and for much more I owe him a measure of gratitude I can only imagine repaying by offering such support to students of my own—but which I have trouble envisioning, given the standards for excellence he has shown me. His work is a testimony to both his enduring fascination with Faulkner and his support of others' efforts to read Faulkner anew.

My parents, Jim and Nancy Lurie, contributed a great deal both directly and indirectly along the way of this project. To them both I wish to express my utmost appreciation. Of my father I should say that, like those of other writers before me, he overcame his misgivings about a son's long indenture to writing (while also not being "of a bum progenitive") and gave unqualified, loving support. My mother, who died while I was in the middle of work on this study and to whom it is dedicated, strongly encouraged appreciation of visual expression and artistic meaning. She remains an inspiration for any act of hard work and imagination and is present in the most genuine moments of such an effort here.

There are several other individuals and parties whose help added significantly to the project. John Paul Riquelme offered insight and advice at key junctures throughout the stages of work; his role in the beginning of its life as a book, as near its end, was instrumental. He too provides a model of scholarly life and activity that I admire deeply and a friendship that I value even more. Leland Monk's input was essential to ensuring that the project treated film as a real entity—and not just as a theoretical model or idea. His affection for and understanding of film's history and no less important aesthetics are animating presences throughout.

A number of friends and colleagues offered support in the form of readings of chapters as well as, and perhaps more importantly, moral support. Among them are Jonathan Mulrooney, Mark Eaton, Laura Johnson, and Rebecca Schoff. Jonathan has glided effortlessly to a position as a professional colleague yet still helps maintain a vital, ingenuous, *non*professional perspective. Mark is a fellow-traveling Americanist and has been an optimistic and encouraging— indeed, hopeful—voice over our long friendship. Laura was a wonderfully sensitive reader of chapters in draft form and a no less gracious and cherished colleague. Rebecca came through famously with a last-minute, highly astute reading of the book's conclusion. Without them I would not be where I am today with this work and otherwise.

My anonymous reader at the Johns Hopkins University Press provided invaluable suggestions for the manuscript's revision. In particular, his advice about the use of Faulkner's original text of *Sanctuary* and the invitation for a more expansive conclusion led to some of the more important readings in the book. Carol Zimmerman, senior production editor at the Press, patiently and clearly answered several important questions toward the project's end. Humanities editor Michael Lonegro helped with his correspondence and attentive ear.

I would like to thank the administration of the Special Collections of Mugar Library at Boston University. Sean Noel and his staff were extremely helpful in my reading the gangster and pulp novels on which my discussion of *Sanctuary* draws. I would also like to thank the reader at *American Literature,* whose promptings toward history helped strengthen my chapter on *Absalom, Absalom!* considerably when it was still in article form. In particular I thank the journal's managing editor Frances Kerr for her focused, good-natured approach to our work, the effects of which are still evident here. The editors of *American Literature* as well as of the journal *Études Faulknériennes* have also kindly granted permission to reprint materials that appeared originally in those journals.

The late stages of preparing the manuscript benefited from the support of the News International Research Fellowship in Film Studies at Keble College, Oxford.

My final and most important thanks are for Kristin. Her understanding and support are indeed remarkable, on which my daily happiness and very well-being, let alone any scholarly endeavors, depend. Just as remarkable though are her deep intelligence and perhaps better knowledge of the importance of everything beyond this book. There are many and more significant meanings of immanence that define our time together. She is the love and the real vision in my life.

Vision's Immanence

Adorno's Modernism and the Historicity of Popular Culture

William Faulkner hated the movies. Or so he was fond of saying and apocryphal accounts of his life have made famous. Joseph Blotner reports that, assigned to a screening of a Wallace Beery wrestling picture when he went to work for MGM, Faulkner cut the session short with the assertion that he knew how it would end.[1] Faulkner also despised the popular magazines, if not the short stories he frequently chose to submit to them. In a letter to the editors at Scribner's from early 1930, he explained why he thought the magazine should publish his story "Red Leaves": "Not because it is a good story; you can find lots of good stories. It's because I need the money" (Selected Letters, 46). In another letter from 1932 to Harrison Smith, Faulkner refers to his work "whoring again with the short stories" during a period when he wanted to work on a novel (Selected Letters, 59).

Despite these protests and their suggestions of a distaste for the products of mass culture, however, Faulkner was keenly aware of the methods, types, and formulae of the popular art of his period. As the following discussion suggests, this awareness is clear throughout Faulkner's fiction of the thirties, in particular in the four novels that are the subject of this study. Comprising the central texts of his mature modernism, these works repeatedly address the circumstances of modern mass cultural production. The conflation here is deliberate. That is, an account of Faulkner's 1930s novels that addresses their engagement with mass culture must also consider that engagement as constitutive of Faulkner's development as a modernist. As a writer deeply aware of his historical moment, Faulkner produced a modernism that reflected not only his high-art ambitions but his concern with the attitudes and tastes of the market for commercial art as well. His modernism developed, that is, in part because of his critical response to popular culture. Faulkner may well have hated film, as he claimed. He certainly cared little for Hollywood (though there seems a clear distinction between his contempt for Hollywood and his regard for silent art film)[2] or for the short story market for magazines. Yet despite this antipathy, Faulkner's novels in the thirties show continued involvement with a popular art that defined its forms and its cultural role differently than did the high modernism with which he is regularly identified.

That Faulkner was aware, like any modern writer, of the popular culture around him is apparent, a fact that was crucial to his approach to his four most important novels of the thirties: *Sanctuary* (1931), *Light in August* (1932), *Absalom, Absalom!* (1936), and *If I Forget Thee, Jerusalem* (1939). His own extensive work producing material for the culture industry includes the several stories he submitted and published throughout the decade, his interest in selling the rights to his novels to the film studios, and above all, his work in Hollywood as a screenwriter.[3] All of these examples point to Faulkner's direct involvement with the consumer art he claimed to disdain. A fifth novel from the period—*Pylon* (1935)—examines journalism as a commercial, popular mode of writing that differed meaningfully from what Faulkner deemed more serious literature. Appearing at first glance as an alternative to popular culture, Faulkner's modernism is, in fact, heavily mediated by his relationship to it, a relationship that included envy, fascination, frustration, contempt—and that produced some of the most powerful as well as the most unsettling effects of his writing.

Although this study means to show the ways in which Faulkner's approach to popular culture contributed to his development as a modernist, the relationship between modernism and mass art has often been conceived rather differently. Earlier models of modernism stubbornly denied the connection between modernist and popular art. Both Andreas Huyssen in *The Great Divide: Modernism, Mass Culture, Postmodernism* and Theodor Adorno in his theoretical work generally argue for modernism's strict autonomy. In particular, both believe that modernism derives its identity (and its aesthetic and cultural value) from its opposition to the simplistic, escapist pleasures and commercial impulse of mass art. Lamenting commercial art's susceptibility to instrumental uses, Adorno writes, "What is involved in this process can best be shown by looking at low-brow art and entertainment, integrated, administered and qualitatively changed as they are today by the culture industry . . . [T]here is at least a parallel here between the masses' relation to art and their relation to real consumer goods" (*Aesthetic Theory*, 24). In contrast to consumer art, modernism's act of turning "inward" through its attention to characters' interior lives and its pleasure in the anti-utilitarian play of language and form prevent its ready consumption. Against the sense of popular art as a consumable product, Adorno posits the fundamentally negative social role of all art, and especially of modernism in its nonmimetic ("non-identical") aspect. For Adorno "every work of art spontaneously aims at being identical with itself. . . . Aesthetic identity [in modernism] is different, however, in one important respect: it is meant to assist the non-identical in its struggle against the repressive identification compulsion that rules the outside world. It is by virtue of its separation from empirical reality that art can become a being of a higher order, fashioning the relation between the whole and its parts in accordance with its own needs" (*Aesthetic Theory*, 6). This "non-identical" struggle, present in all art but epitomized for Adorno by the modernist work, allows modernist art to resist commodification. As Lambert Zuidervaart describes this aspect of Adorno's theory, "Certain modernist works have sufficient experiential depth and technical progressiveness to resist the commodification of consciousness" (*Adorno's Aesthetic Theory*, 42).

Huyssen's position on the difference between modernism and mass art appears similarly unforgiving. Orienting his discussion from Flaubert, Huyssen uses Emma Bovary as the model of a reader who overinvests in her reading of popular romance novels. Flaubert himself, by contrast, through his repudiation of sentimentality and his rigorous devotion to style, became "one of the paradigmatic master voices of an aesthetic based on the repudiation of" commercial art produced for and consumed by the masses (45). Referring to the "core of the modernist aesthetic," Huyssen offers an account of modernist autonomy and separation from reality similar to Adorno's. "The [modernist] work is autonomous and totally separate from the realms of mass culture and everyday life," he writes (53). Elsewhere Huyssen extends what, for him, is a critique of modernism, asserting that as a "reaction formation to mass culture and commodification" (57), modernism denies its relation to "the matrix of modernization which gave birth to it" (55).

Theories of modernism's separation from mass culture have had a long history. Their orienting point is difficult, if not impossible, to trace, but it includes several high-profile statements and critical schools. In hindsight, it appears that certain eras and cultural contexts lent themselves to the view of modernism's "vertical" position above popular art, and this insistence has included both celebratory and more skeptical positions. In their heralding of the detached aesthetic uniqueness and edifying nature of literature, the American New Critics resolutely denied even the possibility that a high-art school like modernism (including, and at points especially, that of a writer like Faulkner) might involve itself with art for the masses. Other critics like Clement Greenberg, in his once-canonical and widely influential essay "Avant-Garde and Kitsch" from 1939, strenuously asserted the categorical and qualitative difference between a challenging, demanding modern form of painting, appreciable only by an educated and refined viewer, and a debased popular version of "poster art," consumed—but not genuinely "felt"—by the public. Explaining these differences by way of a rather broad view of history and urban development, Greenberg writes,

> The peasants who settled in the cities as proletariat and petty bourgeois learned to read and write for the sake of efficiency, but they did not win the leisure and comfort necessary for the enjoyment of the city's traditional culture. Losing, nevertheless, their taste for the folk culture whose background was the countryside, and discovering a new capacity for boredom at the same time, the new urban masses set up a pressure on society to provide them with a kind of culture fit for their own consumption. To fill the demand of the new market, a new commodity was devised: ersatz culture, kitsch, destined for those who, insensible to the values of genuine culture, are hungry nevertheless for the diversion that only culture of some sort can provide. (10)[4]

Writing in the 1940s and 50s, Greenberg sought to encourage greater interest on the part of what he saw as an American taste resistant to the less innately pleasurable or "beautiful" visual aesthetic of painterly modernism.[5]

The move from a laudatory emphasis on modernism's superiority over commercial culture to an awareness, particularly in a neo-Marxist vein, of the elitism of views like Greenberg's was a short one. Yet even in the interests of questioning such supposed elitism, theorists like Fredric Jameson often maintained or repeated the terms of cultural division that Huyssen and others have used. Showing the standard view of modernism's autonomy in his account of postmodernism, Jameson points to "the older (essentially high-modernist) frontier between high culture and so-called mass or consumer culture" (*Postmodernism*, 2). According to Jameson, modernist authoritarianism and elitism gave way to a range of cultural practices that came to be identified as postmodern and which, unlike modernism, had in common as their "fundamental feature" a populist blending of high and low art. Whether referring to it as a "frontier" or a "great divide," earlier theorists of modernism have stressed its separation from the realms, production, and orientation of mass art.

Huyssen's particular view of this separation is useful in returning this discussion to Faulkner. Though Huyssen shares with Adorno and others a view of the distinction between modernism and popular culture, he claims that Adorno and other theorists take a more rigid approach to the question than he. "My point," Huyssen writes, "is that the champions of modernism themselves were the ones who made [its] complex history into a schematic paradigm" (55). To a degree, Huyssen is right in his account of Adorno's uncompromising critique of mass culture. Yet in such moments he also overlooks a key component to the workings of Adorno's aesthetic theory: the dialectical cast to both his perspective and his manner of articulating it. Adorno's thinking about modernism includes definitions which appear to work against one another but which, as is often overlooked, function complementarily. Articulating those definitions and their specific relevance to Faulkner suggests a use of Adorno "against himself," as it were. Doing so, however, remains true to both the content of Adorno's thinking and to his own theoretical method. "Critical theory," writes Guy Debord, "must be articulated in its own language. This is the language of contradiction, which must be dialectical in its form as in its content" (*Society of the Spectacle*, paragraph 204). Approached in this manner, Adorno offers a useful way to describe how Faulkner's writing addresses, in Huyssen's words, "the matrix of modernization which gave birth to it."[6]

Above all, what my study seeks to draw attention to is precisely this aspect of Faulkner's modernism: the way that, through its encounter with mass cultural strategies and forms, his writing shows a deep awareness of the modernization around it. Most specifically, and often most provocatively, this occurs through Faulkner's imaginative use of formal and representational modes of the mass

arts, above all, the cinema. Although direct and indirect references to particular films or texts occur throughout Faulkner's thirties fiction and inform the
discussion that follows, what I find most compelling as a way of reading
Faulkner's modernism is its inflection by what we might call the "film idea,"
the manner of impression and visual activity his novels emulate from the
cinema. Pursuing such an approach, however, informed though it is by recent
scholarship (and in particular by reconsiderations of modernism, postmodernism, and mass culture),[7] requires a caveat. Describing Faulkner's way of
including elements of film or other examples of mass culture, I do not suggest
that these sources appear necessarily positively or as a way to politically "re-
deem" his high-art elitism (as might an earlier cultural studies). The critical
approach suggested by recent debate and that my study pursues is attention to
the fluid, creative, and critical use to which Faulkner puts the cultural phenomena of his era.[8]

Adorno's notion of "identity" is particularly helpful for orienting my consideration of Faulkner. If all art, particularly high art, maintains its "non-
identity" and presumes to have nothing to do with the reality that surrounds it,
it ceases to maintain what Adorno would describe as another necessary component of art: its *retention* of what it is not. "In its difference from the existent,
art of necessity constitutes itself in terms of that which is not a work of art yet is
indispensable from its being. The emphasis on the non-intentionality in art . . .
indicates that art became aware, however dimly, that it interacted with its
opposite. This new self-conception of art gave rise to a critical turn" (*Aesthetic
Theory*, 11). This self-conscious similarity *and* difference is what confers on art
its "negative" relation to society. Without its trace of reality, art would too
nearly approach its ideal of self-identity; it needs to retain the hint of the reality
from which it differs in order to distinguish itself as a separate (negatively
critical) entity. Without an index of the circumstances that surround its production, moreover, art loses another key element for Adorno's conception of
the aesthetic: the marker of its historical specificity. "[I]n all dimensions of its
productive process art has a twofold essence, being both an autonomous entity
and a social fact" (*AT*, 8). Despite its apparent autonomy, art must not deny its
social and historical identity—which in the case of modern works of art includes the "pressure" of conformity, homogenization, and the market. Modern art is valuable in this way in that it reveals its influence by modern technical
and economic forces. "The fact that art has a critical edge in relation to society
is itself socially determined," Adorno writes. "It is a reaction to the numbing

pressure of the body social . . . it is tied up with the progress of the material forces of production outside" (*AT,* 48).

Important to Adorno's theory, and what connects it to my reading of Faulkner, is Adorno's claim that art performs its own version of cultural critique. In "Cultural Criticism and Society," Adorno advocated for the necessity of art to reflect on its position *in* culture, to include an awareness of itself as part of the same society that produced it. Describing the way in which "[a]s a result of the social dynamic, culture becomes cultural criticism" (28), Adorno argues for cultural critics' and artists' engagement with the objects of their criticism. Declaring that "[n]o theory, not even that which is true, is safe from perversion into delusion once it has renounced a spontaneous relation to the object" (33), Adorno makes clear the need for cultural criticism to avoid the appearance of transcendence or a position outside of the culture of which it is a part. Failure to do so results in the false sense of superiority that adduces to cultural criticism (and, often, to Faulkner). For modern art, this process would include acknowledging the "material forces of production." As Adorno puts it, "Rooted in society, these procedures and experiences are critical in orientation. Such truly modern art has to own up to advanced industrial society rather than simply deal with it from an extraneous standpoint. The mode of conduct and the formal idiom of modern art must react spontaneously to objective conditions" (*AT,* 49).

Adorno's notion of the "spontaneous" reaction of modern art to its circumstances contributes significantly to understanding Faulkner. Unlike other forms of culture (including those prominent in the 1930s such as proletarian literature and social realism), modernist artworks reveal Adorno's idea of art "owning up" to its historical reality indirectly—through veiled references, for example, or, more importantly, as manifested in artistic form. "Many authentic works of modern art," Adorno claims, "while anxiously avoiding a thematic focus on industrial reality . . . allow that reality to come back with a vengeance" (*AT,* 49). In Faulkner's thirties fiction, modern industrial reality—in the form of commercial cultural production, generic types and forms, and prefabricated, popular attitudes and tastes—all "come back with a vengeance." Appearing throughout the novels of this period and pointing up many of the most invidious patterns of contemporary thought, the consumer cultural elements of Faulkner's fiction reveal his critical take on the "objective conditions" of his work as a writer. The role of those conditions often manifests itself in parody or allusion, appearing in Faulkner's use of generic types from fiction, such as the gangster, or in stereotypical representations of race and gender drawn from early film. The presence of mass culture in these novels is also often indirect, traceable, as Adorno says of much modern art, on the level of form. Sections of *Sanctuary*, for instance, appear as deliberate, even self-conscious reproductions of the diction and style of hack fiction as well as the accessible realism of popular writing. *Sanctuary*, though, also demonstrates a decided split in its use of language: "low" cultural slang and idioms jostle with classical allusion and stylized, high-modernist lyricism. Above all, representational strategies in *Sanctuary* and Faulkner's other thirties novels draw attention to their resemblance to a modern, technical, and increasingly visual mass culture. Temple Drake in *Sanctuary* and Joe Christmas in *Light in August* both offer themselves up to an objectifying, mass-media "gaze" that informs their sense of identity and that is manifested textually in the narrator, as well as in the actions of other characters. In a manner that recalls the cinema, processes of imaginative "projecting" structure the several acts of narrating Thomas Sutpen's story in *Absalom, Absalom!* Rosa Coldfield's language in her chapter of *Absalom*, as well as Faulkner's descriptions of the Mississippi River in the "Old Man" section of *If I Forget Thee, Jerusalem*, further approximate the experience of viewing a film. All of these examples suggest the way Faulkner's formal strategies respond to, or even reproduce, aspects of the modernization that surrounded them.

More important to Adorno's theory of modernist form and to my reading of Faulkner is the role of tension and discontinuity. For it is this dimension of modern art that, above all, marks its historicity. As the first novel I consider, *Sanctuary* offers several examples of modernist "dissonance." In the case of Popeye and its gangster story, *Sanctuary* makes some of Faulkner's most overt references to mass cultural fare. Moreover, in his own comments on the novel, Faulkner suggested his sense of it as a novel written to pander to market tastes.[9] Yet undermining Faulkner's statements about its being written in order to court scandal and thus promote sales, *Sanctuary*—particularly its original version—includes several examples of the formal innovation and fragmentary narrative structure that had characterized Faulkner's earlier high-modernist works, *The Sound and the Fury* (1929) and *As I Lay Dying* (1930). In its multiple flashback technique, shifts in narrative point of view, and self-consciously lyrical use of language, *Sanctuary* uses several experimental strategies that define Faulkner's modernism. These strategies thus work against what we will see as the novel's more crassly or brutally commercial practices—often in deliberate resistance to them. "A successful work," as Adorno puts it, "is not one which resolves objective contradictions in a spurious harmony, but one which expresses the idea of harmony negatively by embodying the contradictions . . . in its innermost structure" ("Cultural Criticism and Society," 32). Faulkner's use of modernist *and* commercial devices combine in *Sanctuary* and elsewhere to "negatively embody" their society's contradictions. This combination also contributes to some of the novels' more uncanny effects—an odd, tense suspension in which readers "watch" the various representational strategies contend. Like *Sanctuary, If I Forget Thee, Jerusalem* offers variant literary styles, an opposition that produces an ambivalent "atmosphere" in both novels and a means by which these books allow their materials to reflect critically on one another. In this respect they exemplify a quality Adorno ascribes to modernist works: "The tension in art . . . has meaning only in relation to the tension outside" (*AT,* 8).

In this light and as the orienting point of my discussion, the opening of *Sanctuary* is instructive. For there we see Faulkner's effort to allegorize the two main strands of thirties cultural production—modernism and mass art—as figured in the characters Horace Benbow and Popeye, as well as his placing them in a position of mutual regard. In addition to examining popular cultural materials, an important dimension of *Sanctuary's* cultural criticism is that with this novel Faulkner also shows a critical awareness of his own modernism. In Horace, a figure for the academic modernist, certain tendencies such as linguistic superfluity or an aversion to the physical, sensory pleasures of commodities come under scrutiny. The result is a novel that exhibits an oddly divided or self-regarding habit, figured in the book's opening with Popeye and Horace confronting one another at the spring.

This activity of looking is central to each of the novels I consider, and its pervasive, culturally critical role in Faulkner's thirties writing is expressed by my study's title. Vision plays a particularly important role throughout the thirties novels, both as it appears in characters' acts of looking and as it is reproduced or simulated in the reader's encounter with the texts. Vision's "immanence" throughout the period thus refers to the way I see Faulkner manifest his critical stance vis-à-vis popular culture while at the same time maintaining an engaged relationship with it as an object of inquiry. The voyeuristic pleasure Temple Drake furnishes the male characters in *Sanctuary* is one clear and well-known manifestation of this focus on sight. So too, however, are several other instances of the look in *Sanctuary* and elsewhere. Horace demonstrates his own visual and onanistic preoccupation with his stepdaughter's image in her photograph, as well as with Temple in their interview. Through Faulkner's descriptions of Temple, readers are also encouraged to participate in an imaginative version of looking at her—an activity that through the novel's workings becomes itself subject to critique. Surveillance and the gaze thoroughly condition both characters' and readers' experience of Joe Christmas in *Light in August,* evident in textual operations that track Joe from his first appearance in the novel at the mill. As a child, Joe is subjected to the carceral,[10] institutional gaze of the orphanage and the lunatic scrutiny of Doc Hines; late in the novel, Percy Grimm acts as the apparatus and "eye" of the State. After Joanna Burden's murder, the reader also participates in the activity of surveilling and looking for Joe through the "policing" action of its crime and mystery plot.[11]

Looking is important in other novels as well. Though I do not include it in my study for reasons I describe below, the main action of *Pylon* centers around the activity of watching airplane races and Faulkner's elaborate accounts of characters' like the reporter's and Jiggs's jaundiced visual perceptions. Quentin Compson's encounter with the Sutpen narrative in *Absalom, Absalom!* is described throughout the novel with references to his act of "watching" or "seeming to see" its events. In another of the novel's optical effects, the language in Rosa Coldfield's chapter approximates an experience of reading that is visual. At the end of the decade, the "Wild Palms" section of *If I Forget Thee, Jerusalem* depicts Harry Wilbourne imaginatively "screening" events from his own life like a viewer of a melodrama. In the same novel, the Tall Convict performs a sustained act of looking at the Mississippi River and its mirror-like surface that contributes both to a formation of identity suggestive of Lacan and to the novel's self-reflexive, culturally critical operations.

Beyond detailing the range of visual effects in these novels, it is important to assess the particular role of this visual impulse in Faulkner's thirties fiction and to ask what accounts for it. One answer lies in the increasing role in the first decades of the twentieth century of that supremely visual and reifying form: film. The period of the late 1920s to the late 1930s saw not only the increased consolidation of film production in the hands of studio heads and the development in the industry of an elaborately structured power hierarchy (which placed writers, like Faulkner, at its bottom), but above all and simply, the massive proliferation of movies.[12] Accompanying the broad distribution of a centrally produced, standardized product as well was film's capacity to shape the consciousness of millions of spectators, an aspect of film that for many, including Faulkner, was both a fascination and a concern.[13]

Initially, Faulkner's interest in film had been based on optimism. As indicated earlier, his fiction includes at least a handful of references to what Faulkner considered the artistic value of the medium, especially its silent-era practitioners.[14] Like most Americans in the early decades of the century, Faulkner went to the movies frequently when he was growing up in Mississippi.[15] His long affair with Meta Carpenter, a script supervisor whom he met at the Twentieth Century Fox lot and who for Faulkner embodied Hollywood's potential romance, suggests a fascination with the film industry that played itself out in his life. Faulkner also enjoyed a productive, genuine friendship with the director Howard Hawks, who helped Faulkner with several screenplays and, perhaps more importantly, with his troubled relationship with the studio heads. Later, Faulkner demonstrated what seemed real interest in cinema in his work in Oxford, Mississippi, on the film version of *Intruder in the Dust* (1948).[16]

What drove Faulkner's sharper and more critical interest in movies, however, and what provides the basis for this discussion, was the enormous and at times destructive power of the new medium. This aspect of film had been apparent in its earliest history, exemplified by a director like D. W. Griffith, whose widely influential *Birth of a Nation* (1915) both relied on and disseminated a racist ideology. Based on a notorious and best-selling novel that Faulkner encountered at an early point in his life, *Birth* was a film Faulkner almost certainly saw.[17] Like other movies, *Birth* based its appeal on its capacity to present viewers with a compelling visual simulacrum—in this case, a convincing image of history and the Civil War. Upon its opening in 1915 and for years thereafter (due in part to its re-release in 1930), *Birth* became the most widely viewed film in history. As the first "blockbuster" movie, it accelerated a pattern for film viewing and consumption that had begun in the teens but that only increased in the years that followed, particularly during the rise of the classical Hollywood cinema of the thirties.[18] The thirties also saw Faulkner spend several years participating in the film industry as a screenwriter, an experience that contributed to his understanding of its workings and the nature of its product. During this period, then, Faulkner saw the increased influence of film as a cultural force and as an economically vital, self-contained system, as well as—importantly—his own frustrated effort to find a broad audience for his books.[19] One result was Faulkner's impulse to work out a critical response to film through his novels written in this period. In their repeated visual tropings and negative regard for the movies, that is, Faulkner's novels were in dialogue with a competing medium.

Although none of his novels are actually set in Hollywood or depict the activity of film viewing, two of Faulkner's short stories epitomize his highly critical take on the movie industry. "Golden Land," about a Los Angeles real estate developer and his would-be starlet daughter, and "Dry September," which includes a scene of an aging spinster becoming hysterical at the movies, both show the pernicious effects of Hollywood. The earlier of the two, "Dry September" (which appeared in *Scribner's* in 1931), is overt in its account of the danger produced by film's escapism. References in the story to the cinema house—its polished, rarefied atmosphere used to sell the "silver dream" of romance (*Collected Stories*, 181)—as well as to film's wholly superficial images of beauty and youth strongly link the experience of film viewing to Minnie Cooper's accusations of rape. Her fatal story about Will Mayes appears prompted by her desperate (and financial) need to re-occupy a position as an object of male desire like the images she sees on the movie screen. As a result, Mayes becomes a ready scapegoat for the racist and violent need of the men in the story to protect their idea of white female purity. Faulkner's metonymy of the town square with the cinema seems complete when, on Minnie's way to the picture show and after Mayes's lynching, her crossing the square affords the opportunity for Minnie's visual consumption by the Jefferson men. "She walked slower and slower . . . passing the hotel and the coatless drummers in chairs along the curb looking at her: 'That's the one: see? The one in pink in the middle.' 'Is that her? What did they do with the nigger? Did they—?' 'Sure. He's all right.' 'All right, is he?' 'Sure. He went on a little trip.' Then the drug store, where even the young men lounging in the doorway tipped their hats and followed with their eyes the motion of her hips and legs when she passed" (*CS*, 180). Once inside the movie house, Minnie's recognition of the picture's false promise arrives, ironically and tragically, too late, as she becomes unhinged by hysterical laughter during the movie and has to be ushered from the theater by her uncomprehending friends.

Written later than "Dry September" and after Faulkner's initial forays in Hollywood, "Golden Land" (1935) treats the experience and effects of film viewing less directly. Yet it reveals Faulkner's dark attitude toward the industry even more violently than had the earlier story. Its protagonist, Ira Ewing, does not produce movies or even, we expect, ever go to see them. He does, however, sell real estate in Hollywood, and his daughter is an aspiring actress who changes her name and, the story implies, takes part in a sex orgy to help her film career. Faulkner's story communicates his distaste with the Hollywood scene in these details of its plot, but perhaps more clearly in its descriptive language. One passage in particular reveals its narrator's wholly negative, even apocalyptic vision for film. Driving through the Beverly Hills streets, Ewing passes a scene that reflects Faulkner's mind-set:

> [H]ad he looked, he could have seen the city in the bright soft vague hazy sunlight, random, scattered about the arid earth like so many gay scraps of paper blown without order, with its curious air of being rootless—of houses bright beautiful and gay, without basements or foundations, lightly attached to a few inches of light penetrable earth, lighter even than dust . . . which one good hard rain would wash forever from the sight and memory of man as a firehose flushes down a gutter—that city of almost incalculable wealth whose queerly appropriate fate it is to be erected on a few spools of substance whose value is computed in billions and which may be completely destroyed in that second's instant of a careless match between the moment of striking and the moment when the striker might have sprung and stamped it out. (*CS*, 719)

In a voice that is hard not to hear as Faulkner's own, twice in this paragraph the narrator shows a violent impulse toward destroying the California scene before him. Combined with other references in Faulkner's fiction to the "celluloid germs" and contagion of film images (*Pylon*, 984) or, in his correspondence, to his antagonism for the movie industry, this passage suggests a measure of rage on Faulkner's part toward Hollywood. The urge for a Biblical "good hard rain" to "wash forever from the sight and memory of man" the rootless city is only slightly removed from the more human fantasy of setting a match to Hollywood's figurative but also real economic foundation in film stock.[20]

Incendiary moments occur elsewhere in Faulkner, and one of them at least may add to our understanding of this scene. Darl Bundren's burning of Tull's barn in *As I Lay Dying* seems an act of protest—obviously not of Hollywood, but over his family's treatment of his mother. This passage from "Golden Land," however, suggests Ab Snopes and his act of violent protest in "Barn Burning" (1939). Written after Faulkner went to Hollywood, the story clearly expresses an understanding of exploited labor—an idea Faulkner held about his work for the studios.[21] Ab's statement when he arrives at Major de Spain's, for instance, might well describe Faulkner's feelings toward the various studio heads every time he returned to Hollywood: "I reckon I'll have a word with the man that aims to begin to-morrow owning me body and soul for the next eight months" (*CS*, 9). Ab's feelings of frustration at his financial circumstances suggest a connection to Faulkner's own frustration at his work in Hollywood as well as to what appears in "Golden Land" as a similarly violent, if only imaginary, response to them.

As these examples suggest, Faulkner was highly skeptical of film and its commercial imperative. Yet film was only one of a range of cultural phenomena that Faulkner observed critically in the thirties and that depended on visuality for its effects. Another reason for Faulkner's visual tendencies in the decade may have to do with the fact that social practices as well as cultural forms in the modern period were increasingly shaped by visual experience. Several cultural historians and theorists of modernity have pointed to the particular role of vision as a defining feature of modern social, economic, and aesthetic life, a development occasioned by the increased role of forms like film and photography as well as by whole systems of social relations and organizing. Guy Debord's *The Society of the Spectacle* is especially provocative in this light, as he defines the spectacle as both a material phenomenon (as in commodities and visual forms of culture) and an agent for social ordering: "The spectacle is not a collection of images but a social relation among people mediated by images . . . In all its specific forms, as information or propaganda, advertisement or direct consumption of entertainments, the spectacle is the present *model* of socially dominant life" (paragraphs 4, 6). Consistently elliptical, Debord suggests the ways that vision and socially organized acts of looking serve to unify parts of society (the agents of looking) and exclude others. As he writes, "The spectacle presents itself simultaneously as society itself, as a part of society, and as *instrument of unification*. As a part of society it is specifically the sector which concentrates all looking and all consciousness. Because of the very fact that this sector is *separate*, it is the location of the abused look and of false consciousness" (paragraph 3). Vision plays a singularly important role in the enforcement of rigid lines of separation in Faulkner's South, especially as it concerns questions of race, gender, and social identity, and in ways that strikingly resemble Debord's thinking. In *Light in August*, as we will see, the "abused" look produces a false consciousness for characters and for readers as well.[22]

Aspects of the visual component of southern as well as modern social and cultural reality played a key role in developments of which Faulkner's novels appear acutely aware. It has been suggested, for instance, that male fantasies in the South about black sexual potency and white female purity gave rise to efforts to control black men through surveillance, as well as subtended cultural forms like the plantation romance. Women's role as objects of the gaze in southern social and cultural institutions like the plantation and the romance was similar to their function in the developing mass media—a fact that was not lost on Faulkner.[23] This is evident in his depiction in *Sanctuary* of Temple Drake's mass-media subjectivity, and in Jefferson's cinematic and fantastical response in *Light in August* to Joanna Burden's murder and perceived rape.

Central to Faulkner's thirties fiction was the fact that modern and popular cultural experiences of vision played a role in structuring attitudes about race as well as gender. From the earliest depictions of African Americans in film, stereotypes of black behavior, such as a willing subservience, sexual threat, or physical menace, predominated.[24] These stereotypes obtain in Faulkner's depiction of Joe Christmas, as do descriptions of his movement and appearance that offer a variation on what has been described as the cinematic "spectralizing" of the event.[25] Of particular concern to my discussion of Christmas as well is the way in which blackness appeared as a distorting demarcation and a spur to the eye in popular fiction in the period during which Faulkner was writing. Popular novels about black urban life such as Carl Van Vechten's *Nigger Heaven* (1926) and others of the Harlem School, for instance, played on notions of black exoticism and danger at the same time that they demonstrated a fascination with the image of blackness as a (consumable) spectacle.

The slightly anomalous *Pylon* appeared in the precise middle of the decade and, like *Light in August,* offers a critical account of violent spectacle. Faulkner's novel of air shows, journalism, and modernity (written, he claimed, as a relief from his struggles with *Absalom, Absalom!)* also pays attention to communal perceptual experience and to individual characters' acts of seeing. This is clear in the spectators of the barnstorming as well as, often, in Faulkner's "visualizing" of experiences ordinarily considered nonvisual. In the novel's several accounts of characters reading the newspaper, we find an instance of a strategy that appears at other points in Faulkner's thirties writing: the abrogating of verbal and cognitive processes to what Faulkner depicts as the specifically unreflexive, acritical experience of looking. References to the way "[t]he eye, the organ without thought speculation or amaze, ran off the last word" (850) as the reporter reads, sound, we will see, a good deal like textual and stylistic effects that occur in *Absalom, Absalom!* In this respect, and in its critique of the spectacle of the air show—and especially of the newspaper's "selling" stories of the airmen's death—*Pylon* shares strategies and concerns with other of Faulkner's thirties novels.

Pylon does not, however, treat these same issues as reflexively as do those works. Acts of collective and individual looking figure thematically, for instance, in *Light in August,* but they also shape to a considerable degree readers' engagement with Christmas and with racial typing. The visual mode in *Absalom,* particularly the way in which vision displaces verbal narrative (and functions "without thought speculation or amaze") surfaces throughout the novel, conditioning readers' as well as characters' experience of the Sutpen story. *Pylon* does not quite implicate readers along with characters in its critical treatment of vision as do Faulkner's other thirties novels. We might also say that *Pylon*'s popular cultural elements are perhaps *too* manifest a form of cultural criticism. Its emphasis on spectacle or sensationalism; its use of Hollywood fodder (the courageous pilots, the love triangle, and the use of bold-face "headlines" throughout the text, a practice Faulkner used in his own screenwriting[26]); and its satire of the newspaper and its editor Hagood, who in his insistence on stories that will sell resembles one of Faulkner's magazine editors, are all evident references to mass media and technology. In a similar fashion, *Sanctuary* certainly makes overt uses of popular cultural materials. Yet *Sanctuary* and especially the other novels of my study also approach their use of mass art practices obliquely, alongside (in dialectical relation with) their modernist strategies. In its more direct references to popular culture, *Pylon,* while relevant to a discussion of Faulkner's thirties fiction, helps point up the presence of mass art in what would appear to be the less likely places, for example, in the high-modernist novels. Despite its considerable interests, *Pylon*'s approaches to visual and mass culture are not as veiled and therefore— importantly—as implicative as are those of the other novels from the decade.

My other reason for not including *Pylon* in this study has to do with its position relative to Faulkner's canon. While certainly it is about the "modern" phenomena of technology, newspapers, aviation, and spectacle, as well as about the role in each of a vicious economic imperative and system, *Pylon* is not as recognizably modern*ist* as are the other novels of this period.[27] Set almost completely in unified space (Faulkner's fictionalized New Orleans), and following a series of events that take place over a circumscribed period of time, *Pylon* makes use of few of the narrative and temporal ruptures that characterize high-modernist experimentation.[28] Moreover, in his use of a single narrative voice and perspective, Faulkner offers with *Pylon* a work that, in comparison with his perhaps most famously fragmented narrative experiments *The Sound and the Fury* and *As I Lay Dying,* as well as with each of the novels I consider here, is relatively straightforward.[29] My overriding argument in this study is with those theorists and critics who have claimed that modernists like Faulkner excluded all traces of popular art from their writing, an assertion that is more readily countered with works that are identified with the modernist canon.

In addition to the visualizing of race and the advent of consumerist spectacle, Faulkner's thirties modernism showed an awareness of a range of visual effects and influences. Historical thought as well, in the period before and during which Faulkner produced his modernist fiction, suffered from what he understood as a visual "crisis," one that he recognized was exacerbated by film. Offering revisionist and aesthetic treatments of history, films like *Birth of a Nation* effected a "removal" of history from "the field of vision."[30] Under the guise of a seeming realism, the use of nostalgia and an idealizing vision of the past in films like *Birth* (and others such as Edwin Porter's *Uncle Tom's Cabin* [1903] or Paul Sloane's *Hearts in Dixie* [1929]) obscured history rather than clarified it.[31] In *Absalom, Absalom!*, written during and after his own work in Hollywood and following the re-release of *Birth* in 1930, Faulkner used a repeated reference to characters' acts of "watching" the Sutpen narrative as well as what I call a "visualized" prose style, one that performs an immanent critique of film efforts to narrate and visualize southern history.

Faulkner's final novel of the thirties, *If I Forget Thee, Jerusalem*, squarely and repeatedly confronts patterns of cultural consumption that, at the end of the decade, had solidified into a vast, transnational system. More than any of the novels of the period, *Jerusalem* alludes to a range of popular cultural models: *The Virginian*, Joan Crawford, detective magazines, Greta Garbo, confessional pulp pornography, popular romance, and the domestic film melodrama. Less directly, it also makes critical use of two very different 1937 movies: John Ford's enormously successful commercial release *The Hurricane* and Pare Lorentz's *The River*, made for the WPA. As examples of both documentary and fictional treatments of disasters, these movies offer variations on generic approaches that Faulkner critiques in his own narrative of flooding and catastrophe. In "Old Man"'s story of an escaped convict adrift during a flood and its suggestion of Hollywood conventions such as disaster stories and chain gangs, and with the mass popularity of film melodrama as the backdrop for "Wild Palms," *If I Forget Thee, Jerusalem* considers a cultural landscape that by 1939 had blurred into a bland continuum.[32] In addition to popular films like *The Hurricane*, *Jerusalem* also targets Hollywood vehicles like Crawford's *Possessed* (a 1931 romance involving madness, murder, and suicide), and *Sadie McKee* (from 1934, in which Crawford endures a marriage of convenience while harboring passions for two other men). In *Jerusalem*, Faulkner resists tendencies in pictures such as these toward sensationalizing or a ready emotional escapism, furnishing instead means by which readers confront their own pleasure in stories of natural (or marital) disaster. In the novel's conclusion, where Wilbourne is depicted remembering and "recording" images of Charlotte's body to replay for himself "pornographically" when in prison, Faulkner extends and sharpens this critique. I argue that Wilbourne's position at the novel's end, trapped in the repeated act of consuming his own projective desire, refers readers to their own entrapment by a culture industry that, as Adorno and others show, works to stimulate but never satisfy consumers' longing.

Other theoretical work has suggested a relation between literary modernism and film and visual culture that is similar to my consideration of the visual in Faulkner. In his introduction to *Signatures of the Visible*, Fredric Jameson declares, "The visual is *essentially* pornographic, which is to say that it has its end in rapt, mindless fascination" (1). Suggesting elsewhere a link between the mesmerizing spectacle of film and Marx's conception of the auratic "magic" of commodity aesthetics, Jameson posits an explanation for the visual's uniquely commercial capacities: "Briefly, this view can be characterized as the extension and application of Marxist theories of commodity reification to the works of mass culture" ("Reification and Utopia in Mass Culture,"10).[33] Jameson claims that film lends itself to commercial practices because of its reliance on a purely sensory, largely visual, and ultimately abstracting experience. This manner of defining film by its capacity to provoke an uncritical response is common in theoretical treatments of it, particularly by Frankfurt School thinkers; their position is also useful in describing the critique of film that I argue is immanent in Faulkner's various visual practices.[34]

Jameson is apt here because of his effort to historicize not only properties of film but changes in the way visual activity came to be experienced in the modern period, as well as those changes' social effects. As he puts it, "[T]he only way to think the visual, to get a handle on increasing, tendential, all-pervasive visuality as such, is to grasp its historical coming into being" (*Signatures of the Visible*, 1).[35] Seen as a clear vestige of commodity aesthetics, the privileging of vision as it appears in various modern forms, especially film but also certain high-cultural models, requires a reading of those forms' historically determined nature. One manner of doing this would be to do away with the different categories of culture (Huyssen's "great divide") in an effort to grasp their more significant and historically contingent mutuality. As Jameson put it in an early essay, "[W]e must rethink the opposition high culture/mass culture in such a way that the emphasis on evaluation to which it has traditionally given rise . . . is replaced by a genuinely historical and dialectical approach to these phenomena . . . as twin and inseparable forms of the fission of aesthetic production under capitalism" ("Reification and Utopia in Mass Culture," 14). Jameson's appeal here for a dialectical reading of high and mass art is key. It anticipated work like DiBattista's and Huyssen's reassessment of *The Great Divide;* it also echoes Adorno's famous pronouncement that modernism and mass culture "both bear the stigmata of capitalism, both contain elements of change. Both are torn halves of an integral freedom to which however they do not add up."[36] Jameson's call for an historical and dialectical reading of high and mass culture is important because it suggests a way to see modernism point up reifying tendencies in other cultural forms, such as film and popular culture's emphasis on visual experience.

This historicizing impulse was central to Faulkner's thirties novels and to their culturally critical strategy. The visual and the filmic as they appear repeatedly in Faulkner's fiction, that is, do so as part of his cultural and historical critique as well as in dialectical relation to his modernism. Unlike his models, Faulkner's use of the visual is not reduced to "rapt, mindless fascination." Even when readers are mesmerized by Faulkner's language, as I argue they are by the Rosa section of *Absalom, Absalom!,* their experience of a visual mode occurs in the context of Faulkner's demonstrating or objectifying it, putting the effects of such a type of reading experience on display. A similar effect occurs elsewhere in his writing, as in *Sanctuary,* wherein referential or descriptive writing strategies are put into tension with more abstract, occlusive uses of language. If the visual in Faulkner is not "essentially pornographic" (though in places it is this too), it is because Faulkner allows readers a means of resistance by treating the visual as a textual and aesthetic function, pointing up its tendency toward commodification and reifying.

Like the novels' several visual elements, generic strategies and types figure prominently in Faulkner's interaction with popular culture. Genre is important to my discussion because it was both a successful element in the culture industry's standardizing of its product and another way that Faulkner's novels reflect on the popular culture that surrounded them. This procedure is perhaps clearest in the case of *Sanctuary,* in which gangster, crime, and *roman noir* models heavily inform Faulkner's narrative of Temple Drake, Horace, and Popeye. In Faulkner's novel, however, generic elements such as Popeye's inhuman, synthetic construction, or set pieces like the gangster funeral scene encounter a critical pressure as Faulkner parodies or ironizes them. My discussion of *Light in August* also highlights generic tendencies. Operating frequently as a mystery, *Light in August* is structured so as to draw readers into a search for the killer of Joanna Burden. These effects, as well as references in the book to the way Joe's identity is constructed by his own reading of detective magazines, are at play in the novel's manipulation of genre and its way of implicating readers into its mystery or detective plot.

Absalom, Absalom! shows a marked awareness of genre through its suggestions of historical film and Griffith's *Birth of a Nation* in particular. Notably revisionist in its treatment of history, *Birth* also forged a radical new language for cinema. In doing so, it produced a narrative expansiveness (as well as a market) for the feature film that was to have an unquestionably profound effect on film history as well as on popular conceptions of the South. As such, its impact on Faulkner is hard to dispute. In my chapter on *Absalom* I argue that Faulkner's method in the novel amounted to a literary alternative to cinematic approaches to southern history epitomized by Griffith's film. Characters' romanticizing of the Sutpen narrative, such as those of Rosa Coldfield or Shreve, appear analogous to practices of *Birth* and other films that substituted a romantic and idealized account of historical events for a critical understanding of their causes.

In asserting that Faulkner's modernism was shaped by the popular culture that surrounded it, I draw on other commentary that connects Faulkner to his cultural setting and, importantly, that culture's climate. In *Faulkner and Modernism*, Richard Moreland theorizes the position of the modern southern writer in ways that help clarify the connection between Faulkner and film. Moreland's assessment of the "melancholiac," drawn from Freud's model for loss and mourning, offers a way to understand Rosa Coldfield's fixation on the South and her uniquely modern reaction to the Civil War. In Moreland's reading of the various narrators' efforts to come to grips with the loss of the Old South, Rosa, like Freud's melancholiac, "compulsively repeats a scene of trauma or loss" (28). Recalling the technical dimension of film and the mechanical, repetitive nature of its several depictions of the South, Moreland's comments contribute to my description of a broad-based, cultural "melancholy" toward the war in the period in which Faulkner wrote and of which Rosa's position is highly symptomatic.

Bruce Kawin offers the most sustained reading of Faulkner's relationship to cinema. Looking closely at Faulkner's work on film scripts in Hollywood, Kawin points to ways the screenplays suggest Faulkner's facility with writing for a different medium as well as his ability to produce material that he expected would sell.[37] In his consideration of Faulkner's screenplays such as *The Road to Glory,* Kawin also describes Faulkner as using his screenwriting to work through themes that informed his fiction—in the case of this film, for instance, "the individual's relation to history" (*Faulkner and Film,* 91). In addition, Kawin reads formal elements of Faulkner's novels as literary versions of filmic devices such as Eisenstein's practice of dialectical materialism and montage. Kawin sees Faulkner's narrative impulses as similar to Eisenstein's or Griffith's efforts to associate ideas or to produce narrative tension by the combination of opposites.[38] More than other critics who see affinities between Faulkner's representational practices and those of film, Kawin grounds his reading in an understanding of film's cognitive or philosophical impact.[39]

My own approach is distinct from Kawin's in several ways. The most important of these is my suggestion that Faulkner's cinematic strategies followed an impulse that was not only formal and imitative but critical, an approach that is more evident in Faulkner's serious literary projects than in work he produced with Howard Hawks (or that he wrote to appease studio heads like Irving Thalberg). That is to say: Faulkner's approach to the medium of film and to the particular practices of Hollywood—many of which he observed when working for the studios—differs significantly when he stood at a distance from them in his novel writing. The scripts he wrote show Faulkner as an able storyteller and, in general, willing to subordinate his more experimental tendencies to the need for accessibility or narrative coherence. Faulkner went to Hollywood, as he often stated—and, as Kawin and Blotner both note—to make money. Because he could not easily do so at the same time as expressing his frustrations with the film industry, Faulkner displaced that critique into his novels. It is this that gives his modernist works from the thirties their uniquely dialectical quality: they are engaged with filmic practices at the same time as they invent new versions of the novel form.

I also differ from Kawin in my more extensive appeal to film theory. Film theory is important to the project because it offers ways to sharpen my claim for the filmic properties of Faulkner's writing and to articulate formal affinities between literature and cinema. The assessments of Siegfried Kracauer and others of the spell-binding, mesmerizing effect of film, for instance, contribute to my account of Quentin's and the reader's "cinematic" response in *Absalom* to the idea (and image) of southern history, as well as to my description of Rosa's singularly affecting voice.[40] Daniel Dayan describes film's shaping of narrative through the "glance of a subject," a process that resembles the reliance on the structuring of narrative through the play of glances in *Light in August*. Temple Drake's characterization in *Sanctuary*, as we will see, owes much to practices common in cinema, including early film, which contributed to women's status as the object of male desire. These practices have long been staples of feminist film theory, examples of which contribute to my account of Temple as a popular cultural fetish or icon. Film theoretical accounts of cinematic means of structuring narrative proved especially helpful in explaining what I consider one of the key moments of narration in *Absalom*. Faulkner's effort at the end of the novel to conjoin his "viewing" and narrating subjects (Quentin and Shreve) with the object of their narration (the southern past), I argue, resembles one of the principal unifying strategies of narrative film. Described by film theory as *suture*, the process by which a film's lost "object" is recovered and reincorporated into the body of the text, this effect shares much with the characters' encounter in *Absalom* with a reanimated, uniquely vivid encounter with southern history. Quentin's and Shreve's processes of narration and identification, we will see, recall as well the efforts of early cinema to falsely heal or "suture" social divisions produced by the Civil War.

Other critics also look to Faulkner's thirties work, in particular his writing for the studios and the short story market, as an index of his cultural critique. In "Faulkner and the Culture Industry," John T. Matthews closely reads the World War I story "Turnabout," which appeared originally in the *Saturday Evening Post* (the rights for which MGM eventually paid Faulkner $2,250). In his reading of both the story and Faulkner's script for the film, Matthews sees several self-critical and resistant gestures toward the war genre (a foregrounding of the homosocial aspects of wartime camaraderie, an exposing of the limits of modern martial technology, and a surprisingly antiauthoritarian ending and tone). Matthews also suggests that when Faulkner was asked to change his screenplay for the film version to include a romantic lead for Joan Crawford, he subtly worked out a plot that drew attention to its own contrived nature (the story originally did not include a female character), at the same time that it adhered to Hollywood's conventions. In "Shortened Stories: Faulkner and the Market," Matthews reveals Faulkner's other self-critical and resistant strategies in the pieces he routinely submitted to magazines.

My approach to the novels, though concerned with a similar aspect of Faulkner's relationship to the culture industry, is different from that of Matthews. Working this question somewhat in reverse, I expose the ways in which Faulkner's canonical, high-modernist works reveal traces of the market, particularly of film, even when Faulkner was supposedly writing in opposition to its effects. The difference between my approach and Matthews's is that it shows the way Faulkner's critical awareness manifested itself throughout his writing in the thirties, even in places where it is less immediately apparent and when he did not appear to have the culture industry in view.

In addition to laying a theoretical ground or identifying scholarly influences, an introduction to this study should also point to the contradictions or limitations in Faulkner's engagement with popular culture. For Faulkner was not always certain about his use of mass art or even, more importantly, in full control of that use's effects. Emulating the strategies of best sellers in *Sanctuary*, for instance, Faulkner also demonstrated an acute anxiety about doing so. This is evident in moments in *Sanctuary* that manifest particular ambivalence toward the masses at whom the novel was purportedly aimed. In these moments, and especially in his revisions of the novel, Faulkner demonstrates a certain antipathy toward a mass readership and crowds. His discomfort with writing for the market thus provides a way to read Faulkner's conflicted approach to this novel.[41] In addition to offering moments of what Faulkner called "horrific" practices of writing, *Sanctuary* reveals an impulse toward high-art lyricism or classical allusion. The result of this conflict in Faulkner's approach with *Sanctuary* is a novel that bears the marks of its self-division openly, even on the level of its very sentences.

One of the most troubling instances of the complications surrounding Faulkner's critique of consumer culture manifests itself in his treatment of race. Though *Light in August* reveals the impact of early examples of popular art on received attitudes toward African Americans, the novel ultimately performs many of these same textual and ideological operations. Due largely to its manipulation of the mystery genre and its placement of Joe Christmas at the center of a narrative that prompts the reader's activity of "policing" him, *Light in August* produces a reassuring comfort for its readers, one that unwittingly secures for them a position of false security outside of the novel's incessant violence. The novel repeatedly depicts the victimization of subjects who, like Christmas, Joanna Burden, or Gail Hightower, are brutalized because of their perceived status of racial, regional, or sexual difference. The novel's manner of drawing readers into its narrative action of monitoring and tracking its protagonist, facilitated by its uniquely invasive form of textual omniscience, aligns readers with several acts of looking that detect, and ultimately punish, Joe. In describing Christmas's death, Faulkner's elevated language also produces a position for readers of detached aesthetic contemplation. As a result of these effects, Faulkner's attention to race in the novel constructs a position for its implicitly white readers similar to that of the characters in it, and to whites generally, of freedom from scrutiny or definition as well as from attendant acts of physical and institutional violence. Unlike the social and textual position of blackness, which is heavily coded and relentlessly surveilled, whiteness in the novel remains an invisible, unmediated, and unmarked (and therefore "unremarked") social position.[42]

My critical reading of *Light in August* departs from the approach I take to the other novels under consideration here. Overall, I see Faulkner's novels of the thirties interacting with mass culture in ways that allow them a critical perspective and a formal complexity which, after Adorno, I would suggest is uniquely modernist in its capacity to reflect on the circumstances of its production. Although my reading of Faulkner seeks to provide a context for his modernism in cultural history and might thus be described as "Adornian," Adorno's theory does not appear directly in the individual chapters. Its influence might best be described as a background for an approach to Faulkner that highlights his interest in mass forms of culture and accounts for that interest as contributing to his modernism. My attention to what amounts to a blind spot about race in *Light in August,* or, as we will see, about labor in "Wild Palms," suggests moments in Faulkner's fiction for which my theoretical approach does not claim to account. Endeavoring as he did to expose the limitations of mass cultural production such as a denial of history, the treatment of artworks as consumable mass-market commodities, and the disseminating of stereotypical attitudes about gender and race, Faulkner also reproduced some of the same problems he sought to address. In a perhaps darker manifestation of Adorno's notion of the artwork's "unconscious" reproduction of social and historical conflicts, *Light in August* suggests an example of the way Faulkner did not always avoid the political shadings and troubling ideology of the popular culture he elsewhere succeeded in critiquing.

CHAPTER ONE

"Some Quality of Delicate Paradox"

Sanctuary's Generative Conflict of High and Low

In the opening chapter of *Sanctuary,* Horace and Popeye have an unusual exchange. Regarding each other across the divide of the spring, the two men strive to understand the reason for the other's presence. Feeling threatened by the bulge in Horace's pocket and assuming it's a gun, Popeye demands to know what Horace is carrying:

> "What's that in your pocket?"
> The other man's coat was still across his arm. He lifted his other hand toward the coat, out of one pocket of which protruded a crushed felt hat, from the other a book. "Which pocket?" he said.
> "Don't show me," Popeye said. "Tell me."
> The other man stopped his hand. "It's a book."
> "What book?" Popeye said.
> "Just a book. The kind people read. Some people do."
> "Do you read books?" Popeye said. (181–82)

Given Popeye's own motives for being at the clearing and his business running liquor, his concern over whether Horace is carrying a gun is reasonable; his query about Horace's reading habits, on the other hand, seems less so. The question, though, appears crucial. For even after Popeye's concern over the gun is satisfied, the men continue their confrontation, facing one another in a protracted silence that lasts, inexplicably, for two hours.

What is at stake in Popeye's floating question? And what lies behind the ominous silence that it prompts? The answer, to Popeye at least, is obvious: Horace does read books, as Popeye indicates when he later refers to Horace as "the Professor." Something more, however, lingers in the space between the two men during their vigil, and I suggest it has to do with the nature of Horace's reading. Several possibilities exist for "what book" Horace carries. In his appearances in *Flags in the Dust,* he quotes Keats; at the end of his encounter with Popeye here, he refers to *Madame Bovary* (remarking of Popeye that "he smelled black, like the stuff that ran out of Bovary's mouth" [184]). Horace also invokes, for one of the only times in Faulkner's fiction, the term *modernism*. In a statement of the narrator's aligned with Horace's perspective, Popeye is described as seeming "all angles, like a modernist lampstand" (183). In his reference to works of canonical literature and to modernist aesthetics, Horace exemplifies academic high-mindedness and taste. Even his name recalls a classical tradition, and it is likely that the book he is carrying is an example of the high-art values he represents. Popeye, on the other hand, arrives in the novel and at the spring via a quite different literary heritage. His background lies not in an academic or classical tradition, but in high art's supposed opposite: commercial culture, in particular the crime and detective stories that were immensely popular in the 1920s and 30s. Popeye's position opposite Horace thus figures the cultural circumstances that surrounded Faulkner and his writing of the novel—his position as an author of a European-influenced literary modernism, as well as a writer aware of the market for "hack" fiction.

As Faulkner's language in *Sanctuary* and in this scene in particular makes clear, he was interested in the popular models that furnished a character like Popeye. Popeye's role in the narrative and his interest in Horace's reading, then, become clear if we consider the context for the novel's conception. Published in 1931 but first written in 1929, *Sanctuary* refers not only to canonical authors such as Flaubert (or Shakespeare, Conrad, and Eliot)[1] but also to contemporary works of popular commercial fiction. Above all, Popeye resembles the gangster figure as he appeared throughout the late twenties in publications like *Black Mask* and in novels such as Dashiell Hammett's *Red Harvest* (1929), R. W. Burnett's *Little Caesar* (1929), and Charles Francis Coe's *Me,*

Gangster (1927). Several aspects of Popeye's behavior and appearance suggest characters from these works, each of which appeared at the same time as *Sanctuary* or in the period before it. A bootlegger, murderer, and sexual deviant, as well as a caricature and a grotesque, Popeye shares defining elements of several potboiler criminals depicted in these and other books. His menacing sullenness and unpredictability thus suggest the danger he poses as a character in the narrative, but also, and more specifically, as a representative of a literary type. Details of his appearance, such as his tight black suit and slanted cigarette, his eyes that resemble "two knobs of soft black rubber" (181), and his "little, doll-like hands" (182) imply that Popeye, like the gangster figures from pulp fiction and film, is a manufactured, commercial product.[2] Appearing at the novel's outset, Popeye highlights the presence of consumer culture in the period in which Faulkner wrote; standing across the spring from Horace, he also figures the conflict Faulkner and other writers faced between writing for the masses and producing art fiction.

Faulkner's Two *Sanctuaries*

Important to understanding the meaning of Popeye and Horace's encounter is *Sanctuary*'s compositional history. Though he published it in 1931, Faulkner wrote the original version of *Sanctuary* between January and May of 1929, shortly after completing *The Sound and the Fury* and just before writing *As I Lay Dying*.[3] In the process of revising, Faulkner radically altered what became the published version of the book. The earlier 1929 edition included several elements that distinguish it from the 1931 version, among them a greater use of strategies such as flashback, interiority, and a shifting point of view. The revised text, for its part, contains additional scenes as well as alterations in its opening and narrative structure that contribute to its overall clarity. Moreover, this version also shows a significantly reduced emphasis on Horace. The 1931 edition has for many years stood as the standard text, due in part to Faulkner's own statements about the different versions of the book, the most infamous of which is that it was "a cheap idea . . . deliberately conceived to make money."[4] More recently, scholars have come to read the two versions of the book together and, as Noel Polk puts it, "as a single intertext" ("The Space Between *Sanctuary*, 34).[5] In his 1932 Preface to the Modern Library *Sanctuary*, reprinted in the Library of America edition of the novel, Faulkner distinguishes the revised edition of the novel on the basis of aesthetic merit; of the second version, he said he hoped it "would not shame *The Sound and the Fury* and *As I Lay Dying* too much" (1030). Yet while he here implies that the published edition of *Sanctuary* more closely resembles his pre-1931 high-modernist works (and as such stands as the "better" version), the novel Faulkner produced through his revisions in fact departs in significant ways from both of those examples as well as from the original text, particularly the original's own more recognizable modernism. Less "Faulknerian" than the earlier version, the 1931 text highlights the role of Popeye and, by extension, the novel's cultural backdrop: the commercial and crime fiction that Popeye's presence invokes. The later version is notable for the streamlining of its story and its often more straightforward depiction of the novel's world. The original *Sanctuary,* for its part, is appreciably more inward-looking. Above all, it offers more of Horace's perspective on events and his Quentin-like preoccupations with his sister and with his stepdaughter's sexual purity. Put another way, the revised edition pushes attention outward from Horace's subjectivity to external realities such as the action of the narrative and, importantly, the broader context of the book's writing.

One of the clearest ways it does this is through its change in the opening, which shifts emphasis toward Popeye in two ways, each of them significant. The first is structural. The 1929 version starts, not with the scene at the spring, but with Horace crossing the town square in Jefferson and noticing the figure of a man jailed for murdering his wife (and even longing for something of his calm and security in the prison).[6] In this version, the scene of Popeye and Horace at the spring occurs further into the novel, in the middle of the second chapter. Appearing there, it follows Horace's departure from his home with Belle and thus occurs in a causal sequence. In the original text we know, in other words, why Horace is at the spring, as well as his state of mind upon arriving there. Structurally and thematically, the confrontation with Popeye is less prominent in the novel's first version, since it occurs in a way that subordinates it to the book's overall emphasis on Horace and his reactions to his marriage and events in Jefferson.

In the revision, Popeye figures from the opening as an important character—equal in significance to Horace and an effective counter to him. This is true in part because in the revision we do not immediately know that Horace is the book's protagonist. In addition, and more subtly, the revised edition shifts perspective to Popeye, thus granting him a measure of agency and, as we will see, a not unimportant capacity to wield a scrutinizing, interrogative mode of "looking." The first time we encounter Popeye in the original is when Horace sees Popeye's straw hat reflected in the water of the spring (*Sanctuary: The Original Text*, 21). Following this, Faulkner maintains Horace's perspective as he sees Popeye "standing beyond the spring, his hands in his coat pockets, a cigarette slanted from his pallid chin" (*SO*, 21). As this paragraph and the rest of the scene continue, the prose maintains Horace's perspective on Popeye and events. The 1931 edition, by contrast, opens with the scene at the spring and immediately situates perspective with Popeye: "From beyond the screen of bushes which surrounded the spring, Popeye watched the man drinking. A faint path led from the road to the spring. Popeye watched the man [. . .] emerge from the path and kneel to drink from the spring" (181). Horace is not named here, but Popeye is; thus our entry into this version of the novel is through Popeye and his act of secretly watching Horace, a fact that Faulkner's narrator stresses.

I have pursued this comparison for several reasons, the main one having to do with Faulkner's shift in emphasis in the revised edition. As he does throughout the novel, Popeye figures more centrally in the revision's opening, a fact that not only highlights Popeye's role in the narrative but also suggests his symbolic or allegorical meaning. Noel Polk notes this difference in the two editions, attributing to it a key dimension for my understanding of the book. Stressing Faulkner's shift in the revision's second paragraph to Horace's perspective on Popeye, Polk writes,

> [Horace and Popeye's] mutual vision of each other helps explain, in ways the original scene does not, the mysterious and significant two hours during which they sit, motionless, staring at each other across the spring. . . . In this way Faulkner places the thematic relationship between Popeye and Horace more directly at the center of the novel's meaning than that between Horace and Temple. That is, in the revised text Faulkner directs us at the outset to weigh Popeye and Horace in the same scales. ("Afterword," 303–4)

It is precisely this equal measure of Popeye and Horace's meeting that is crucial to the later novel's meaning. Specifically, the idea of a "mutual vision"—an orienting moment in the narrative that stresses both men's action of visual appraising—figures in the scene's and the novel's importance (as does, by implication, an appraisal of the visual). In addition to appearing as a confrontation, one that produces a palpable tension between Horace and Popeye, their meeting also depends on a figurative and literal reflection. It is this structure of reflection and "mutual vision," to borrow Polk's phrase, that I argue characterizes not only Popeye and Horace's exchange but the action and rhetoric of the novel generally. In Faulkner's revision, because Popeye acquires a degree of agency he and Horace both engage in a process of thoughtful and critical reckoning. The nature of that reckoning relates to the fact that the two men find themselves inhabiting the same "space"—textually, spatially, and, most significantly, culturally. Isolated at the clearing throughout their encounter in a "suspirant and peaceful following silence" (181), Horace and Popeye occupy a faintly unreal, seemingly timeless space, one in which Horace comes face to face with what appears to be his cultural opposite. Faulkner's description, however, indicates the way in which Popeye stands more as Horace's double: reflected together in the same pool, the two men are connected.

This combining of popular and high-cultural elements continues throughout *Sanctuary*, and it goes a long way toward producing the novel's indeterminate status. Neither a high-art experiment like Faulkner's other fiction of the period, nor simply his hack version of a commercial genre like the gangster story (as he ironically claimed it was), *Sanctuary* is a self- conscious and uniquely striking combination of both, a novel that uses opposed approaches to its materials and thus becomes a distinct kind of modern—as well as modernist—work.[7] Throughout *Sanctuary*, as its opening suggests and the ensuing discussion illustrates, Faulkner uses recognizable elements of popular fiction and film at the same time that he demonstrates the hallmarks of his modernist literary strategy. The result is a work that invites recognition of the ways these seemingly opposed forms of cultural production were related and followed from the same historical circumstances. Viewed in this light, the novel and its unlikely combination of elements—like the faintly surreal encounter between Horace and Popeye at the spring—appear less willfully obscure.[8] Rather than offering an example of modernism that mystifies itself or seals itself off from everyday life such as commercial culture, as several theorists have described, *Sanctuary* shows a version of modernism that actively engaged with the popular art and consumer culture of its period. As he was to do increasingly in his novels from the thirties, with *Sanctuary* Faulkner offers a discursive use of commercial and modernist practices in the same text, one that suggests, not the dualistic nature of popular and modernist art, but their mutual identity and constitution.

One backdrop for this consideration is a discussion of modernism that sees its relationship to mass art in strictly oppositional terms. Andreas Huyssen, in

The Great Divide: Modernism, Mass Culture, Postmodernism, describes theoretical efforts to set modernism against its supposed cultural counterpart or "other." According to Huyssen, because of the antagonistic relationship between modernist and mass art, modernism uncompromisingly denied itself any contact with the practices or materials of popular culture and hence with the commercial reality it targets. As he puts it, "Only by fortifying its boundaries, by maintaining its purity and autonomy, and by avoiding any contamination with mass culture and with the signifying systems of everyday life can the [modernist] art work maintain its adversary stance: adversary to the bourgeois culture of everyday life as well as adversary to mass culture and entertainment" (54). Elsewhere Huyssen describes the modernist "nightmare of being devoured by mass culture through co-option, commodification, and the 'wrong' kind of success," as well as the need of "the modernist artist . . . to stake out his territory by fortifying the boundaries between genuine art and inauthentic mass culture" (53).[9] At least part of what motivated Faulkner in writing *Sanctuary* was precisely the "wrong" kind of success: commercial gain. Nor did his novel demonstrate anything like a clear boundary between what Faulkner himself considered an art novel and a work that also pandered to the demands of mass culture. For Huyssen and others, modernism took its "adversary" stance against popular culture by assuming itself to be completely autonomous and self-sufficient. Constrained to work with the popular strategies of his day, with *Sanctuary* Faulkner worked this adversarial formula in reverse, as he co-opted the practices of mass culture for the purposes of exposing and questioning them.

Faulkner did possess the skepticism about mass culture that Huyssen attributes to him and other modernists. But in Huyssen's characterization of those writers, including Faulkner, he overlooks much of what distinguishes Faulkner's modernism from that of other American authors of his era. As Huyssen put it, "[M]ajor American writers since Henry James, such as T.S. Eliot, Faulkner and Hemingway, Pound and Stevens, felt drawn to the constructive sensibility of modernism, which insisted on the dignity and autonomy of literature, rather than to the iconoclastic and anti-aesthetic ethos of the European avant-garde which attempted to break the political bondage of high culture through a fusion with popular culture and to integrate art into life" (167). Though Faulkner may have "insisted on the dignity" of literature in other places, *Sanctuary* does not appear to be one of them. His use of "low," popular, even pornographic strategies in this novel served his "constructive" sensibility precisely by engaging him with commercial culture and through it, with everyday life. In opposition to Huyssen's claim that "[t]he autonomy of the modernist art work . . . is always the result of a resistance . . . to the seductive lure of mass culture, abstention from the pleasure of trying to please a larger audience" (55), *Sanctuary* takes as a constitutional element the very figures, plot lines, and narrative strategies that had already pleased audiences for popular fiction and film.

When he wrote *Sanctuary*, and especially when he revised it, Faulkner was clearly driven by the need for money. As his comments about the novel indicate, in his approaches to *Sanctuary* Faulkner unapologetically took up what he saw as standard approaches of commercially successful fiction. His motives for doing so certainly had to do at least in part with what he claimed in the Preface for the 1932 edition of the book—to sell copies.[10] His real interest with the novel, though, also had to do with giving readers "more than they had been getting" in popular fiction of the period. As he wrote in a letter about the novel's conception, "I made a thorough and methodical study of everything on the list of best-sellers. When I thought I knew what the public wanted, I decided to give them little more than they had been getting: stronger and rawer—more brutal" (Faulkner quoted in Blotner 1984, 233–34). With *Sanctuary*, Faulkner did give the public what it wanted, as the book's commercial success indicated.[11] Yet in this remark we find a key indication of Faulkner's larger ambitions with the book, his interest not only in imitating consumer culture but in examining or testing it. Part of that approach is produced by Faulkner's other discursive mode—his use in *Sanctuary* of a modernist practice that contrasted with the commercial approach he took to the book. The novel's modernism is evident in both the 1929 and the 1931 versions, and it includes several strategies: a self-consciously stylized prose and use of figurative language, a subjectivizing of time and temporality, a fragmented narrative structure, the use of stream of consciousness technique, an emphasis on interior states of mind (other characters' as well as Horace's), and a number of high-art allusions that show Faulkner designing his work to be understood as "literary." I offer a fuller account of these strategies later in this chapter. In light of them, *Sanctuary* may be seen to demonstrate a relationship between modernism and mass culture that is not generally acknowledged in models like Huyssen's "great divide" or Jameson's "frontier." As we will see, the combination of *Sanctuary*'s modernist elements with its more commercial approaches provides the novel with a quality that is both powerfully unsettling, and, following theories of textual pleasure, distinctly modern.

Gangster Grotesquerie

Faulkner's motives for his use of popular forms in *Sanctuary* were likely not solely critical. As he acknowledged, his approach to the book included efforts to sell it. Yet in his use of commercial forms, Faulkner offers variations on the materials he took up that unmistakably question those models' formulae or patterns.

What amounts to a parody of mass culture in *Sanctuary* can be seen if we consider Faulkner's treatment of Popeye. One quality that defines Popeye, for instance, may be described as his abstractness, an aspect of his characterization that connects him to specific gangster novels of the period. Evident throughout *Sanctuary* is Popeye's detachment from his surroundings and even from his partners in crime, produced not only by his constant disdain for other characters and his denigrating comments to anyone he comes near but also by the deliberate artificiality with which Faulkner depicts him. Machine-like, synthetic, and brittle, Popeye is less a full characterization than a function. In this respect, Popeye resembles the hero of Dashiell Hammett's early novels, the Continental Op. As an outsider investigating the city of Personville in *Red Harvest* (a novel that appeared in serial form in the crime magazine *Black Mask* before it was published as a novel in 1929), the Op demonstrates consistently muted responses to events. Throughout the novel and in the face of sudden paroxysms of violence, the Op almost never manifests an emotional reaction.[12] Like the Op, Popeye lacks a complete subjectivity or human sensibility. Curiously detached, Popeye's flatness or lack of an even illusory subjective fullness is highlighted during his and Horace's encounter. In a statement that follows from Horace's perspective, the narrator remarks that Popeye "had that vicious depthless quality of stamped tin" (181)—an observation that implies Popeye's two-dimensional characterization, like that of many pulp characters, as well as the pulps' mass-produced quality. This quality is evident too in descriptions of the scene that suggest its artificial or technological feel and thus its link to other forms of modern, technical media, despite Popeye and Horace's encounter in a natural setting. Appearing to Horace "as though seen by electric light" (181), Popeye and the language used to describe him approximate the mechanical apparatus used by film. With this reference and another to the way Popeye's hat "jerked in a dull, vicious gleam in the twilight" (183), Faulkner gives Popeye a machine-like or metallic glow, faintly suggestive of the movies or of mass-produced consumer items.[13]

In his mechanical or inhuman nature, however, Popeye resembles above all the hero of R. W. Burnett's seminal gangster novel *Little Caesar*. Like *Red Harvest*, *Little Caesar* enjoyed a wide financial success and was a novel that Faulkner may well have known. Cesare Rico Bandello is a character who is notable to other characters in the book for qualities that, while different from Popeye's, nevertheless connect him to Faulkner's gangster. Burnett's narrator maintains that it is because of Rico's determining characteristic—his intense self-discipline and single-minded focus on his work—that he fails to appeal to the imaginations of the people around him.

> [Rico] had none of the outward signs of greatness. Neither the great strength and hairiness of Pepi, nor the dash and effrontery of Ottavio Vettori, nor the maniacal temper of Joe Sansone. He was small, pale, and quiet. . . . In other words, the general run of Little Italians could find nothing in him to exaggerate; they could not make a legendary figure of him because the qualities he possessed they could not comprehend . . . Rico's great strength lay in his single-mindedness, his energy and his self-discipline. The Little Italians could not appreciate qualities so abstract. (*Little Caesar*, 161–62)

Seen thus, Rico is a different kind of hero, one who is uninspiring to others because of his abstract or unreal status.[14] Popeye shares Rico's single-mindedness and tense self-discipline, qualities, as we will see, that Faulkner emphasizes or even distorts. Like Rico's, Popeye's fearsomeness comes, not from a physically imposing presence (both men are described as pale and diminutive), but from their constant watchfulness and their violent and volatile temper.

Popeye also shares Rico's intense focus and cold utilitarian functioning. Impervious to others' pleas, like Temple's for a ride to town, and always at the ready with his "artermatic" pistol, Popeye moves slowly and with deliberate calculation. Like Rico, Popeye's physically unprepossessing presence forces him to rely entirely on extraphysical, prosthetic threats—such as a corncob or a gun. In their mechanistic behavior, both characters may be said to embody modernity—specifically, the modern mass culture that produces them and of which they are examples. The two men even share a temperament, one of constant, nervous watchfulness and self-scrutiny. Rico, like Popeye, doesn't drink, contributing to the fact that he was "always keenly alive" and to the fact that he "lived at a tension. His nervous system was geared up to such a pitch that he was never sleepy, never felt the desire to relax" (*Little Caesar,* 132). Popeye's own high-strung sensibility is on display throughout *Sanctuary.* Routinely placed outside of action or dialogue, "leaning against a post" or looking through the smoke of a slanting cigarette, Popeye displays a constant tautness. Faulkner not only borrows this quality from Burnett's Rico but parodies it in the extreme quality of Popeye's jumpiness or agitation. This is evident in the anecdote Tommy tells of Popeye shooting his dog when he surprises Popeye (192), or when he cringes against Horace in fear of a passing bird (183).

Rico and Popeye share other qualities as well, among them an acute narcissism. Burnett pays careful attention to the details of the way Rico presents himself through his jewelry and clothing (*Little Caesar,* 110); Rico also compulsively, methodically combs his hair (31, 36, 49). As the narrator indicates, "Rico was vain of his hair" (31). Popeye's absurd last line on the scaffold, "Fix my hair, Jack" (*Sanctuary,* 398), offered after he uses his last request to send for hair lotion, seems another parody of Burnett's characterization of Rico. Finally, Rico is preoccupied with the images of "society girls," figures who, like Temple Drake for Popeye, appear "insolent [and] inaccessible," exert a powerful fascination, and are seen from a distance as they emerge from limousines (*Little Caesar,* 79). Of particular interest for Rico is the story he reads in a magazine of one such girl who falls in love with a bootlegger. He is, we are told, "fascinated by a stratum of existence which seemed so remote and unreal to him" (78). In *Sanctuary*'s account of Temple's "fall" from debutante to Popeye's forced sexual partner and the nymphomaniac girlfriend of the gambler Red, *Sanctuary* offers the same pop cultural fantasy of sexual and class transgression as the one Rico reads about in his magazine.

Faulkner reproduces several other elements of the gangster genre as exemplified by *Little Caesar* and other novels. For example, *Sanctuary* includes a staple scene from pulp fiction: the gangster funeral or banquet. In his rendering of Red's funeral, Faulkner combines them in a way that resembles the funeral scene's combination of gravity and humor.[15] Even the faintly comic fight that breaks out and that overturns Red's coffin resembles the fight between Killer Pepi and Kid Bean in Burnett's banquet. Another staple of the gangster novel is the distorted or grotesque quality of the gangster evident in physical description. Hammett's gangsters routinely display a marked deformity or physical idiosyncrasy: Max (The Whisper) Thaler's voice, never audible above a horse whisper, or a side-kick who has no chin (49). At the start of *Red Harvest*, Hammett describes Elihu Willson in a way that suggests a kind of geometric inhumanness: "The old man's head was small and almost perfectly round under its close-cut crop of white hair. His ears were too small and plastered too flat to the sides of his head to spoil the spherical effect. . . . Mouth and chin were straight lines chopping the sphere off" (13). Later we find another of the novel's descriptive passages that distorts its human subject: "He was a portly, white-mustached man with the round undeveloped forehead of a child" (61). Faulkner seems to mimic these descriptions when he writes of Popeye, "His nose was faintly aquiline, and he had no chin at all. His face just went away" (*Sanctuary*, 182), or when he refers to "his face like the face of wax doll" (182). James Naremore points to this quirk in Hammett, indicating that "Hammett liked to describe his crooks in terms of some principle of deformity . . . creat[ing] the feeling of a cartoon" ("Dashiell Hammett and the Poetics of Hard-Boiled Fiction," 71, n. 10). In his parodic treatment of the gangster, Faulkner literalizes this cartoonish impulse, repeating Hammett's habit of distorted representation in Popeye and naming his gangster after a newspaper comic.[16]

Other characters demonstrate Faulkner's similar use of gangster fiction strategies. Ruby Lamar, for instance, in her constant self-sacrificing devotion to Lee Goodwin, is a model of the fallen-yet-virtuous woman. In his 1929 gangster novel *Louis Beretti*, Donald Henderson Clarke invokes this ideal in his description of Ma Beretti, suggesting as he does so that it was already a worn image. "Ma Beretti was a magnificent and unconscious monument to . . . wifehood and motherhood about which writers and public speakers have sentimentalized" (18).[17] This account of Ma Beretti points up a quality of the gangster and crime novel which, perhaps above all, *Sanctuary* reproduced. For here Clarke, like several pulp writers, displays a self-consciousness about his genre that is also clear in Faulkner's approach to *Sanctuary*. The element of parody in Faulkner's treatment of the pulps, that is, was evident in many of the crime and gangster stories themselves. *Little Caesar*, for instance, seemed acutely aware of its similarity to the movies and was well aware of the entertainment value of its materials. In a key moment of the story, when Joe Massero reacts in horror to a story in the paper about the murder of one of his gang members, his girlfriend placidly and indifferently looks through the paper for a movie (92)—a comedy, notably, which moments later Joe agrees to see in order to feel better. Both kinds of "stories" (gangster and comedy) thus appear in the novel as journalistic and mass media representations. Another scene further demonstrates *Little Caesar*'s self-consciousness about itself as consumer culture. At the gang's banquet celebrating Rico's establishment as its leader, a group of newspaper photographers arrive; their assignment is to take pictures for a Sunday magazine article depicting how " 'different classes of people live in Chicago. See? Last week we featured Lake Forest' " (129). At such moments Burnett seems well aware of the appeal of the gangster story, self-consciously linking his novel to other modern cultural forms like the Sunday lifestyle supplement.

This self-awareness is evident in *Louis Beretti* as well. When Louis finds himself the object of Louise Pedersen's fascination, he understands that she arrives at her understanding of Louis from what she has read in books—specifically, gangster stories like *Louis Beretti*. "Louis knew there was nothing romantic about himself, although he didn't use the word romantic" (62). Like these moments in Clarke and Burnett, Hammett's *Red Harvest* displays an awareness of itself as a generic work. Hammett's hard, slangy diction and spare prose are hallmarks of his writing, immediately recognizable and often parodied—even by Hammett himself. The Op of *Red Harvest* makes regular references to speech, foregrounding Hammett's concern with language. After listening to Charles Proctor Dawn's long-winded manner, he says, "He knew a lot of sentences like those" (164). Elsewhere, after Elihu Willson addresses a group of gangsters in a speech, the Op opines, "It wasn't a bad oration" (136). An awareness of language and its effects is evident in moments such as these that betray Hammett's interest in and awareness of his own style. As Naremore puts it, "[Hammett's] language . . . pushed toward a kind of self-parody" ("Dashiell Hammett," 58). *Sanctuary* obviously makes its own use of a tough gangster vernacular, one that is also self-conscious or parodic. Popeye, again, exemplifies this quality, routinely cursing other characters or using locutions like "shut it" (274), "Jack" (398, 183), and "whore" (212). One of the qualities of the potboiler Faulkner takes on, then, in addition to its gangster idiom and its various set pieces, is the hard, cynical attitude toward itself as a commercial product and its own gestures of self-parody.

In Faulkner's case, the issue was finding a way to take that parody even further, a positioning that took the form of resistance to the generic mode at the same time that he used it. In addition to *Sanctuary*'s extreme quality—its "rawer" and "more brutal" version of the potboiler- -this resistance appears in specific approaches and scenes. One of those is Faulkner's ironic use of the "biography" or confessional format found both in Clarke's *Louis Beretti* and in another popular gangster novel of the period, Charles Francis Coe's *Me, Gangster* (1927). Both exemplify a kind of gangster *Bildungsroman,* in which the protagonist's story traces his involvement in crime from early childhood, a deterministic approach that emphasizes the impact of the character's environment and draws readers into seeing events from the gangster's perspective. As Louis Beretti says, " 'I'd probably been a boy scout if I'd been born in a boy scout neighborhood' " (61). Instead, he grew up in a neighborhood populated by small-time criminals and had experiences—such as his first sexual encounter at fourteen with a neighbor's wife—that led him away from moral rectitude. Coe's novel uses a first-person narration to bring readers imaginatively "closer" to its gangster hero, involving us with his thoughts and emotional experience. The novel opens with an admission of wrongdoing and then maintains its first-person confession for the remainder of its protagonist's ruin and (inevitable) redemption, when he marries and forswears a life of crime.

Faulkner's short "biography" of Popeye at the end of *Sanctuary* seems a nod to earlier deterministic models for gangster narratives like Clarke's and Coe's. In Faulkner's case, however, his use of this approach is two-sided. Like other borrowed elements of the gangster novel, Faulkner's use of Popeye's "biography" ironizes it as a formal element in the novel. For Popeye's life story that appears at the novel's end is obviously insufficient as a means to "explain" him. Rather than offering readers any real sense of understanding Popeye, the material about Popeye's past, which appears after the main events of the novel and then only as a brief sketch, brings *Sanctuary* around to a more recognizable generic form; gangsters, Faulkner seems to acknowledge, have troubled pasts.

Faulkner's strategy with Popeye, however, also reveals the ways in which his own version of the gangster novel resists generic ways of operating. As we have seen, Popeye's first appearance in the book describes him as possessed of "that vicious depthless quality of stamped tin" (181). In such moments, Faulkner deliberately renders Popeye as two dimensional. One effect of this is to undermine the processes of identification or empathy encouraged by, for instance, Coe's confessional model in *Me, Gangster* or Clarke's life story in *Louise Beretti.*[18] Faulkner gives us Popeye's life history belatedly, at the very end of the novel; it comprises a scant few pages and appears willfully stock.[19] Like his "depthless" image, Popeye's characterization and biography remain insistently shallow—an index of Popeye and of the novel as examples of consumer culture.

Temple and Novelistic Voyeurism

Like Popeye, Temple Drake is one of the novel's self-referential "products" of commodified pleasure. Temple appears in the narrative and through Faulkner's language as an object of both the reader's and the male characters' gaze; as such, she performs a function akin to that of women in the popular visual media of film and advertising. That Temple is customarily the object of the gaze is apparent in the first mention of her in the text, which refers to others' acts of seeing her: "Townspeople taking after-supper drives through the college grounds or an oblivious and bemused faculty-member or a candidate for a master's degree on his way to the library would see Temple, a snatched coat under her arms and her long legs blonde with running" (198). Focusing on a specific body part—as do cinematic and mass media representations of women—this passage is typical of Faulkner's descriptions of Temple (199, 206, 376). It also exemplifies the novel's demarcation of Temple as a figure who functions as an object of male visual contemplation.[20] We are told on the next page of the ways in which the town boys, lingering outside the college dances, "watched her enter the gymnasium upon black collegiate arms"; later in the night "they would watch her through the windows" (198). The voyeuristic experience Temple provides other men in the novel is well known, and it is hardly limited to these relatively innocuous glances. They include the following more specifically scopophilic and nefarious examples: Tommy watching her undressing at Goodwin's, which we see through his perspective; Goodwin and Van's competitive leering at her on the porch and their threatening visit to her room; later, Popeye's sublimated pleasure in watching Temple's sexual encounter with Red; and most suggestively, Clarence Snopes's act of spying on Temple through the key-hole to her room.[21]

Significantly, Temple herself is complicit in the presentation, or *representation* of herself as an object of male voyeuristic pleasure. In the sequence of Tommy's spying on her through the window to her room, Temple evinces a particularly modern and popular-cultural sensibility. Sitting on her bed undressing, Temple would seem to be unaware of the fact that she is being looked at; Tommy, at least, is under the impression that she can't see him spying. This privacy or solitariness, however, is only apparent. For the passage makes clear Temple's awareness, even when she is alone, of a scrutinizing male gaze. When she raises her skirt to take her watch from the top of her stocking, "she lifted her head and looked directly at him, her eyes calm and empty as two holes" (226)—despite the fact that Tommy is hidden. Tommy here regards Temple through a crack in a sheet of tin nailed across a missing pane of glass. He is not detectable, and yet Temple "looks directly at him." Her awareness of an invisible male presence looking at her as she undresses, evident again after she removes her dress and "looked straight into Tommy's eyes" (227), suggests the way Temple's identity has been conditioned by her experiences and by modern technical modes of representing women such as photography and film. The description of her "eyes calm and empty as two holes," in particular, suggests a hollowness to Temple's identity outside of her function as an object of the male gaze. The particular detachment she reveals in the face of this disembodied gaze contributes as well to the sense of Temple's possessing a kind of cinematic object-status that is clearly related to the generalized agency of the look. Like Tommy's gaze, dispossessed of a particular presence—yet nevertheless pervasively *there* in Temple's consciousness—the gaze of the movie camera is detached, objective, and lifeless, as well as constitutive of a "mass-mediatized" subjectivity. Temple exists, in other words, as though she were constantly being looked at, not only by individual men but by the anonymous legions of viewers afforded by cinema and for whom the filmic apparatus acts.[22]

As with his use of other popular cultural strategies, Faulkner's visual mode of depicting Temple draws attention to the way such strategies operate and thus may be said to parody or question them. Faulkner's treatment of Temple as the object of the male look, for instance, also reveals the ways in which such visual experience is commodified. Among the novel's several instances of male voyeuristic activity around Temple is a passage that connotes the painful longing associated with vision, commodities, and fetishism. Having watched Temple undressing and then what he thinks are several acts of sexual ravishment as Popeye and Goodwin emerge from her room, Tommy is described as "writh[ing] slowly in an acute unhappiness" (227) or "rocking . . . in a dull, excruciating agony" (232). Following these descriptions, which themselves suggest the discomfort of frustrated desire, we find at the close to the chapter another description of the diffuse, unsatisfied feelings Temple's presence provokes. As Tommy walks away from the house in which she lies sleeping, he looks back at it: "From time to time he would feel that acute surge go over him, like his blood was too hot all of a sudden, dying away into that warm unhappy feeling that fiddle music gave him" (233). Tommy's feelings here, clearly an indication of a frustrated sublimation and sexual longing, approximate the sensations experienced by consumers—whether they look at the out-of-reach commodities in shop windows or the eroticized images of pornography.[23] In this respect, Tommy's reaction imparts the sense of Temple as an object which, like other fetishized consumer products, provides a spur to desire as well as its frustration.[24]

The text reveals the decidedly visual pleasure Temple affords characters in other places as well. At the same time, however, and importantly, it does so in a manner that implicates the reader in the act of consuming her image. Complicating Temple's function as a commodity, these scenes add to Faulkner's examination of popular cultural effects and strategies. One of these scenes occurs during Goodwin's trial, a section in which Temple occupies an especially public and visible position. When Temple takes the witness stand and comes before the collective gaze of the trial's onlookers, Faulkner presents an unusually detailed account of her appearance. Significantly, the passage also refers to the crowd at the trial that watches her:

> From beneath her black hat her hair escaped in tight red curls like clots of resin. The hat bore a rhinestone ornament. Upon her black satin lap lay a platinum bag. Her pale tan coat was open upon a shoulder knot of purple. . . . Her long blonde legs slanted, lax-ankled, her two motionless slippers with their glittering buckles lay on their sides as though empty. Above the ranked intent faces white and pallid as the floating bellies of dead fish, she sat in an attitude at once detached and cringing. (376)

Against the array of specific details of color and light attached to Temple (her black hat, red curls, rhinestone pin, platinum bag, tan coat, knot of purple, glittering buckles), as well as the signature detail of her "long blonde legs," stand out the pale, white faces of the trial's crowd. Associated with the rotting bodies of dead fish, the audience reveals Faulkner's sense of the ways in which certain acts of looking are corrosive—not only to the object of the gaze, but to the viewing subject as well.[25] Readers' own experience of "looking" at Temple (effected by references to her appearance or to characters' perception of her) is implicated in the unsavory voyeuristic pleasures enjoyed by the onlookers at the trial as well as by the novel's more depraved characters in other scenes. Though Faulkner does not depict Temple's rape, for instance, he nevertheless involves readers in imaginative acts of violating her privacy or even her body elsewhere-as when we, along with an anonymous male character, overlook her relieving herself in the woods near Goodwin's (242).[26] Faulkner's treatment of Temple in these passages pushes readers toward a consideration of their experience of reading and of imaginatively watching, looking at, or consuming her—similar to those of Tommy, Popeye and Snopes, or the Jefferson crowd.

Drawing attention to Temple's image, as well as to characters' and readers' activity of looking at or "consuming" it, Faulkner shows the contradictory impulses that inform his treatment of her and of the novel. Other sections of the book further complicate Temple's sexualized status and thus the novel's ostensible prurience. We have seen how Temple's presence evokes longings and sensations in the manner of commodities and the ways in which her identity seems structured along cinematic lines. Such moments rely on a clear offering of Temple's image for characters and readers alike. With Temple elsewhere, however, Faulkner uses a mode of narrative that undermines the illusions of clarity or "availability" that define her appearance otherwise. These sections instead offer more demonstrably abstract and modernist strategies that stand out against the novel's sensational cultural practices and that, along with Faulkner's self-consciousness about those strategies, undermine them.

Temple and Modernist Spatial Form

This abstracting method is evident in a number of passages from the early portion of *Sanctuary,* in particular several scenes set at Goodwin's. When Temple arrives at the bootlegger's house, her experience is rendered through a range of disorienting effects, such as the fragmenting of space, breaks in narration, and a corresponding obscurity or confusion on characters' (and readers') parts, that suggest part of *Sanctuary's* modernism. In her frenetic running, Temple moves in ways that fail to correspond to the structure of Goodwin's house—or for that matter, to the structure of any house. Through the hallway to the kitchen, from the backyard to the front porch, Temple's movements are not only frantic and unexpected but unrecognizable within a unified spatial construction. In addition to being disorienting, her "modernist" movement through space offers an alternative to the novel's use of Temple as a spectacle or display.

Several sequences demonstrate this strategy. Following Temple and Gowan's arrival at Goodwin's, at the point when Gowan tries to silence Temple, she initiates one of her many flights through the house.

> She broke free, running. [Gowan] leaned against the wall and watched her in
> silhouette run out the back door.
>
>   She ran into the kitchen. It was dark save for a crack of light about the fire-
> door of the stove. She whirled and ran out the door . . . (213)

The prose here is deceiving. As Gowan watches her, Temple at first appears to
run "out the back door" of the house. While this door may connect to the
kitchen, we are temporarily dislocated, having expected Temple to leave the
house altogether. As the passage continues, the confusion surrounding Temple's movement increases, as does our understanding of her fear at being
trapped in Goodwin's house. Once outside, Temple "saw Gowan going down
the hill toward the barn," Gowan having crossed (but this we are left to pre-
sume) from the front of the house outside it to the barn in the back. Next,
without telling us that Temple has re-entered the house, the narrator indicates
that "she moved quietly on tiptoe . . . crowded into the corner . . . and began to
cry" (213). Occurring within the space of a few lines, these movements lack a
clear relationship to contiguous or coherent space. Later, Temple performs
another of these spatial dislocations. Having walked onto the front porch,
Temple flees from Van's sudden grasp. "Still smiling her aching, rigid grimace
Temple backed from the room. In the hall she whirled and ran. She ran right
off the porch, into the weeds, and sped on" (223). "Backing" from the porch
where Van and the other men sit and into the house, Temple would ordinarily
first reach the kitchen, which in descriptions of other characters' movement,
including that of Temple herself, is connected to the back porch (Popeye
approaching Ruby, 184; Tommy hiding the jug, 186).

    Earlier, we find the clearest example of the abstract and modernist construc-
tion of space Faulkner crafts in this section. In her first movements through
the house, Temple makes her way up the darkened hall. When she discovers Pap
on the back porch, Temple approaches him boldly, but still with a sense of
foreboding:

> "Good afternoon," she said. The man did not move. She advanced again, then
> she glanced quickly over her shoulder. With the tail of her eye she thought she
> had seen a thread of smoke drift out of the door in the detached room where the
> porch made an L, but it was gone. (207–8)

After seeing Pap more closely and starting in response to his clotted, clay-like
eyes, Temple hears a voice say to her, " 'He can't hear you. What do you want?' "
Reacting,

[s]he whirled again and without a break in her stride . . . she ran right off the porch and fetched up on hands and knees . . . and saw Popeye watching her from a corner of the house, his hands in his pockets and a slanted cigarette curling across his face. Still without stopping she scrambled onto the porch and sprang into the kitchen, where a woman sat at a table, a burning cigarette in her hand, watching the door. (208)

The detail of Ruby's cigarette here is key, showing Faulkner's deliberate effort to mislead readers as to the source of the smoke Temple had first seen with the "tail" of her eye. The disjointed structure of the house, signaled by the "detached room where the porch made an L," is rendered even more extreme in this passage through the difficulty in locating the source of either the smoke or the voice that addresses Temple.[27]

What prompts this deliberate misleading on Faulkner's part? It may follow his effort to force the reader to share Temple's dislocation in the unfamiliar and threatening environment at Goodwin's. Another, reason, however, may have to do with what I have described as Faulkner's conflicted approach to this novel. Using strategies associated with popular and generic fiction elsewhere in the book, and foregrounding the novel's use of Temple earlier as an image or commodity, in sections such as these at Goodwin's Faulkner pursues a more modernist and obscure narrative technique.[28] That both practices are evident in the novel—the association of Temple with the visual pleasures of the commercial cinema and commodity fetishism, and the modernist fragmenting of space—marks *Sanctuary* as unusual. For in the novel Faulkner pursues narrative and aesthetic practices together that earlier commentary has suggested occupy mutually antagonistic cultural positions. Thrown together here, those practices not only stand out in greater relief; they jam against one another and undercut what were supposedly stable textual and generic expectations. This "collision" of elements, however, generates enormous energy and reflexive force, allowing readers to recognize (and thus resist) the novel's more generic or sensationalist pleasures.[29] This contrast also, as we will see presently, helps debunk the modernist conceit of separateness or autonomy.

Temple Subjectivized: *Sanctuary*'s Modernism as Process

Other sections of *Sanctuary* go even further in their modernist innovation and, as a result, in exceeding generic expectations. As such they illustrate Faulkner's larger ambitions with the novel. Set in Memphis after Temple's abduction and rape, these passages offer yet another variation on the book's representation of her. Unlike passages that suggest Temple as a commodified object of desire, these passages treat her state of mind, subjectivizing her experience of time and focusing on her tenuous feelings of identity. Faulkner's formal and stylistic flourishes, evident in several of these passages, contribute to important departures in this section of the book from its emphasis earlier on Temple's image. The modernist properties of these sections emerge slowly but decidedly; it is this aspect of *Sanctuary*'s "becoming modernist," its use of different modes at different points, that places its treatment of Temple in Memphis at odds with its more conventional representational practices.[30]

Much of this treatment of Temple has to do with Faulkner's seemingly deliberate act of de-centering the reader's gaze. Temple's appearance at the dance, in the bedroom at Goodwin's, or later in the courtroom scene rely on a simulation of the act of looking that presumes a unified, putatively male subject position and a corresponding clarity and unity of the visible object, strategies on which the pleasures of both realist fiction and conventional cinema depend. Following the scenes at Goodwin's, Faulkner's further undermining of such realist practice reveals itself as Popeye and Temple arrive at Miss Reba's. The passage that describes their approach to Memphis is ambiguous as regards the narrative point of view, but several details suggest that it belongs to Temple's traumatized consciousness. It also offers a clear illustration of Faulkner's movement between representational strategies. As the two characters arrive in the city, we find a passage that begins by attending scrupulously to the outward, physical surface of the setting but that, at its end, obscures its own "photographic" realism:

> They reached Memphis in the afternoon. At the foot of the bluff below Main Street Popeye turned into a narrow street of smoke-grimed frame houses with tiers of wooden galleries, set a little back in grassless plots, with now then a forlorn and hardy tree of some shabby species—gaunt, lopbranched magnolias, a stunted elm or a locust in grayish, cadaverous bloom—interspersed by rear ends of garages; a scrap-heap in a vacant lot; a low doored cavern of an equivocal appearance where an oilcloth-covered counter and a row of backless stools, a metal coffee-urn and a fat man in a dirty apron with a toothpick, stood for an instant out of the gloom with an effect as of a sinister and meaningless photograph poorly made. (277)

What is "sinister" here in part is Faulkner's manipulation of perspective, his blurring of focus like an unsteady cameraman. Initially, we are given a strictly objective account of the physical scene through the vista of the city, the gradual accumulation of physical details, and their notable, increasing specificity (the low door, the row of stools, the counter, the apron, the toothpick)—only to have it taken away from us at the passage's end. Faulkner here offers a camera-like attention to surface detail, but then blurs or erases that very photographic clarity at the passage's close. One effect of this maneuver is to signal to readers that in this setting and in the section of the book that follows, a clear, objective picture of the sort we associate with the camera and with realism will not obtain. This urban landscape, rare in Faulkner's Yoknapatawpha novels but common in the crime and detective fiction from which *Sanctuary* draws, is rendered hazy in the simile of the photograph. Invoking the mechanical apparatus that Faulkner's earlier depictions of Temple suggest—as she is "tracked" by Popeye, Tommy, or the boys from Jefferson—Faulkner here renounces the use of a camera-like literary method to represent her.

Much of that blurring of perspective follows from Temple's unsteady frame of mind, an element that is clear in other parts of the passage and that brings us away from a position of looking *at* Temple and into her point of view. The "shabby" and "forlorn" trees, while surely a part of the prevailing atmosphere of Memphis and Miss Reba's neighborhood, also conform to Temple's condition—particularly through the evocation of violation or dismembering in phrases such as "lopbranched." Faulkner's version of Eliot's wasteland or Fitzgerald's valley of ashes appears in this "scrap-heap," suggesting the collapse of Temple's understanding of meaning or "sanctuary" that constitutes one of the novel's central concerns. The oxymoron, a provocative figure in many of Faulkner's novels, here also appears in the service of rendering her state of mind—the trees' "cadaverous bloom" connoting the psychological death-in-life that Temple is experiencing.

As this section of the novel continues, it further undermines its earlier treatment of Temple, revealing the effects of her constant exposure to the assaultive acts of both rape and the gaze. One description refers to those events and suggests a clear connection between Temple's rape and the book's manner of placing her as the object of the look. Lying in bed, bleeding, and naked, Temple hears "the rhythmic splush-splush of the washing board" as Minnie, downstairs, tries to wash the blood out of her clothes. As she hears this reminder of what has happened, Temple "flung herself again in an agony for concealment, as she had when they took her knickers off" (279). Due to her repeated exposures to the look—effected by both Faulkner's textual strategies and by several characters—Temple finally becomes painfully desperate for privacy. Her nakedness here produces an "agony" not unlike the trauma she has experienced with Popeye, suggesting a connection between visuality, exposure, and rape.

As another of the novel's self-reflexive moments, Temple's pain at being looked at here is a trauma that the novel acknowledges. Like the scene at the trial, but unlike the popular models the novel draws from, *Sanctuary* here implicates itself in the act of providing a certain kind of visual and textual pleasure. Having "treated" readers earlier to the image of Temple "match thin in her scant undergarments" (227) when we viewed her through the window with Tommy, Faulkner here shows how Temple's undressing causes her distress. Unlike the scene at Goodwin's, this moment at Miss Reba's discloses the discomfort Temple experiences at being seen. As such, this passage refers readers to their own pleasure or experience of watching Temple—like Popeye's from across the bed, when Temple "would wake to smell tobacco and to see the single ruby eye where Popeye's mouth would be" (334). Unlike Popeye, invisible to Temple in the dark, readers are revealed in their act of watching Temple through her reference to her distress. This reference also prefigures Temple's later exposure to Horace's probing eye during their interview scene. Submitting Temple to his questioning, Horace effectively searches her body as well as her memory for the traces of her assault.[31] With references to Temple's "agony for concealment," Faulkner further alters the object-status to which she has been consigned.

The process of subjectivizing Temple continues throughout the initial stages of her recovery, and attending that change are some of the most lyrical and abstract sections of the book. As time passes and day turns to evening, Temple's experience in the room at Miss Reba's takes on all the hallmarks of a high-modernist rendering of subjective, personalized time. Even in its focus on clocks and light, this short section of the novel resembles Faulkner's effort at subjectivizing time in places such as the Quentin section of *The Sound and the Fury* (or Joyce's in all of *Ulysses*). Like Quentin's watch and the clock in the Compson kitchen, the clock in Temple's room is broken; though running, it "had only one hand . . . lending to the otherwise blank face a quality of unequivocal assertion, as though it had nothing whatever to do with time" (281). Temple here is both in time and "outside of time," hearing the clock ticking but operating according to a temporal reality that is uniquely her own.

Another passage conveys Temple's frame of mind through a wildly extravagant and, as it gathers momentum, increasingly abstract prose. Faulkner's use of language here typifies modernism's self-consciously poetic strains while effectively connoting Temple's shattered psyche and distorted sense of time. Moreover in so doing, it moves beyond a realist attention to physical detail to a decidedly modernist, universalizing perspective. Lying in bed, Temple sees that

> A final saffron-colored light lay upon the ceiling and the upper walls, tinged already with purple by the serrated palisade of Main Street high against the western sky. She watched it fade as the successive yawns of the shade consumed it. She watched the final light condense into the clock face, and the dial change from a round orifice in the darkness to a disc suspended in nothingness, the original chaos, and change in turn to a crystal ball holding in its still and cryptic depths the ordered chaos of the intricate and shadowy world upon whose scarred flanks the old wounds whirl onward at dizzy speed into darkness lurking with new disasters. (283)

In ways that anticipate the near-vertigo and mesmerizing play of Faulkner's later, even more abstract prose strategies in *Absalom, Absalom!,* this paragraph eclipses the light in Temple's room at Miss Reba's and, very nearly, the linguistic sense of the passage. Yet while it spins itself out into a contemplation of shapes, negative space, and speed, it nevertheless maintains a tenuous link back to Temple. This includes her physical state as well as her mind-set, suggested through references to "scarred flanks," "old wounds," and "new disasters." In its high modernist trappings, this passage departs radically from the more straightforward representational practices Faulkner had earlier used to depict Temple.

Finally, this section significantly alters the visual terms with which we have encountered Temple earlier. Catching sight of herself "in a dim mirror, a pellucid oblong of dusk set on end, [Temple] had a glimpse of herself like a thin ghost, a pale shadow moving in the uttermost profundity of shadow" (281). Like the blurred photographic image of the Memphis street, Temple's image here appears to both the reader and to Temple herself as shadowy or indistinct. Finally possessed of the gaze herself, Temple here engages in the act of looking; yet she does so in a manner that reflects her hazy state of mind. The significance of this moment is that, although Faulkner reverses the action of seeing and allows Temple to wield the look, he does so in a manner that both maintains a sense of Temple's consciousness and offers her a measure of protective distance. Unlike other examples of looking at Temple that are keyed to a male perspective, this instance of Temple looking at herself "de-materializes" her image, divesting it of its object-status and its capacity to provide a certain kind of visual pleasure.

Modernist Immanence

Through the last sections of this discussion, I have suggested that Faulkner's treatment of Temple reveals two very different representational practices at play in the same text, those associated both with modernism and with commercial fare like potboilers and film. According to traditional theories of modernism, such works denied themselves any "contact" with popular forms of narrative such as pulp fiction and the narrative cinema. Yet this division founders in *Sanctuary*'s depiction of Temple. Following her initial appearance as a commodified object of desire and the gaze, Temple prompts several of the novel's flights into high stylization. Synesthesia, the fragmenting of narrative and of space, the rendering of an interior state of mind or a subjective experience of time, a self-conscious use of figuration—all are hallmarks of modernism, as well as of Faulkner's modernist strategies in particular. Appearing alongside more generic narrative strategies from elsewhere in the book, Faulkner's modernist treatment of Temple creates a sharper awareness of both practices, allowing them to stand out, as it were, in relief. The use of varying strategies offers readers not only two distinct experiences of reading or of "seeing" fictional narrative but also a way to note their interplay and the conflict produced by the novel's oppositional styles. This critical interplay of styles and modes suggests a clear example of a modernism that interacted with, as opposed to denying, its supposed cultural "other."

It also offers a version of what Adorno describes as "immanent criticism." Unwilling in *Sanctuary* to deny himself what Adorno calls a "spontaneous relation to the object," with this novel Faulkner engages the practices of commercial culture in several ways. Though not a cultural critic per se, Faulkner's manner of taking up popular art, evident in his reproduction of the gangster genre or his sensational use of sexuality and rape, suggests his pointed awareness of popular cultural forms. In Faulkner's variations on his generic materials through exaggeration or parody, and in his use alongside them of high modernist stylizations, with *Sanctuary* he offers a version of Adorno's pronouncement, "As a result of the social dynamic, culture becomes cultural criticism" ("Cultural Criticism and Society," 28).[32]

Key to this culturally critical turn was Faulkner's refusal to fall back on a position of what Adorno describes as a false "transcendence" or superiority. One of the ways *Sanctuary* avoids that stance is its willingness to subject its modernist aspects, like its popular cultural elements, to scrutiny, an approach that is occasioned in the way the novel treats its protagonist. Horace's situation at the opening of the book—positioned opposite Popeye, the novel's most demonstrably generic element and the harbinger of its popular cultural status—informs his role in much of its subsequent action. In several ways, as we will see, Horace suggests an allegorical figure for the modernist artist and sensibility. Though that capacity will reveal his (or Faulkner's) discomfort with a character like Popeye as well as, elsewhere, with the novel's version of the masses, it also shows Faulkner's self-consciousness about his own literary practices. In this respect, the book takes an oppositional stance not only toward popular or commercial art but toward its own high-art modernism as well.

One of the places that stance reveals itself is in Horace's behavior at Goodwin's. In these sections Horace offers a version of the modernist sensibility and, in particular, an approach to language that Faulkner was also in the process of establishing in his writing. Horace's excessive garrulousness and his academic air suggest the formal properties of modernism and of Faulkner's own developing literary habits, such as its fluid, unpunctuated prose and its supposedly detached position vis-à-vis quotidian or commercial activity. Sitting on the porch, for example, discoursing about Little Belle, "progress," and the grape arbor, Horace sounds to Ruby slightly absurd. " 'That fool,' the woman said. 'What does he want . . .' She listened to the stranger's voice; a quick, faintly outlandish voice, the voice of a man given to much talk and not much else' " (188). Horace's "quick, outlandish" voice stands as the marker of his foreignness to the environment at Goodwin's, the novel's "real world" or popular-generic element. The narrator further notes Horace's speaking manner as he continues talking. "The stranger's voice went on, tumbling over itself, rapid and diffuse" (189), suggesting a self-consciousness on Faulkner's part about his emerging style.

In the original version of the novel, Horace himself remarks on the separation between him and what he terms "reality." At the close of the original text, in a letter to Narcissa, Horace reflects back on what drew him to the Frenchman's Bend in the first place, the act that involved him in Temple's case and that exposed him to the gangster and bootlegging world. "I ran [to Goodwin's]. Once I had not the courage to admit it; now I have not the courage to deny it. I found [there] more reality than I could stomach, I suppose" (*SO*, 281). Excised from the 1931 edition, this statement suggests an important element of Faulkner's awareness, as well as Horace's, of the differences between Horace's rarefied sensibility and the hard-scrabble, underworld life of Frenchman's Bend. The difference between Horace and the reality of the underground world that is marked in his comment, as well as by the distinctness in Horace's language, also reflects on Faulkner's cultural position. Because of Horace's abstruse rhetoric or florid voice, he appears somewhat effete—a designation that might have suited Faulkner's identity as a modernist, but one that was at odds with the image of himself as the hack writer churning out material for the market that he also tried, if ironically, to present.

This aspect of Horace surfaces in other parts of the novel as well. His metaphysical musings, for instance, upon returning home from Miss Reba's seem surprising in a novel that also makes use of sensationalist pleasures and titillation: "The voice of the night . . . had followed him into the house; he knew suddenly that its was the friction of the earth on its axis, approaching that moment when it must decide to turn on or remain forever still: a motionless ball in cooling space, across which a thick smell of honeysuckle writhed like cold smoke" (332–33). Two figural devices common to Faulkner's modernism—synesthesia and the oxymoron—appear in this passage, as does the universalizing perspective that adduces to Horace and that identifies him as an aesthete. Faulkner's free indirect discourse suggests Horace's impulse to retreat into a cosmic consideration rather than admit the reality and horror of Temple's rape. Faulkner's handling of that separation with Horace, though, is notable. References to Horace's verbosity, or examples such as this of his incapacity to cope with the events of the novel, reveal Faulkner's awareness of the gap between the literary and the real. Addressing that gap self-consciously, or thematizing it as he does with Horace, Faulkner exposes rather than maintains the divisions between mass culture and high art on which earlier models of modernism relied.

Doing so, Faulkner also suggests modernism's dependence on mass culture for its identity. This dependence becomes clear in the way Horace exemplifies the modernist denial of physical or sensory pleasures. In an essay on Joyce and modernist aesthetic theory, Garry Leonard describes Stephen's behavior in *Portrait of the Artist as a Young Man* in ways that recall Huyssen's reference to the modernist "fear" of pleasure associated with commodities. Leonard sees Stephen as a figure for the modernist artist, aware of, but always on guard against, the stimuli of urban and commercial life. As such he typifies the difference between modernist aesthetics and their commercial counterparts. "[C]ommodities insist on being enjoyed," asserts Leonard, "the result of which is that '[w]ith the rise of mass media and the advent of commodity culture, modernist aesthetics come under a peculiar form of pleasure" ("Modernism, Aesthetic Theory, and the City," 80). Modernist aesthetic experiences, Leonard implies, insist on *not* being enjoyed as a means of distinguishing themselves from commodities. Either as part of the experience of reading or as represented in narrative, physical pleasure—particularly erotic pleasure—must, in Leonard's and others' accounts, be suppressed in the modernist text.[33]

Several moments in *Sanctuary* manifest a similar stance toward sexuality and the physical. Horace, like Stephen, finds flesh offensive and limits his own physical interactions with other people. He leaves his wife because he can't stand the smell of the shrimp she cooks every Friday, and his own illicit desires for his stepdaughter are sublimated into his onanistic contemplation of her photograph. Horace's muted erotic longing is evident in his sexless marriage with Belle and, while at Goodwin's, in his reactions to Ruby Lamar. His revulsion at physical, fleshly experience is most clearly demonstrated, finally, when he vomits in response to contemplating Little Belle's photograph while recalling Temple's rape (333).

These moments suggest the ways in which modernist practices and aesthetics, embodied by Horace and unlike popular commodities such as pulp fiction and pornography, define themselves by the denial of bodily or sybaritic gratification. Yet *Sanctuary* also constantly titillates the reader with the suggestion, if not the actual proffering, of pornographic or erotic pleasures. The most obvious examples are the active presence of Temple and the text's foregrounding of her erotic role—an element that distorts into caricature in scenes of her begging for sex with Red (344–45). More subtly, it includes several references to corrupting or illicit acts, ruptures in the narrative and in Horace's veneer of self-control that ironize the modernist denial of the sensory.

Horace demonstrates the incapacity of modernist strategies for denying the body and for maintaining a rigid separation from manifestations of "the real" in a number of ways. In the first place, Horace demonstrates several instances of physical longing, especially for Temple and Little Belle as objects of desire, as well as reveals a more perverse erotic interest in his sister. Our first encounter with Temple includes an oblique reference to both Horace and to the modernist, "disinterested" response to erotic and/or sensory stimuli: "Townspeople taking after-supper drives through the college grounds or an oblivious and bemused faculty-member or a candidate for a master's degree on his way to the library would see Temple" (198). Despite his and other modernist efforts to deny physical sensation and pleasure, Horace is clearly affected by the presence of women like Temple, suggested here and evident in his fascination with her story and in his preoccupation with his stepdaughter's adolescent sexuality.

Most pointed in this regard is Horace's interaction with Temple when he interviews her at Miss Reba's. Earlier I described the way this scene suggests Horace's repetition of the act of exposing Temple. Ostensibly for the purpose of getting information, Horace's visit with Temple is rendered in such a manner as to draw attention both to her erotic presence and to Horace's response to it. As such, the scene clearly compromises a modernist denial of pleasure. Sitting up in her bed, with the shoulder of her nightgown repeatedly slipping down, Temple has to be reminded by Miss Reba to "cover up [her] nekkidness" (327). Throughout the interview Horace's interest in the act of the rape is evident, as is Temple's discomfort at feeling asked to reproduce the sexual details of the experience. "Now and then Horace would attempt to get her on ahead to the crime itself, but she would *elude him* and return to herself sitting on the bed" (327; emphasis added). Seeing her in this condition and hearing Temple's story, Horace is both intensely fascinated and profoundly shaken. Walking the Memphis streets after Temple finishes her story, Horace witnesses a scenario that reveals much about his state of mind:

> In an alley-mouth two figures stood, face to face, not touching; the man speaking in a low tone unprintable epithet after epithet in a caressing whisper, the woman motionless before him in a musing swoon of voluptuous ecstasy. (332)

Set in the unsavory atmosphere of an alleyway, this passage evokes the sordid world and the settings of pulp fiction. It also, I suggest, reflects on the broader workings of the novel. Like the opening scene of Horace and Popeye face to face across the spring, this passage offers a reflexive positioning of two figures, one of whose violence or lasciviousness renders him "unprintable" (as Faulkner said his publisher originally considered *Sanctuary* to be).[34] Against that figure, and rendered in a very different manner, is the motionless woman. The description of her reaction renders her in the elevated (and eminently printable) language of poetry, the assonance of "musing swoon of voluptuous ecstasy" producing a moment of aurally pleasing lyricism. Yet the woman's own pleasure in the face of the man's verbal torrent signals a capacity to be stimulated or even aroused by a "low" or unprintable language. The false division between high and low that Horace exemplifies and that he strives to maintain is compromised here in his imagination, as it is throughout the novel. In moments such as these, Faulkner foregrounds but also undermines the high/low cultural divide as he makes clear that Horace's efforts at the denial of physical experience, modernist or otherwise, of necessity fail.

Faulkner, Horace, and the Masses

As I have been describing it, *Sanctuary*'s combination of discursive modes suggests a variation on notions of modernism that insist on its separation from mass art. Its interrelation of high and low elements reveals a modernist work that rather was deeply marked by its involvement with the commercial mode of cultural production that surrounded it. Viewing it in this way allows a reading of modernism that, as recent cultural theory has suggested, recognizes its more complicated and engaged relationship to the popular culture with which it was contemporaneous.

Writing a novel that implied his awareness of the market, however, affected Faulkner in ways that he did not entirely control and that emerge at particular points in the narrative. At such moments, *Sanctuary* reveals a strain produced by its formal split or aesthetic self-division. Evincing Faulkner's varied motives for his approach to the book, these sections manifest an antagonism toward the novel's representations of the masses that might suggest a variation on the modernist "anxiety" about commercial activity.[35]

Anyone familiar with Faulkner's expectation that he could earn a living writing knows that he was not especially troubled by the prospect of financial success. As his extensive correspondence with his agents and editors demonstrates, Faulkner was routinely frustrated that his books, even his high modernist novels, did not sell. Notwithstanding Faulkner's sense of himself as a professional writer as well as a serious artist, *Sanctuary* includes elements that, in a manner that certainly differed from his earlier novels, could appear as a form of pandering. Those elements, combined with his highly ambivalent comments in his Preface as well as later statements about *Sanctuary*, suggest a relation to this novel that was at odds with that to his other books.[36] As such, scenes that depict the masses merit scrutiny for what they reveal of Faulkner's attitude toward those types as potential readers. In its derisive treatment of characters like Clarence Snopes or other figures for the "public," *Sanctuary* suggests a measure of irony, if not toward itself, then toward novels it resembled or toward certain readers (notably those who to that point had ignored Faulkner's books). At the same time, these sections maintain the defining quality of Faulkner's method evident throughout the novel: the peculiar combination of high-art and popular practices that I argue distinguishes it and that affords readers' critical reflection on the similarity, as well as difference, in modern cultural forms.

The novel's antagonism toward the masses is suggested, perhaps not surprisingly, in scenes of public spaces. On the way to Oxford to look for Temple, Horace rides the train with members of what he plainly considers the vulgar herd. Implicit in a passage describing Horace's regard of his fellow travelers is a thinly veiled contempt, expressive of an attitude bordering on violence:

> The man and the woman got on, the man carrying his rumpled coat, the woman the parcel and the suit case. He followed them into the day coach filled with snoring, with bodies sprawled half into the aisle as though in the aftermath of a sudden and violent destruction, with dropped heads, open-mouthed, their throats turned profoundly upward as though waiting the stroke of knives.
>
> [Horace] dozed. The train clicked on, stopped, jolted. . . . Someone shook him out of sleep into a primrose dawn, among unshaven puffy faces washed lightly over as though with the paling ultimate stain of a holocaust. (295)

In addition to suggesting hostility toward its subject, the language of this passage manifests many of the contradictions and tensions that *Sanctuary* demonstrates formally and throughout its narrative. Although it depicts a prosaic, squalid scene, its language is elevated. Phrases such as "primrose dawn" and "paling ultimate stain," self-consciously poetic and, in the case of the former, faintly Homeric, reveal the novel's high-art or literary pretensions. The passage referring to the sleepers' upturned throats, keyed to Horace's perspective like earlier descriptions of Popeye, recalls Conrad's *Lord Jim*—another canonical modernist text.[37] Rhetorically as well, the image of cleaning or "washing" the faces of the travelers implies the novel's impulse toward aestheticizing its materials—in this case, representatives of an "ugly" reality. But even at these moments, Faulkner's language is conflicted: the means of cleansing his representatives of the masses is accomplished through the contradictory image of a "stain."

Most significantly, in depicting the members of the crowd and their coarseness ("rumpled coat," "bodies sprawled," "unshaven puffy faces"), this passage also registers an antipathy that suggests itself in a language of mass annihilation. Horace's perspective, through which this scene aboard the train is oriented, figures him here not only as the mass's critic, a position he occupies throughout the novel, but as their executioner as well.[38] (And if Horace is correct in his criticisms of the town's hypocrisy, he is also extreme in his superiority and sanctimoniousness.) Later, returning from Oxford, this arrogance manifests itself when Horace encounters Clarence Snopes. Viewed from Horace's perspective, the description of Snopes reveals Horace's conception of himself:

> "Ain't this Judge Benbow?" [Snopes] said. Horace looked up into a vast, puffy face without any mark of age or thought whatever—a majestic sweep of flesh on either side of a small, blunt nose, like looking out over a mesa, yet withal some indefinable quality of delicate paradox, as though the Creator had completed his joke by lighting the munificent expenditure of putty with something originally intended for some weak, acquisitive creature like a squirrel or a rat. (299)

Because Horace is in on it, the "joke" told by the Creator at Clarence's expense confirms Horace's privileged social position: God, in Horace's conception, is like him—an elitist. Like the earlier passage, Faulkner's prose here manifests several contradictions as well as suggesting Horace's smugness. The derisive irony in the reference to Clarence's "majestic" sweep of flesh keys to Horace's perspective, as do the more obviously condescending, naturalizing metaphors (Clarence allied with the mesa, the rat). Yet here again we find the element of contradiction, the "quality of delicate paradox" that characterizes Faulkner's strategies throughout the novel. The diction of "Yet withal" and "munificent expenditure" as well as the sophisticated handling of imagery—the pastoral and visual evocation of "looking out over a mesa"—convey a genuine majesty, even an intimation of the sublime. As such, they demonstrate a poetic subtlety and treatment of language that is at odds with the prosaic or mean character of the passage's subject—Clarence Snopes or the travelers of day-coaches. The interpenetration of high and low modes of literary production that characterizes these passages, even those that suggest Faulkner's discomfort with the masses (or perhaps with mass markets) reveals Faulkner's divided and contradictory approaches to the novel. Viewed thus, it suggests the contradictions in Faulkner's position writing in the thirties, circumstances that confronted Faulkner and other writers in the modern period and that manifest themselves in the novel's uniquely divided style.[39]

Faulkner's awareness of the masses is evident in other places as well, revealing his clear disregard for the effects of commercial art. The audience for Goodwin's trial, for instance, resembles the readership for mass-market fiction, particularly in their taste for a certain kind of entertainment or story. Presented to the townspeople as a kind of spectacle, Goodwin's trial resembles commercial forms of entertainment which, Faulkner makes clear, base their appeal in low forms of pleasure and serve as a diversion from everyday life. Earlier, we noted Faulkner's "exhibition" of Temple on the witness stand as an object for the gaze of readers and the trial audience alike. During the trial, Popeye's assault of Temple is vividly recalled with an exhibition of the bloody corncob, much to the audience's satisfaction. Twice we hear their reaction to details of Temple's testimony, which expresses itself in a sigh, a "collective breath hissing in the musty silence" (378, 379).[40] Due to the fascination it provides its audience, the trial makes clear the townspeople's longings, as do the events that follow it when the mob attacks Goodwin. In burning Goodwin for Temple's rape and Tommy's murder, the townspeople clearly execute the wrong man. Yet their act of vigilantism provides an outlet for the prurient and sensationalist appetite that the trial stimulates.

Readers of the novel possessed a similar interest in sensational subject matter, and that interest allies them with Faulkner's depiction of the trial crowd. The same group that gathers in the courthouse to watch the trial, for example, appears earlier in the novel as they gather in the town square on the day Tommy's body is found. In town to trade and (significantly) to shop, the members of the crowd become eager onlookers at Tommy's body and at the violence enacted on it by Popeye. Clustered in front of various shops, these visitors also partake of consumer culture of the type the novel resembles; on a break from their work, they demonstrate a particular kind of cultural taste:

> The sunny air was filled with competitive radios and phonographs in the doors of drug-and music-stores. Before these doors a throng stood all day, listening. The pieces which moved them were ballads simple in melody and theme, of bereavement and retribution and repentance metallically sung, blurred, emphasised by static or needle—disembodied voices blaring from imitation wood cabinets or pebble-grain horn-mouths above the rapt faces. (257)

Moved by "simple" ballads and by disembodied "metallic" voices, the members of the throng share much with the market for the culture industry. Faulkner identifies them here as the kinds of consumers who prefer an imitative, mechanized cultural product to something original or unique. They are moved by the stories of innocence lost that, in addition to their luridness, animate *Sanctuary* and underpin Goodwin's trial. Itself an imitation of commercial and generic fiction, *Sanctuary* tells a story of "bereavement" and shares with the radio ballads—as well as with gangster novels such as *Me, Gangster*—sentimental elements in its protagonist and, at its ending, in Popeye. Though the novel draws attention to, and thus also resists, its use of commercial elements, it is crucial to see the way it offers the same kinds of mass-market pleasures as those Faulkner attributes to products of the culture industry and that are enjoyed by the novel's crowds.

Realism and the Marketplace

It is for this reason, perhaps, that the book ends as it does. For toward its close, *Sanctuary* performs a shift in method that further ensures its appeal to the mass market. In its final section, and through several of Faulkner's additions to the original version, *Sanctuary* makes a deliberate move toward realism and toward mainstream fiction that is at odds with the formal play it demonstrates earlier and that had contributed to its modernism. This shift within the novel is present to a far greater degree in the revised edition, and it corresponds to Faulkner's revision strategies with *Sanctuary* generally. As indicated earlier, the original text more often relies on a modernist emphasis on the play of perspective and the rendering of interiority, particularly Horace's. His musings on his family's past, on his relationship with Narcissa, on the jailed murderer, and on Little Belle occupy a far greater degree of the original. Many of these were deleted in the revision, freeing the novel from Horace's dominating perspective and allowing a more direct account of the narrative. In its later chapters that take place in Jefferson, *Sanctuary* confers a unity and clarity to its events which, I suggest, play to its audience's taste for an accessible style and a straightforward narrative structure.

The difference in narrating strategies in the Jefferson sections becomes clear immediately if we compare them to other parts of the book. The first time we see the Jefferson area, we find a narrative method that is strikingly different in function from those in Memphis or in the novel's opening chapters.

> On the next afternoon Benbow was at his sister's home. It was in the country, four miles from Jefferson; the home of her husband's people. She was a widow, with a boy ten year's old, living in a big house with her son and the great aunt of

her husband; a woman of ninety, who lived in a wheel chair, who was known as Miss Jenny. She and Benbow were at the window, watching his sister and a young man walking in the garden. His sister had been a widow for ten years. (195)

As this chapter opens, we immediately find ourselves in a narrative register different from the novel's more visible modernism. To begin, we have a series of simple declarative phrases, structured paratactically so as to provide information evenly and directly. In its forthright, casual tone as well as in its specific content, the passage marks a shift from the cryptic, information-withholding manner of the novel's opening. Details of location, age, and description are immediately forthcoming; characters' names and their relationships are established. Even specific measures of geography such as space and distance figure in the passage, as do expository details. In sum, this chapter and the Jefferson section of the novel operate under the auspices of a fully articulated narrative realism.[41]

It is only necessary to recall the deliberate obscurity of the novel's opening chapters or of its sections set at Goodwin's or in Memphis to trace the differences in narrative method. The next chapter whose events take place in Jefferson opens in a similarly clear manner:

Benbow reached his sister's home in the middle of the afternoon. It was four miles from town, Jefferson. He and his sister were born in Jefferson, seven years apart, in a house which they still owned, though his sister had wanted him to sell the house when Benbow married the divorced wife of a man named Mitchell. (253)

Temporal details here, as well as information about property and the legal status of Horace's married life, further the sense that this portion of the novel will furnish conventional novelistic terms of its characters' lives.[42] This method continues, generally, throughout the Jefferson sections of the book, narrated as they are by a restrained, third-person voice that eschews many of the Faulknerian and modernist excesses of figuration, abstractness, and fragmentation.

The straightforward narrative method reaches its apotheosis in a passage late in the novel that describes Horace's entrance to the courtroom—a space that, as defined by its role in the public sphere, is rendered in a manner that is sharp-edged and readily accessible:

[T]he square was filled with wagons and cars, and the overalls and khaki thronged slowly beneath the gothic entrance of the building. . . .

The broad double doors at the head of the cramped stair were open. From beyond them came a steady preliminary stir of people settling themselves. Above the seat-backs Horace could see their heads—bald heads, gray heads, shaggy heads and heads trimmed to recent feather-edge above sun-baked necks, oiled heads above urban collars and here and there a sunbonnet or a flowered hat. (374)

Among its many details of setting (including styles of architecture and clothing), this passage is significant for its attention to the external details we associate with and expect from realism. The second paragraph, especially, makes a particular insistence on the external visual details of the crowd's heads, references that correspond to an external gaze looking at clearly demarcated objects in space.

If Faulkner's treatment of the public space of the novel relies on a sharply photographic or realist representation, it is important to see this shift in relation to the novel's narrative. For there is a correspondence between the events of the book's conclusion and the manner in which they are depicted. Accessibility here is key—for both the townspeople to the courthouse, and for the readers into the novel's last section. It is in the courthouse where, as we have seen, the reader's pleasure in the sensational aspects of the story is both figured and repeated in the reactions of the crowd. Here we see that figure for the novel's readers ushered in "beneath the gothic entrance" of the courthouse to the trial's (and the novel's) retelling of the gothic events of the crime. As he does so, Faulkner decisively cuts to a use of realism. Whereas *Sanctuary* opens with modernist opacity and demonstrates fragmentation and stylization in its middle sections, it ends with a move Faulkner makes to re-engage his readers.

The final section of the book also reveals, for my analysis, one of Faulkner's single most significant revisions. Beyond his shifts in style and representational method, the revised version of the novel includes its arguably most sensational scene: Goodwin's lynching. Unlike the novel's other acts of violence (Temple's rape; Tommy's or Red's murders), which are revealed only indirectly, Goodwin's burning death at the hands of the Jefferson crowd appears vividly and directly. Clearly, and in ways the original version of the novel had not, the lynching scene functions to titillate readers. Beyond any scene in the original text, it includes visceral and graphic details.[43] Faulkner's suggestion that, with the revision, he removed that material which he thought readers would find offensive is worth noting in this context. This is implicit in his statement in the "Preface" that he "saw that [the original text] was so terrible that there were but two things to do: tear it up or rewrite it" (1030). Yet as the lynching scene suggests, the revision of *Sanctuary* becomes in certain ways even more "terrible" than the original.[44] The addition of Goodwin's killing provides the book with a literal outburst of violent energy as well as a dramatic outcome to its prior action that the earlier version of the novel had declined. It also suggests a capitulation on Faulkner's part something like Horace's at the end of the book. Like Horace, who comes to recognize the townspeople and their tastes for a certain kind of "story," Faulkner, with the ending of the novel, demonstrates his awareness of a reading market that wanted its narrative pleasure to be a certain way: readily accessible, "consumable," and shocking.

In making the shifts he did, Faulkner strove to provide the novel with the clarity and drama that it had lacked through much of its narrative, both in the early sections of the published version and, importantly, in the original edition of the text. Doing so amounted to Faulkner's recognition, like Horace's after the trial, of "reality"—in Horace's case, the realities of injustice and of the townspeople's taste for violence and scandal; in Faulkner's case, the realities determining cultural production in the modern period.

Faulkner's response to those realities, however, was more resistant than Horace's. For at the same time as he provided readers with a more "commercial" reading experience, Faulkner used *Sanctuary* to comment on his readers' tastes. With his moves to realism and to a more streamlined and sensational narrative, Faulkner effected a means to address his readers as well as a departure from the novel's earlier modernist strategies. Doing so allowed Faulkner to have it both ways—to produce a novel that would appeal to the mass market, but one that also included aspects of his modernist practice and a mode of writing that was different from generic fare. This combination allowed the book its unique identity as well as its powerful position for cultural critique: *within* the modes and forms of fiction toward which that critique was directed.

Coda: Popeye, Temple, and the Luxembourg Garden

In order to see the novel's overture toward the market, it is helpful to recognize fully the narrative and generic variations that appear in its final chapter. Here Faulkner provides readers with something he deliberately denied them at its opening. In Chapter XXXI, the novel's short "biography" of Popeye seems to furnish its readers with everything they might have expected in a sentimental, first-person gangster narrative. It offers a range of information that fills out Popeye's depiction in a conventional novelistic manner and suggests the causes for his criminality.

Popeye's life history is another of Faulkner's more meaningful additions to the published version of the book. For Popeye's background story does a great deal to humanize him (or at least, it appears to); it also adds considerably to the book's resemblance to its models in commercial fare. As such, this section appears part of Faulkner's effort to make the book more marketable. Included in the description are the following elements of Popeye's background: a physical disability (Popeye's arrested development, revealed in his failure to walk or speak until he was four years old); a pathology (Popeye's sadism, evident in his vicious treatment of animals); a life history, including his parents' troubled work experience; and a story of family dysfunction, complete with an abandoning father and a negligent caretaker (Popeye's grandmother) (388–93). In short, the chapter about Popeye provides the background and dimension to Popeye that Faulkner's earliest depiction of him had denied. When we first encounter Popeye, he seems entirely two-dimensional, and Faulkner's characterization of him is notably cryptic and opaque. Here, at the novel's end, he acquires psychological and emotional "depth."[45]

Viewed in the light of Faulkner's interests with *Sanctuary,* its additions and the shifts in representational practice in its closing chapters amount to what might well be another dimension of its immanent form of cultural criticism. With *Sanctuary,* as with later novels, Faulkner sought to present readers with both the narrative pleasure they knew from popular cultural forms and a commentary on them. He presented those pleasures through different narrative practices within the same text, and he did so in a manner that allowed those practices to reflect on one another. Faulkner also, though, took measures to bring the novel to a mass audience. Giving readers a way into the story by way of a simple style or a sentimentalizing of Popeye through his life history, Faulkner recognized, would contribute to the book's success. As Joyce Carol Oates says of sentimentality and its impact on a mass audience, it "is but one form of brutality" (124). The appearance of Popeye's history is a logical outcome of Faulkner's extraordinary ambitions with the novel, and especially with the revision. For it brings the novel closer to Faulkner's sources and thus to possessing mass-market appeal, and it also facilitates his particular form of cultural critique.

This assessment of Faulkner's cultural circumstances and his approach to them provides a useful way to understand the novel's close—its move in the last chapter from Popeye's generic story to Temple in the Luxembourg Gardens. For the book's ending shows a marked contrast in setting, atmosphere, and language from much of the novel generally, and in particular its treatment of Popeye. Significantly, Popeye's final words in life and in the novel appear in the same chapter that discovers Temple on a Paris park bench. Popeye's comment to the sheriff on the scaffold, "Fix my hair, Jack" (398), as well as his use in his last days of a mass-produced hair lotion—a product, "Ed Pinaud," that he asks for by name (395)—are in the register of the common and the everyday. Like most of Faulkner's treatment of Popeye they use the slang idiom employed by commercial fiction as well as the brand-names of consumer products. Abutting these references is a passage set in the epicenter of modernist high culture, one that Faulkner exalted in a manner that evokes Flaubert and that reveals both a tenderness and rigor toward its effects of language:

> It had been a gray day, a gray summer, a gray year. On the street old men wore overcoats, and in the Luxembourg Gardens as Temple and her father passed the women sat knitting in shawls and even the men playing croquet played in coats and capes, and in the sad gloom of the chestnut trees the dry click of balls, the random shouts of children, had that quality of autumn, gallant and evanescent and forlorn. From beyond the circle . . . filled with a gray light of the same color and texture as the water which the fountain played into the pool, came a steady crash of music . . .
>
> In the pavilion a band in the horizon blue of the army played Massenet and Scriabin, and Berlioz like a thin coating of tortured Tschaikovsky on a slice of stale bread, while the twilight dissolved in wet gleams from the branches, onto the pavilion and the somber toadstools of umbrellas. Rich and resonant the brasses crashed and died in the thick green twilight, rolling over them in rich sad waves. (398)

In addition to a Flaubertian irony directed toward the army band, the passage is noteworthy for its alliterative play of sounds, its expressionistic details of color (such as the "thick green twilight"), its moments of synesthesia, metaphor, and delicate diction—in short, a decidedly belletristic method. The Luxembourg Gardens scene, as well as Faulkner's own remarks about it, stands in sharp contrast to the literary practice we find surrounding Popeye in his last appearance. Composed when Faulkner himself was in Paris and before he wrote *Sanctuary,* the Luxembourg scene originally stood as an unrelated set-piece or tableau, a fact that might account for the scene's displaced feel. In a letter to his mother in 1925 about this passage, Faulkner had declared,

I have just written such a beautiful thing that I am about to bust—2000 words about the Luxembourg gardens and death. It has a thin thread of plot, about a young woman, and it is poetry though written in prose form. I have worked on it for two whole days and nights and every word is perfect. I haven't slept hardly for two nights, thinking about it, comparing words, accepting and rejecting them, then changing again. But now it is perfect—a jewel. (*SL,* 27)

What Faulkner also called a "prose poem," this "perfect . . . jewel" exemplifies a very different approach to writing than he took through much of *Sanctuary,* in particular the sections that treat Goodwin, Miss Reba, Red—and above all, Popeye. Though he is not with Temple and her father in the Luxembourg Gardens, Popeye and the language that attaches to him is still, at the novel's close in Paris, lingeringly *there.* Bearing the trace of Popeye's rough colloquial and his affinity with mass-market synthetic products, the novel's coda is part of a deliberately jumbled, heterogeneous blend of practices and styles. Like the novel's opening and the silent confrontation between Popeye and Horace at the spring, it offers the opposition between high and low cultural sites and modes of production.

By the time he wrote and, especially, revised *Sanctuary,* though, this juxtaposition of modernist high-art and commercial culture was exactly what Faulkner sought. In the last chapter, with a prose poem about the Luxembourg Gardens and references to consumer products, Faulkner simply performs a short-hand version of what he had done throughout the novel. In placing a modernist and high-art aestheticizing of language against a use of mass-cultural found objects and terms, Faulkner focalizes the tension he had produced across the novel's earlier sections and in passages like its opening that dramatize the confrontation of modernism and mass culture. Doing so, he offers a novel that can not be fully accounted for by binary terms such as "modernist" or "popular." With its different stylistic and representational strategies, *Sanctuary* offers a version of modernism aware of, and open to, the "modern" art that surrounded it.

This aspect of *Sanctuary* and its ending also bears a striking resemblance to terms for modernity that Roland Barthes describes in *The Pleasure of the Text.* Barthes provides a suggestive way to close my discussion, offering as he does an alternative model for my efforts to describe the unique, strange effects and properties of Faulkner's text. For Barthes, textual pleasure inheres not in purely transgressive or pornographic practices; what he values is the moment of contact between the sanctimonious, privileged text and its "other":

Sade: the pleasure of reading him clearly proceeds from certain breaks (or certain collisions): antipathetic codes (the noble and the trivial, for example) come into contact . . . As textual theory has it: the language is redistributed. Now, *such redistribution is always achieved by cutting*. Two edges are created: an obedient, conformist, plagiarizing edge (the language is to be copied in its canonical state, as it has been established by schooling, good usage, literature, culture) and *another edge*, mobile, blank . . . which is never anything but the site of its effect: the place where the death of language is glimpsed. These two edges . . . are necessary. (6–7)

Barthes' meditation on textual pleasure, in its attention to the interpretive space or "edge" produced by different novelistic styles, describes well Faulkner's dual strategies in *Sanctuary*. His model of "redistribution" concludes with a notion of textual division that contrasts directly with models of modernist autonomy: "Whence, perhaps, a means of evaluating the works of our modernity: their value would proceed from their duplicity" (7).

It is this description of the modern novel—its "duplicitous" or split character—that offers a uniquely apt way to consider *Sanctuary*. In it we have seen the various styles with which Faulkner works. What's more, we can see the ways in which those styles' difference or even opposition contributes to the novel's ability to reflect on itself and its mode of production. Using popular forms self-referentially, Faulkner allowed readers to recognize those forms. Bringing them into relief against the novel's high-art or modernist elements also gave readers a critical and analytic distance from them—something that neither the pulps themselves nor the more rarefied high-modernist texts, whose only relation to mass culture was through its denial, accomplished on their own. Equally important, the conjunction of different literary modes or "edges" in *Sanctuary* confers a distance from its at times elitist and aestheticizing high modernism, evident in several sections and embodied in Horace Benbow. Earlier conceptions of modernist autonomy or separateness apply well to those works that actively seek to deny the experience in modernity of commercial, quotidian life, including consumer culture. Yet their refusal to acknowledge commercial art denied those works an investment in the specific cultural realities and history of which they were also a part. Faulkner's engagement with aspects of popular art allows us to claim of *Sanctuary* a more genuine involvement in its own historical moment. As well that engagement prevents the impression of a false transcendence of the cultural and historical circumstances that produced it.

Faulkner's suggestions of canonical writers like Conrad and Flaubert clearly exemplify Barthes's reference to a work's "conformist, plagiarizing edge," a quality of *Sanctuary* evident, as elsewhere, in the Luxembourg Gardens scene. His stylistic flourishes, moreover, produce the novel's stamp of literariness and sophistication. Lyrical passages describing Temple in Paris or Memphis and the novel's literary allusions furnish its refined pleasures, its high-art seam or "edge." *Sanctuary*'s "mobile" edge, conversely, is its use of language in passages and sections that treat Popeye and the book's generic materials. Popeye's rough colloquial subverts the novel's literary elegance, amounting to what Barthes calls the "death of language": moments when the aura of literariness is destroyed.

Used against one another or in opposition, the novel's two "edges" provide *Sanctuary*'s unique interest and energy, producing a tension that casts a mesmerizing spell over the whole of the novel. Held in a kind of suspension, like the two-hour silence forced upon Popeye and Horace in the opening, readers occupy a vaguely defined interpretive position from which we observe the novel's various textual operations and their at times jarring, highly charged dissonance. In addition to its specifics of plot or even theme, we are aware, throughout the novel, of this atmosphere or discord. As with its treatment of its characters, *Sanctuary*'s use of different modes keeps its readers at a distance, refusing the operation of drawing them into an illusory reality or a sense of identification with its characters but preventing, as well, the refined satisfactions of high art. Without a firm grip on the mode of reading, jostled repeatedly out of a clear relationship to the text by its own shifts in method, readers stand back from the novel's elusive and unsettling operations. Reading *Sanctuary* or, more precisely, "watching" its languages and its strategies play out, we are witness to an ongoing interaction between high and mass-cultural forms that provokes a more acute awareness of each strategy and an understanding of them as different, but *related,* aspects of modernity. Doing so allows readers to view the reifying products and processes of mass culture, such as Temple's eroticized presence or Popeye's generic function, from a distance rather than consume them uncritically or whole.

As part of the novel's split, modernism is also subject to its critical gaze. Faulkner's identifying of Horace with modernist practices and his willingness to expose modernism's conceit of purity suggests his interest in questioning his own high-art literary habits and identity. Aware of the tendency of modernist texts to deny their involvement in cultural and historical realities, Faulkner shows modernism in its position as one of several literary discourses at play and in contention during the period of modernization. More than his other early novels, finally, *Sanctuary* shows popular culture's willingness not only to be looked at by modernism, its opposite or cultural other, but also its ability and willingness to look back.

"Get Me a Nigger"

Mystery, Surveillance, and Joe Christmas's Spectral Identity

Faulkner introduces Joe Christmas to *Light in August* through the appraising eyes of other characters. Appearing unexpectedly at the mill one day, Joe stands before Byron Bunch and the other workers until they notice him. They do not stop their work, "yet there was not a man in the shed who was not . . . watching the stranger in his soiled city clothes" (422). Following this initial glance, the men take in enough of an impression of Christmas to decide that he deserves to be "run through the planer" in order to take the "arrogant and baleful" look off his face (421). What is also clear in Joe's introduction is the fact that his way of carrying himself is a performance offered as a spectacle for public scrutiny and judgment. " '[T]hat's a pretty risky look for a man to wear on his face in public," says one of the workers. "He might forget and use it somewhere where somebody won't like it" (421)—which, of course, he already has. In his earliest appearance, in both Jefferson and in the novel, Joe's presence is an affront to the other characters that inspires contempt and mistrust, and that, as the foreman suggests, provokes a violent response. Even before his actions, Joe appears to those who look at him to merit punishing.

That Joe is introduced through the scrutinizing look of a group of white men is instructive, as is the implicit connection between that act of looking and its attendant action of violent discipline. Faulkner renders that act visible—that is, he shows readers the men's act of looking at Christmas. Like several passages and other parts of the book, this scene also provokes the reader's own act of looking at Joe. As the novel's subsequent action and Faulkner's structuring of it make clear, Joe is defined by his position as the object of the gaze—of various characters, but more subtly and pervasively, of readers as well. Like the men at the planing mill, we are positioned by and within the novel so as to wield a surveilling, domineering, and, ultimately, a punishing look, one that addresses itself to Christmas and at the same time secures our position external to the novel's events. Throughout the novel we are positioned as looking *at* and, most often, looking *for* Christmas in an implicitly violent way.[1]

In the following pages, I argue that the process of searching for and surveilling Christmas is analogous to an experience that Faulkner's readers' had already had well before the appearance of the book. As a result of treatments of race in many popular depictions of African Americans, as well as of a southern ideology that saw blackness as a threat, readers of *Light in August* had come to assume black guilt and to take the need for its violent suppression and punishment as a matter of course. The act of looking both for and at black men in a certain manner—as a threat to white women and as a spur to white male control—presumes the kind of violent and sexual acts for which Christmas is ultimately, but at least in part wrongly, punished. That Christmas's identity is not in fact black or even necessarily racially mixed is part of the novel's rhetoric. So too are the ways Joe Christmas's race plays on readers' expectations. Preconceptions on the part of people in Jefferson and on the part of readers about black behavior had figured in earlier writing and films; *Light in August* points to those sources both within the world of the novel and outside it. It is those assumptions about African Americans, and not their connection to "real behavior," or to real blacks, that Faulkner's novel mobilizes and examines.

In the process of doing so, however, the novel produces, perhaps unwittingly, several of the same surveillance practices and ways of conceiving race that it exposes. Joe Christmas, as we will see, is relentlessly the object of a range of controlling and observing glances. As the recipient of a look that is most often specified as white and male, as well as of Jefferson's collective and imaginary vision, Christmas is a clear example of the way the figure of the black man is seized upon as a spectacle in southern social praxis as well as in popular forms such as the romance, popular fiction, and the cinema.

In the imagined rape of Joanna Burden and in the town's conviction about his race, Joe embodies the white community's fears about black licentiousness, a hysteria that asserted itself outside of the novel in the need for white control of African-American men and in popular cultural depictions of blacks as lustful or savage. In addition to revealing these overlapping and mutually dependent types of looks, the novel offers examples of Joe's interpellation that construct his identity in the reflected light of a certain idea of race. The interpellating gaze appears in various guises: in Percy Grimm as a representative of the apparatus of state power; in the carceral, objectifying eye of the orphanage and Doc Hines; and in specific examples of then-contemporary popular culture such as commercial fiction or pulp magazines.

In addition to these instances, Faulkner involves the reader in the novel's sustained act of looking at Joe. Through Faulkner's use of generic strategies, most notably those of the mystery or detective story, readers are drawn into the narrative process of "looking for" Christmas and thus are implicated in the text's construction of him as surveilled, gazed upon, or "policed." Displaying the fervid and chimerical social vision of the crowd at the fire at Joanna Burden's and revealing its "cinematic" belief in the myth of the black rapist, Faulkner elsewhere encourages readers to view Joe like the sensationalized and "spectralized" figures of film. More pointedly, Joe Christmas evokes specific behaviors and characteristics of African Americans that informed representations of them in early cinema, notably and above all in D. W. Griffith's influential epic, *The Birth of a Nation*. Encouraging readers to take part in the activity of aestheticizing and visualizing, Faulkner also keeps readers detached from Joe's tragedy at the novel's end. An unintentional outcome of these strategies is that *Light in August* produces a particularly troubling effect, which, in its production of a false comfort for readers and a liberal "freedom" from the narrative's violent and suppressive events, is unique to the novel form and to Faulkner's novelistic practice with this book especially.

Romance, Film, and the Spectacle of Black Rape

In the novel's second chapter, the men at the planing mill notice smoke coming from what they correctly assume to be a fire at Joanna Burden's house. At work on a Saturday, as they are accustomed to being, they regard the fire as a legitimate motive to stop work early. Byron, the other men assume, will also leave work early to enjoy what appears as a largely escapist pleasure: " 'I reckon Byron'll quit too, today,' they said. 'With a free fire to watch' " (434). Byron does not quit, however, and so with this exception the men travel eagerly out to the Burden place to see the "free fire," a source of entertainment and distraction.

Once at Joanna's, along with the other townspeople, the men engage in an act of collective vision directed at both the fire and, when it dies, at the man they assume is responsible for it: an African American whom the sheriff's deputy produces from the surrounding cabins. "They were gathering now about the sheriff and the deputy and the negro, with avid eyes upon which the sheer prolongation of empty flames had begun to pall, with faces identical one with another. It was as if all their individual five senses had become one organ of looking, like an apotheosis" (614). This passage emphasizes the role of visual experience—the five senses changing to "one organ of looking"—as it describes the object of the townspeople's looking as well as the assumption of the apprehended "negro's" guilt.

The "apotheosis" of collective sight that the fire and the apprehended man furnish may well be compared to another source of visual pleasure, one whose popularity was contemporary with *Light in August* and that the novel elsewhere references. Like the cinema, the fire plays the role for the town of distraction from the deadening routine of work. Faulkner's language likens the role of the fire to a visual, sensational display that, also like film, includes a dimension of fantasy and projected longing. Once Joanna's body is discovered, Faulkner indicates the prurient element to the crowd's interest in the crime:

> Among them [were] the casual Yankees and the poor whites and even the south-erners who had lived for a while in the north, who believed aloud that it was an anonymous negro crime committed not by a negro but by Negro and who knew, believed, and hoped that she had been ravished too: at least once before her throat was cut and at least once afterward. The sheriff came up and looked him-self once and then sent the body away, hiding the poor thing from the eyes. (611)

Aware of the crowd's caustic voyeurism and its fixation on Joanna's body, the sheriff has it removed. In addition to this emphasis on vision, Faulkner's account of the crowd further suggests a cinematic quality as it traces the towns-people's attitude toward the murder. Faulkner deliberately points to the different forms that attitude takes, moving from the crowd's "knowledge" of the rape through a less firm "belief" to, finally and most revealingly, the basis for conviction in longing and "hope." In Faulkner's account of it, the crowd's reaction reveals its basis in projections of unconscious feelings and desires as well as in fears about unbridled black lust. This process was crucial to the way early cinema both produced and relied upon a "projected," ideologized sense of race. In this scene Faulkner suggests that what matters more in the crowd's reaction to Joanna's murder is not what exactly took place but what the townspeople imagine occurred. Like the operations of the cinema, and in particular certain examples of film that informed Faulkner's novel, watching the fire provides an opportunity for projections of imaginary conceptions of the murder as well as of social reality. The ravishing of white innocence by black lust was a particularly forceful element of the southern imagination and, as we will see, of early film.[2]

Well before Faulkner wrote *Light in August*, the figure of the violent and threatening Negro played a forceful role in both southern and national attitudes about race. Pervasive throughout popular culture, many of those attitudes were crystallized and exploited by D. W. Griffith in his wildly influential *Birth of a Nation*, a film that I suggest bears a strong relationship to aspects of Faulkner's novel.[3] The movie's characters and imagery, though they made a significant impact, themselves drew on a myth of black sexuality and unbridled lust that had its basis in earlier cultural manifestations of southern ideology. Critical accounts of the structure of the romance, for instance, pay careful attention to the genre's use of the myth of black sexual aggression and an attendant emphasis on the agency of the look. Miranda Burgess sees the romance genre, with its insistence on the absolute purity and innocence of the southern lady, as the source for the racist myth of black potency and, by extension, for whites' fear and their need for social control: "In the antebellum historical romance . . . the heroine was the 'Southern lady' or plantation mistress, simultaneously constructed to be absolutely pure and absolutely helpless. . . . But the lady's purity also required the sexualization of black bodies—the male as a threat to her purity, justifying the control of black male bodies" ("Watching Jefferson Watching," 96). Because of its investment in black *and* white men's common wielding of the desiring look, Burgess argues, the romance gave rise to ever more repressive social practices: "The conjunction of the two male looks . . . necessitates the control of the black man by the white man. . . . Hence the genre of romance is inseparable from notions of surveillance and the controlling gaze" (96–97).[4]

Drawn from southern social practice and cultural belief, the threat posed by black men to white women had seen several popular cultural manifestations before Faulkner's novel. In *Birth of a Nation*, for instance, the former slave Gus's fatal pursuit of Flora Cameron presented an image of blackness at its most "bestial"; similarly, the mulatto Silas Lynch's consuming lust for Elsie Stoneman corresponded to whites' worst fears about interracial marriage.[5] To southerners, the mulatto most insidiously manifested the threat of blackness, and other film versions of the sinister or tragic mulatto had already appeared in the period before Griffith's film. *The Debt* (1912) and *In Slavery Days* and *The Octoroon*, both from 1913, played on notions of the mulatto's "tainting" with black blood.[6] Above all, depictions of the mulatto exposed white anxiety over the prospect of miscegenation, a fear that infused Griffith's film and that Faulkner exposes in various ways in *Light in August* (and even more shatteringly in *Absalom, Absalom!*).

Joe Christmas's threat to Jefferson and his presumed rape of Joanna are directly traceable to the received notions of blackness that appear in Griffith's film in Silas and, particularly, in the would-be rapist Gus. Just as the Jefferson crowd assumes of Joanna's "Negro" murderer, Griffith shows Gus as violently attracted to white women. Though Gus does not succeed in assaulting Flora (she jumps from a cliff to her death before he can reach her), his story is connected to Christmas's because of both characters' presumed sexual longing, as well as their experience of being castrated for an act of sexual transgression.[7] Several scenes from *Birth* show black lust and the longing for interracial marriage as one of the overreaching political goals of northern approaches to Reconstruction as well as, ultimately, the cause for redress by the southern Ku Klux Klan. Indeed, it was the film's ideology of white female purity under threat by newly empowered freed slaves that, Griffith believed, provided the necessary unity of northern and southern whites. Other aspects of Griffith's film emphasized black aggression, evident in the confrontations between freed blacks and the Camerons that contributed to another stereotype, the "black buck," that was to have an impact on future film depictions of African Americans. *Broken Chains* (1916), another early feature, played on the same image of blacks as murderous and aggressive that had appeared in *Birth of a Nation*. A series of films from the 1920s about the "savage" African, including *West of Zanzibar* (1928) and *Diamond Handcuffs* (1928) drew on the stereotype of black brutishness.[8] *Fair and Equal*, an ironically titled movie made in 1915 but not released until 1925, depicted the same themes of racial intermarriage and black sexual violence as had *Birth*.[9]

The Popular Cultural Negro

While these examples of early cinema included negative stereotypes, the precedent for the dark or disturbing black presence that Christmas resembles began well before Griffith's *Birth of a Nation,* or even before the medium of film. Thomas Nelson Page, in stories like "Marse Chan" (which appeared in the *Century Magazine* in 1883 and earned him a national reputation) and his novels such as *Red Rock* (1898) and *Burial of the Guns* (1894), contributed to the rise of the Old South myth, in particular the notion of the difference between pacified, "loyal" slaves and more upstart or violent African Americans. Page also contributed to disenfranchisement campaigns in the South[10] and showed a mentality similar to that evinced by Griffith when he wrote in 1905 of the "ignorant and brutal young Negro," whose longing for racial equality meant simply "the opportunity to enjoy . . . the privilege of cohabiting with white women" (*The Negro: The Southerner's Problem,* 112-13). Leslie Fiedler points to the threat of black violence and rebellion and its basis in a late-nineteenth-century form of popular culture: "Down through the history of the minstrel show, a black-faced Sambo (smeared with burnt cork, whether Negro or white, into the grotesque semblance of the archetypal nigger) tries to exorcise with high-jinks and ritual jokes the threat of black rebellion and the sense of guilt which secretly demands it as penance and purge" ("The Blackness of Darkness," 89). In addition to appearing in minstrelsy, menacing, violent blacks figured as a central part of *Birth of a Nation*'s source: Thomas Dixon's widely read and virulently racist novel *The Clansman.*[11] Dixon's novel, a book that Faulkner knew from childhood, was a popular success that showed readers black and mixed-race characters that pandered to their worst fears.

In addition to evoking earlier popular conceptions, Joe's alternately sexual and brutal involvement with Joanna also followed patterns of depicting African Americans that appeared in fiction of the same period in which Faulkner wrote *Light in August.* In particular, Christmas resembles the image of the more specifically urban type common in the Harlem school of the twenties. *Nigger Heaven,* published in 1926 and enormously successful, epitomized the stereotyping of blacks in commercial fiction.[12] Carl Van Vechten's portrait of the street Negro drew on ideas of black exoticism; like Faulkner's text, if in different fashion, it also emphasized the notion of blackness as spectacle. In a description of one of the novel's heroes, Anatole Longfellow, walking down Seventh Avenue, Van Vechten writes, "He wore a tight-fitting suit of shepherd's plaid which thoroughly revealed his lithe, sinewy figure to all who gazed upon him, *and all gazed*" (3; emphasis added). Longfellow's "lithe" body and his alias, the "Silent Creeper," further suggest the mysterious, stealthy presence of African Americans that Faulkner uses in his descriptions of Joe (evident, for instance, in the passage depicting Joe climbing the rope from his window at McEachern's "with the shadowlike agility of a cat" [524].) Though displaced into a southern and rural context, Joe Christmas seems drawn from Van Vechten's account of the urban black.[13] Van Vechten's novel, published six years before *Light in August,* showed the potential for a white author to capitalize on the literary market by producing racial stereotypes. It is this stereotyping that, in turn, Faulkner's novel both exposes and critiques.

Faulkner's choice of the supposed murder weapon further suggests an urban and popular cultural backdrop for Joe. As several examples demonstrate, the razor was the typical weapon of choice in popular depictions, if not in actual cases, of black violence. In *Nigger Heaven* the African-American character Mary thinks of the razor as a "Negro" weapon: "She recalled what she had once been told . . . that Negroes never premeditate murder; their murders are committed under the reign of passion. . . . Negroes use the instruments that deal death swiftly: knives, razors, pistols" (90). Hoke Perkins discusses the razor as a weapon in several of Faulkner's novels, and he establishes its centrality in popular narrative when he describes Faulkner's use of it as "a way of bonding the high with the low" ("'Ah Just Cant Quit Thinkin'" 226).[14] The image of the razor as a "black" weapon was also a part of late-nineteenth-century commercial art. J. Stanley Lymon cites a postcard from 1897 depicting a black wedding; the caption under the drawing reads, "Check yo Razor at de do" ("Black Stereotypes Reflected in Popular Culture," 111). Lymon also points to lyrics from popular songs, one of which refers to four "items" commonly found together: "A watermelon, a razor, a chicken, and a coon" (111).[15] Along with Joe's "soiled city clothes" noticed by the workers at the mill (422), his supposed use of the razor in the murder, and his ubiquitous raked hat (421, 545, 565), Joe's fifteen-year wandering along an endless street that delivers him to Jefferson further establishes his association with the urban milieu of popular culture and fiction.[16]

Christmas's Mass-Cultural Identity

In addition to evoking sources outside it, events within *Light in August* also refer to popular cultural models in constructing Joe. Significantly, several of them reveal the way Christmas's sense of self is conditioned by his encounter with commercial culture. On the day Joanna is killed, Joe is described reading a detective magazine in the forest. Sitting in a clearing with his back against a tree, Joe reads "a magazine of that type whose covers bear either pictures of young women in underclothes or pictures of men in the act of shooting one another with pistols" (479–80). That the description of the magazine sounds like the cover of an issue of *Black Mask* (or *Spicy Detective* or *Spicy Mystery*) is suggestive.[17] In the first place, it connects Joe's potential act of murder directly to the representations of crime depicted in magazine fiction: on the same day he reads the magazine, Joe, we are led to believe, uses the razor to slice off Joanna's head. The reference here to a pulp magazine also offers an instance of Joe's interpellating by the dominant culture and its manifestation in a mass-cultural "gaze."[18] The effect of Joe's reading on his state of mind is clear. He proceeds intently, calmly, "reading the magazine straight through as though it were a novel (480).[19] Giving himself up to the spell of reading, he

> turned the pages in steady progression, though now and then he would seem to linger upon one page, one line, perhaps one word. He would not look up then. He would not even move, apparently arrested and held immobile by a single word which had perhaps not yet impacted, his whole being suspended by the single trivial combination of letters in quiet and sunny space. (481)

The narrator indicates that Joe's identity, his "whole being" is somehow "impacted" by his reading the crime magazine. As an extension of his reading, then, the murder is made to appear as Joe's acting out a role he takes up following his internalizing of images in popular cultural sources[20]—much as he appears to do with others' perceptions of him as black. Joe's motives are perhaps not readily attributable to the nefarious influence of a burgeoning and sensationalistic popular culture. At the same time, however, there is more in Faulkner's language in this scene to suggest at least an indirect connection between Christmas's reading and the crime. As he pauses and looks into the "sunshot leaves," Christmas speculates on an as-yet-unnamed act: "'Maybe I have already done it,' he thought. 'Maybe it is no longer now waiting to be done'" (481).

Accompanying that sense of fatality is a curious but suggestive passage. After Christmas muses that "'it is no longer waiting to be done,'" Faulkner's narrator fashions a tableau. "It seemed to him that he could see the yellow day opening peacefully on before him, like a corridor, an arras, into a still chiaroscuro without urgency. It seemed to him that as he sat there the yellow day contemplated him drowsily" (481). Looking ahead into the day, Christmas sees a long, corridor-like projection of light that leads to a photographic image. Describing that image, Faulkner uses a term from painting ("chiaroscuro"), but as well from filmic *mise-en-scène*. What Joe sees himself entering, and what Faulkner's language evokes, is a cinematic still. Also significant in this passage and its language is the way Joe is looked at, or "contemplated" by the day. In its emphasis on Joe's position as scrutinized, the passage strongly emphasizes his status as an object of the look—and of a particularly disembodied stare at that. As in the scene of Temple Drake undressing at Goodwin's in *Sanctuary,* Joe is here described in ways that suggest his awareness of being seen as well as the ways in which such seeing constitutes his identity. Like Temple, the "apparatus" or presence by which Joe feels watched is the collective popular cultural gaze, constructed by magazines of the type he reads in the forest. Imagining himself as the object of an anonymous look, Christmas gives himself over to its agency.[21]

The action of Joe's being looked at and its role in contributing to his identity in fact occurs throughout the novel. Starting with his earliest memories of Hines and of the dietician, Christmas is aware of others' acts of looking at him. That such a process constitutes his identity is clear in a moment early in his life that reveals Joe's thinking about Hines's constant scrutiny: "With more vocabulary but not more age he might have thought *That is why I am different from the others: because he is watching me all the time* He accepted it" (501). As with Joe's passivity in the forest scene, here he is shown "accepting" the organizing, identity-conferring agency of Hines's stare. That interpellating, observant eye pursues Joe through his youth, and it is generally figured as all-seeing and maleficent. Later in his youth, returning to the McEachern house the night after his encounter with the African-American woman in the shed, Joe sees a light in the kitchen. "He went on, crossing . . . toward the kitchen light. It seemed to watch him, biding and threatful, like an eye" (516). Throughout the novel Faulkner's language is insistent on Joe's specular, objectified status. This is perhaps nowhere clearer than in moments when the language conspires to depict Joe as alone and isolated but also, at the same time, "accompanied," visualized, or seen. On the night Joanna is killed, in the period between when he reads the magazine in the forest and when he returns to Joanna's, Joe wanders the streets of Jefferson. Describing him, Faulkner emphasizes the action of gazing:

He went on, passing still between the homes of white people, from street lamp to street lamp, the heavy shadows of oak and maple leaves sliding like scraps of black velvet across his white shirt. Nothing can look quite as lonely as a big man going along an empty street. Yet though he was not large, not tall, he contrived somehow to look more lonely than a lone telephone pole in the middle of a desert. In the wide, empty, shadow brooded street he looked like a phantom, a spirit, strayed out of its own world, and lost. (482)

This passage is notable for its emphasis on the act of looking. There is some-one, that is, who is insistently present at this moment to see Joe, to note how lonely or how much like a phantom or spirit he "looked." While all descriptions of character are furnished for readers' acts of visualizing, they are not routinely, self-consciously identified as such. Faulkner's language here refers to the presence of an unwavering, pervasive gaze, one that adduces not only to the reader but, through the focalizing strategy of the prose, to a pres-ence internal to the narrative. We have seen Joe's awareness of being looked at by the workers at the mill, by his environment in the forest scene, and by watchful gazes such as Hines's that constitute his identity as "different" (an assessment that seems confirmed by the narrator's description of Joe as alien, "strayed out of its own world"). Here that gaze displaces itself into the lan-guage of the text.

It is also significant that this passage occurs immediately after the narrator takes note of the presence in Jefferson of the cinema: "At seven o'clock [Joe] would have passed people, white and black, going toward the square and the picture show" (482). The description of Joe walking in the street earlier in the evening draws attention to his shirt's white surface and the "sliding" of dark shapes or shadows across it; as such it approximates the movie screen and the play of light and shadow on it. Represented by Faulkner's language as like the screen image, and regarded by the narrating "eye" of the authorial voice, Joe is figured here as an object of a gaze that is both authoritative and cinematic (we might say authoritative *because* cinematic).[22] Dwelling on Joe's image, the passage offers a likeness of characters' appearance in film, one that, as we will see, also derives from Joe's phantom-like presence. Alongside both the refer-ence to the picture show and the suggestions in this section of the images of the cinema, Faulkner's prose evokes the all-pervasive, interpellating gaze of the dominant culture that stares at Joe and that considers him unclassifiable or "different" as well as phantasmal and threatening.[23]

Joe's Spectralizing

In light of these emphases on the act of looking, it is significant that in our first direct encounter with Joe we do not completely see him. Chapter 5 begins in an atmosphere of darkness, one that only deepens and that takes on further shades of (mass-cultural) menace as it progresses. "It was after midnight," the chapter begins. "Though Christmas had been in bed for two hours, he was not yet asleep. He heard Brown before he saw him" (474). Unlike his appearance at the mill or later in Byron's narrating of his story, Christmas is not presented here through others' perceptions of him. Referred to directly by the narrator, Christmas is "present" in the narrative in a way he has not been to that point. He's not much more visible, however: shrouded in darkness, he can neither see nor be seen. In the action that follows, he silences a drunken Brown by beating him, coldly and repeatedly ("he struck Brown again with those hard, slow, measured blows, as if he were meting them out by count" [474]). Joe's threatening aspect only increases when, in the next moment, Faulkner makes another gesture toward the charged, oddly reified murder weapon—the razor, with its connotations of black violence pulled from commercial culture. "Without removing his left hand from Brown's face he could reach with his right across to his cot, to his pillow beneath which lay his razor with its five inch blade. But he did not do it. Perhaps thinking had gone far enough and dark enough to tell him *This is not the right one*" (475). Appearing in the novel directly for the first time, Christmas is thoroughly constructed as a murderous and dangerous figure. Through Faulkner's cryptic references, hinting at the murder which has yet to take place (*"This is not the right one"*), he is presented at the outset as a likely criminal.

Christmas is also offered as another in a sequence of images of black or "black-like" characters that, as we have seen, readers had encountered in various mass-cultural representations. Their resemblance to *Light in August* is enhanced by Faulkner's descriptive method in scenes like this with Joe. In his depiction of Christmas here, Faulkner is careful to keep the details of his appearance hidden. There is no external description of his face or body, so Christmas appears—and remains—a shadowy, vague entity, less a fully realized physical presence than a textual trace or cipher. At the outset of his story Christmas is a construction, that is, whom Faulkner encourages readers to *not* see or know definitively, but rather to associate with representations of the type of character he resembles. As chapter 5 ends, we are required to suspend our witnessing of Joe's movements. Breaking away from Christmas's approach to Joanna's house, Faulkner opens a broad gap in which readers spend subsequent chapters anticipating the completion of the action, a gap filled not only with the wandering, fugitive presence of Joe Christmas but with readers' received, stereotypical and popular vision of the menacing Negro. That Faulkner declines to clearly delimit Joe's appearance contributes to his ghostly presence, an impression that allows him not only to "haunt" those precincts of the novel in which he does not directly appear, but as well to blend with readers' conceptions of blacks that blur beyond the edges of the novel.

Other aspects of the way Faulkner narrates Joe's story contribute to what I describe as its filmic and associative effect. One narrative method that gives this impression involves the way Christmas's actions or movement extend beyond the parameters of what is ordinarily understood as the discreteness of the "event." Events in Joe's narration, that is, are not limited to a self-contained narrative or spatial unit.[24] This occurs, for instance, in the passage following Joe's beating by Max and the stranger he discovers in Bobbie's room. After getting up and drinking a bottle of whiskey, Joe makes his way out of the room where he has been lying and then out of the house. "He stepped from the dark porch, into the moonlight, and with his bloody head and his empty stomach hot, savage, and courageous with whiskey, he entered the street which was to run for fifteen years" (563). This "event" of Joe's leaving the house outruns itself, expanding beyond the act of stepping into the street and into indeterminate regions of space and time. Becoming phantasmagoric in its fluidity, this passage depicts Joe in such a way that his presence becomes impermanent and "de-realized," and so further cinematized for readers and their filmic conception of Joe, particularly of him as a threat.

In addition to his affinity with the filmic stereotypes we have seen, Joe's "spectral" movement in moments like these further contributes to his resemblance to the spectralized figures of cinema. And his de-materialized body and movement extend from this passage: "The whiskey died away in time and was renewed and died again, but the street ran on. From that night the thousand streets ran as one street, with imperceptible corners and changes of scene, broken by intervals of begged and stolen rides . . ." (563). Faulkner's method in these places adds to Joe's vague, otherworldly presence, contributing to a conception of Joe as a figure for cinematic method.[25] Like other moments of Faulkner's text that recall film, though, these passages serve a critical and objectifying end. That is, they allow us to recognize their similarity to film and, significantly, to recognize the notions of blackness that attended film images generally and those in movies like *Birth of a Nation*.

Surveillance and the Stagings of Mystery

Joe's haunting, shadowy presence produces much of the novel's disquieting force, at the same time establishing its resemblance to, and reflection on, practices of popular media like film. In addition, Christmas's "spectralizing" also contributes to what I offer as the novel's other main narrative strategy for depicting him. From the point when he first appears as an inscrutable, unknown presence at the mill, through his interaction with Brown and his subsequent disappearance from the narrative, Christmas is steadfastly looked for, anticipated, "sought," or imagined. Introducing Christmas into the novel in this way—a technique that, as we will see, deliberately plays on conventions of the mystery plot—Faulkner provides an exercise for readers of surveillance or watching. Conspicuously absent (as an adult) from the narrative when Faulkner makes his long forays into Christmas's past, or when he diverts the narrative into Hightower's or Joanna's backgrounds, Christmas exerts a powerful hold on readers' imagination as well as a consistent pull on their attention or readerly "gaze." Even when not present, Christmas incites the reader's desire to "catch" or see him.

One of the ways the novel engenders this desire is through its use of generic strategies. Among the monumental works of Faulkner's high modernism, notable for its density and formal play, *Light in August* also makes use of violent and sensational elements like murder, dismemberment, and policing. As well as challenging readers intellectually, that is, the novel actively draws them into its potboiler story and operates as an exercise in detection and pursuit. Joe is offered as the supposed perpetrator of a crime we hear of from the novel's outset and the resolution—and punishment—of which we spend the rest of the narrative anticipating. The fire that appears at the end of the first chapter hints at the violence that has occurred before the novel opens. Though Faulkner doesn't completely explain events, we fully expect to return to that violence and to discover its causes. The earliest direct hint of Joanna's death appears in the text a short time later when one of the men at the mill remarks, " 'I don't remember anything out that way big enough to make all that smoke except that Burden house," to which another responds, "Maybe that's what it is ... My pappy says he can remember how fifty years ago folks said it ought to be burned, and with a little human fat meat to start it good" (434). Closer to the truth of events than they know, the men initiate a crime story that produces a likely suspect.[26]

This generic detective-story quality takes its clearest shape in chapter 4, when Byron reveals to Hightower the facts of the murder. Through a calculated strategy, Faulkner defers the revelation of Joanna's death for several pages, hinting first, through Byron's faltering narration, at Christmas's and Brown's involvement in the fire. In Byron's manner of narrating, Faulkner combines a revelation of the murder with an emphasis on Christmas's assumed race. Piquing Hightower's curiosity with several variations on "you had not heard yet" or "you aint heard yet" (456, 464), Byron prompts both a keen interest in the details of the murder and a firm connection between Christmas and the fire. That Faulkner intends for readers to pick up the thread of Christmas's connection to the fire is clear in Hightower's elliptical response. " 'Oh,' " he says. " 'The house that burned yesterday. But I don't see any connection between—Whose house was it? I saw the smoke, myself, and asked a passing negro, but he didn't know" (455–56). Though Christmas is not the "passing negro" Hightower encountered, Faulkner deliberately includes him to draw readers' attention to the racial identity of the criminal. And although Hightower does not yet know the nature of the events at the fire, the reader has begun to—and wants to know more. The mystery plot, as several critics have called it, has been initiated.[27] Readers will wait several chapters to arrive at its full conclusion, though, experiencing first a complicated set of deferrals and expectations. The next chapter, chapter 5, begins with a hint of narrative revelation, introducing us to Christmas only to leave him when he approaches Joanna's house and, we gather, is about to commit the murder. Following the break after chapter 5, which ends with Joe's darkly prophetic refrain "*Something is going to happen. Something is going to happen to me*" (486), but with no further information about the murder, readers spend another five chapters and more than a hundred pages before we "see" Christmas again in the context of the Joanna narrative, and longer than that before we return to the actual crime (in chapter 12).

This elaborate structure deliberately keeps us guessing about the murder. There is a crucial difference to *Light in August*'s version of the mystery though. We do not read Joe's story for the ending in the sense of an ordinary detective or crime novel; we know who is responsible for the fire—or rather, we believe we do—as well as who produces what other maleficence the novel's atmosphere and its narrative workings lead us to expect. If our reading act is not fully driven by a need to "know" as it is in classical detective or mystery narratives, it is nonetheless compelled by something more chilling: an anticipatory unease about the nature of what will occur, both to the victim of the novel's violence and to the criminal.[28] This unsettling, "prospective" aspect of Christmas is implied in his earliest appearance in the novel, in which it is clear that something fatal attaches to him. After Christmas arrives at the mill and is hired, the men take note of his "foreign sounding" name. For Byron at least, it sounds like a warning:

> It seemed to him that none of them had looked especially at the stranger until they heard his name. But as soon as they heard it, it was as though there was something in the sound of it that was trying to tell them what to expect; that he carried with him his own inescapable warning, like a flower its scent or a rattlesnake its rattle. Only none of them had sense enough to recognize it. (422)

As Faulkner conveys it, there is a sense of urgency about Christmas's appearance, a warning "if other men can only read it in time." Faulkner's language, in its inversion of the flower's scent to a warning of danger, enhances the sense of events as unnatural or foreboding that we expect from Christmas's story. Joe Christmas's name connotes as well a pending martyrdom that the events of the novel will both require and explain. As Carolyn Porter puts it, "By virtue of his name . . . Christmas cannot be a minor character, so the reader adjusts his expectations to encompass the possibility of tragedy" (*Seeing and Being*, 244). The "inescapable warning" that Byron attributes to Christmas's name, if lost on the men at the mill, can hardly be lost on readers. The interest Christmas generates at the novel's start, then, carries with it the sense of suspense that surfaces in all mystery stories and on which Faulkner's novel, like others of its genre, depends.[29]

In addition to its practices of mystery or detective fiction, *Light in August* seeks to grip its readers through strategies that reveal Faulkner's willingness to use other popular cultural pleasures and structures of thought. At the same moment that the novel first reveals Joe's mixed-race identity, for instance, it also sensationalizes the crime. In the scene at Hightower's in which Byron relates the events of the murder, he establishes both Joe's potential mixed-race status and the crime's lurid nature. In doing so, he implies that the two facts are related. Joanna Burden was not only murdered, Byron reports, but decapitated. In addition to this grisly fact, Byron's narration includes the detail that the man who discovered her body failed to prevent her head from separating grotesquely from Joanna's body. After pausing significantly (and dramatically) for emphasis, Byron indicates, " 'And he said that what he was scared of happened. Because the cover fell open and she was laying on her side, facing one way, and her head was turned clean around like she was looking behind her' " (466).

As Faulkner presents the crime, its sensational aspect appears necessarily linked to its racial dimension. The detail of Joanna's severed head arrives in the text, that is, only *after* Byron reveals to Hightower what to him is the most important aspect of the story. At the start of his narration he states, " 'I knowed you had not heard yet. I knowed it would be for me to tell you.' " He then cautions Hightower: " 'About Christmas. About yesterday and Christmas. Christmas is part nigger' " (464). That Joe's racial identity precedes any details of the story suggests the importance it plays in Byron's and the town's consciousness. That importance was also, Faulkner understood, present in the consciousness of readers. Scenarios of narrating and listening proliferate in this section of the novel, "stagings" of the act of storytelling that treat, repeatedly, the detail of Christmas's race as the linchpin or high point of their narrative. Highlighting the scenario of narration, Faulkner points to readers' own act of reading or listening to the story of the murder. In so doing, he also emphasizes what, to its listeners, are its most salient elements.[30] Hightower sweats and anguishes over Byron's telling; sitting rapt and immobile, he performs the spell-bound state that the murder story effects on all its audiences (464–72). The narrative of a murder of a white woman by a black man, the novel signals in these moments, is a particularly compelling story.

In Joe Brown's narrative of the crime he also provides a clear indication of the story's allure. After his apprehension by the sheriff, realizing that he himself is a suspect in the case, Brown resorts to what he knows will command his audience's attention. Relating this part of the story to Hightower, Byron explains:

"I reckon he was desperate by then. . . . Because they said it was like he had been saving what he told them next for just such a time as this. Like he had knowed that if it come to a pinch, this would save him . . . 'That's right,' he says. 'Go on. Accuse me. Accuse the white man that's trying to help you with what he knows. Accuse the white man and let the nigger go free. . . .'

'Nigger?' the sheriff said. 'Nigger?'

'It's like he knew he had them then.' " (470)

Byron, of course, is right. Brown does "have" the audience, indicated by the fact that the sheriff immediately suspends his questioning of Brown and sends for the bloodhounds with which to search for Christmas. Faulkner too, though, has succeeded in capturing *his* audience's interest. With his insertion of race into an already sensationalized crime, he makes use of a stereotype by which readers of the novel will be fascinated and drawn in, like Brown's audience for his story. In framing the story of the crime with both Byron's and Brown's narrating, Faulkner highlights the reception of the sensationalized murder story. Hightower's tortured but enthralled attention and the town's outrage at Brown's story (like earlier at the fire) offer models for readers' own responsiveness and fascination. Operating reflexively, these scenarios of storytelling and spectacle also point to readers' investment in the story's sensational elements and their taste for racially exploitative narrative.[31]

In this manner, Faulkner implicates readers in a particular kind of narrative pleasure.[32] As we have seen, this experience had, before *Light in August*'s publication, contributed to the popularity of cultural forms such as mysteries, early films, and other racially inflected novels. Having been led from the story's beginning to expect an act of violence to attach to Joe, we are structurally bound into some of the same reactions and expectations as those evident in Faulkner's various representations of the crowd.[33] One moment in the novel clearly reveals this structural effect as well as the place in it of stereotypical roles such as the violent or threatening black. Late on the night of the murder, Joe is walking down the road from Joanna's when he stops two teenagers in a car. Immediately, the young man and woman are terrified. "[The] two young faces seemed to float like two softcolored and aghast balloons, the nearer one, the girl's, backshrunk in a soft, wide horror" (608). After Joe asks them for a ride, "They said nothing at all, looking at him with that still and curious horror" (608). After "the girl began to make a choked wailing sound," her companion warns her not to give them and their alarm away. The episode suggests the way Joe "automatically" instills fear in the people he encounters. This suggestion is misleading, however. For it is not until after the teenagers drop him off that the text reveals the source of their fear: the gun Joe carried without even knowing it was in his hand (610). Without this knowledge, our reading of the episode and of Joe's "fearsome" appearance follow from the text's construction of a particular way of looking at him.[34] Withholding the knowledge of the gun, Faulkner forces readers to see Joe here as do the teenagers and the community: as a menacing, violent Other.[35]

Light in August and the Police

Important to the novel's presentation of Joe as a racialized and generic threat is, in addition to the violence associated with him, his apparent inscrutability. At the center of a mystery and crime narrative, Faulkner offers a figure notable for his ambiguity and for other characters' inability to know who he is. What is curious, and ultimately revealing, about that lack of knowledge is the way it seems to infect not only the book's characters but its narrator as well. In the second chapter, for instance, Faulkner's narration deliberately constructs an aura of mystery around Christmas, one that functions to incite readers' desire for knowledge. One of the principal means for doing this pivots on the text's construction of a realm of secrecy that surrounds Joe and that seemingly exists beyond even the narrative's ability to trace or "know" him.

After opening with Byron Bunch's focalized narration of Christmas's first appearance at the mill, the chapter gives way to a more ostensibly omniscient narration that furnishes information about Christmas, Joe Brown, and the other men: "[Christmas] quit one Saturday night, without warning, after almost three years. It was Brown informed them that Christmas had quit. Some of the other workers were family men and some were bachelors and they were of different ages and they led a catholic variety of lives" (428). Rather than maintain this omniscience, however, in its next section the narration switches back to presenting a more limited version of events as seen through the eyes of Byron and the other men. Soon after we learn of Christmas leaving the mill, the chapter reveals that the other men suspect Christmas and Brown of bootlegging. At least, they suspect Brown; Christmas's involvement remains uncertain.

> "That's what Brown is doing. I dont know about Christmas. I wouldn't swear to it. But Brown aint going to be far away from where Christmas is at . . ."
> "That's a fact," another said. "Whether Christmas is in it or not, I reckon we aint going to know." (430)

The text, however, does "know" about Christmas's involvement in the bootlegging. And it could easily indicate as much, given the ease with which it has furnished information about when he quit, who reported his quitting, the other men's "catholic variety of lives," and so on. Not doing so, however, plays a significant role in the text's construction of Christmas. For it confers an atmosphere of secrecy around him that contributes to the novel's generic quality, a manufactured uncertainty that continues though the next pages—and that we see comes to afflict the narrator as well as the characters. After reporting that Brown too has quit the mill, the narrator describes him and Christmas driving through town in the new car. "Now and then Christmas would be with him, but not often. And it is now no secret what they were doing. It is a byword among young men and even boys that whiskey can be bought from Brown almost on sight, and the town is just waiting for him to get caught, to produce from his raincoat and offer to sell it to an undercover man. They still do not know for certain if Christmas is connected with it" (432). Though it is "no secret" what Christmas and Brown are doing, the text maintains its ambivalence about precisely the nature of Christmas's (unlike Brown's) doings.

Here we also find the explicit construction of the text's policing and surveilling knowledge, its diegetic "undercover man" that could easily catch the clumsy and obvious Brown but, supposedly, does not know "for certain" if Christmas is involved in bootlegging. In moments such as these, the novel invites readers, along with its representatives of the law, to take up the activity of policing, producing a structure of thought that is on the lookout for criminal activity and that takes Joe as its principal object. Earlier we find a seemingly deliberate construction of mystery around Christmas's activities. Using Byron's consciousness as a point of departure, the narrator establishes a difference between what Byron knew of Christmas when he first appeared at the mill, and what he comes to know later about his business selling liquor. "This is not what Byron knows now [three years later]. This is just what he heard then, what he heard and watched as it came to his knowledge. None of them knew then where Christmas lived and what he was actually doing behind the veil, the screen, of his negro's job at the mill" (424). No one involved in Joe's story, it seems—the townspeople, the narrator, or the reader—knows Christmas's activities definitively. The reader, however, is "onto" him. Constructed as another surveilling force in the narrative, like the town's undercover detective, we already have our suspicions raised about Christmas and his activities behind the "screen" of his job at the mill—activities which, we will not be surprised to learn, appear far more dangerous and lethal than his operation of bootlegging.

The text's willingness to invoke but then question its own omniscience points up a crucial element in *Light in August*'s racial workings. In these operations, Faulkner's novel produces a specific ideological effect, one that has been elaborately detailed, and radically questioned, by D. A. Miller in his study, *The Novel and the Police*. Key to Miller's thinking about the novel form and omniscience are elements that are highly relevant to Faulkner's novel: self-disciplining, social organization, and control. Like many of the characters Miller treats, but more importantly, like the novelistic *function* Miller discusses, Christmas reveals the way *Light in August* relies on a reader's ongoing activity of policing. In textual operations such as those surrounding Christmas, *Light in August* performs in a manner that Miller says is peculiar to the novel form. Making a distinction of power between knowing or seeing on the one hand, and "doing" on the other, Miller's Foucaultian perspective explains the novel genre's effort to conceal its controlling elements such as omniscience. "Power, of course, might seem precisely what the convention of omniscient narration foregoes. Omniscient narration may typically know all, but it can hardly *do* all. . . . Yet by now the gesture of disowning power should seem to define the basic move of a familiar power play, in which the name of power is given over to one agency in order that the function of power may be less visibly retained by the other" (25). Importantly, in appearing to limit and thereby conceal their own omniscience, novels generate the impression for readers that omniscience is not complete—in the world outside of the novel as well as the world within it. As a result, readers are encouraged (falsely, Miller argues) to believe that there is a social space free from surveillance and the normalizing gaze (162). Such a belief allows readers the fantasy that they themselves inhabit that space and thus escape the probing eye of politial and social organizing, extensions for Miller of efforts at social control. "As it forwards its story of social discipline, the narrative also advances the novel's omniscient world. It is frequently hard to distinguish the omniscience from the social control it parallels" (27).

Positing information about Christmas, only to then reveal the limits on what it can say or "know" about him, Faulkner's text thus fashions an appearance of an omniscience that is incomplete. The immediate and simpler consequence of this is that readers assume the knowledge about Christmas that the narration is reluctant to give them; not willing to be duped, we become the superior detective or "undercover man" who, without the text confirming them, arrives at several conclusions about Christmas's actions.

The second and subtler operation that the text performs here is to hide its own surveilling knowledge. Through such operations, *Light in August* performs like other novels that endeavor to pass off or hide their panoptic and surveilling capacity. As Miller suggests, however, this power is nevertheless all-encompassing.[36] Though the disclosure of Christmas's character or his motives is far from complete, at certain points readers are encouraged to see his actions as criminal; such moments give the appearance of the text's full omniscience or "knowledge." This occurs as the result of various pieces of "evidence" (the razor, Joanna's gun, the drums of whiskey Christmas cuts open in the forest, etc). At the novel's outset, however, the text seems unable to furnish clear information about Christmas's doings. Seemingly innocent of its full policing powers, the text implicates the reader in its surveilling operations and masks its own (and thereby also readers') ability to "know." Masking its power in this way, the novel allows its readers, who nevertheless become deeply involved in the policing effort, to assume a similar innocence toward their efforts to pursue or "see" Christmas. The constructed "non-knowledge" on the narrative's part demonstrated here ultimately contributes to one of the novel's deeper effects: its readers' presumption of innocence and detachment from the narrative's violence, in particular its eventual subjugating of Christmas and others.[37]

Prior to its violent outcome and Christmas's apprehending, however, and after several scenes that imply his guilt, Christmas remains "at large," having committed the murder, we're led to believe, and leaving a trail of indications of his involvement in it. Accordingly, once the crime story commences, the novel introduces its other, more explicit representative of police power. Embodied in the person of Sheriff Watt Kennedy, that power initially appears supreme. Kennedy's appearance in the narrative and in the text acts as a signal moment in the novel's drama of omniscience and detection. For the reader's act of looking at (and for) Joe, and the role in both activities of received and stereotyped notions of blackness, is dramatized in the episode of Kennedy's investigation.

Faulkner's handling of this section of the novel is intriguing. Initially his manner of narrating the scene proceeds along conventional lines, describing the fire and the onlookers and, in typically omniscient manner, registering the characters' thoughts and responses. (It is here that we see the crowd's assumptions about Joanna's murder and hoped-for rape.) This omniscience is also evident in the passage's account of Kennedy's mounting frustration with the situation as the narrative moves readily into his state of mind: "The sheriff also stared at the flames with exasperation and astonishment, since there was no scene to investigate. He was not yet thinking of himself as having been frustrated by a human agent. It was the fire. It seemed to him that the fire had been selfborn for that end and purpose" (613). Unaccustomed to being deterred by a "human agent," particularly a criminal one, Kennedy turns his anger, we're told, on the fire, a nonhuman, genuinely uncontrollable element.

Following that temporary moment of frustration, however, Kennedy acts. Using an investigative power and omniscience that parallels that of the text, Kennedy asks a deputy about who is living in the surroundings. As if to parody the all-pervasive power of omniscience as well as its corollary in Kennedy, though, at this explicit moment of investigation the text shows a notable break in its workings.

> "Who lived in that cabin?" [Kennedy asks.]
> "I didn't know anybody did" the deputy said. " 'Niggers, I reckon. She might have had niggers living in the house with her, from what I have heard . . ."
> "Get me a nigger," the sheriff said. The deputy and two or three others got him a nigger. "Who's been living in that cabin?" the sheriff said. (613)

In its pat, simplistic repetition of the sheriff's order, the narrator's account of the action here draws attention to its seemingly unreal (and faintly absurd) sequence of events. Appearing abruptly and immediately, the sought-for "nigger" fulfills Kennedy's command unrealistically, by novelistic terms, and as if by fiat. The unlikeliness of this action seems all the greater in light of the fact that two pages earlier Faulkner's narrator indicates how difficult it would be for a deputy to discover anyone—black or white—in these surroundings: "This was a region of negro cabins and gutted and outworn fields out of which a corporal's guard of detectives could not have combed ten people, man woman or child" (611).

Until the response to Kennedy's command, events had been described realistically. We find, for instance, detailed description of the crowd watching the fire as well as of objects like the fire engine that arrives at the scene ("It was new, painted red, with gilt trim and a handpower siren and a bell gold in color" [611]). Both of the text's discursive modes in this section—omniscience and realism—falter in the exchange between Kennedy and the deputy, however. Out of his frustration with circumstances, Kennedy responds automatically— but in a manner that Faulkner's text marks as such. His knee-jerk reaction to the fact that "there was no scene to investigate" is to "find a nigger." Obligingly, the text does. But the effect of its manner of doing so is to signal the deputy's immediate, reflexive response to Kennedy's order as *un*real, producing a break in the text's otherwise realist operations.

The deputy's response also draws attention to the play of omniscience, offering a correlation between the way the narrative readily offers characters' thoughts and, just as readily, locates and seizes on a suspect. Kennedy's and the text's efficacy here in producing a "nigger" is instructive. For it serves Faulkner's larger interest in this scene and in the novel generally: exposing the habit of thought that takes black guilt as a matter of course. Importantly, it is also reflexive, pointing readers back to their to own activity of surveilling as well as to their willingness, like Kennedy's, to find an object for their looking through the novel's invocation of the popular cultural "Negro," as through Faulkner's manipulation of the mystery genre. That operation is one that the text puts into play in its opening chapters and repeats in its depiction of policing here, producing a search for "knowledge" that in both cases, Faulkner reveals, attaches itself only too readily to the African American.[38]

The Interiorized Carceral Gaze

Though the episode with Kennedy reveals the text's willingness to both invoke and question its own omniscience, other sections of the novel are more circumspect—and therefore more troubling—in their uses of surveilling. We have seen those passages that provide information about Joe's activities while refraining from naming them, the result of which is that readers perform the act of labeling him guilty. In such moments of masking its omniscience, the novel also conceals its narrative's ongoing effort to identify or know Christmas, efforts which, in turn, more fully implicate the reader in the novel's policing activity. This process of tracing begins early in the novel, in fact, and its covert nature is evident in depictions of the earliest periods of Joe's life. Faulkner's narration of Joe's childhood at the orphanage, for instance, produces several effects of silent, anonymous, but ultimately oppressive monitoring. In a clear example of one of them, the description of the orphanage is notable both for its carceral overtones and its optical metaphor.

Knows remembers believes a corridor in a big long garbled cold echoing building of dark red brick sootbleakened by more chimneys than its own, set in a grassless cinderstrewnpacked compound surrounded by smoking factory purlieus and enclosed by a ten foot steel-and-wire fence like a penitentiary or a zoo, where in random erratic surges, with sparrowlike childtrebling, orphans in identical and uniform blue denim in and out of remembering but in knowing constant as the bleak walls, the bleak windows where in rain soot from the yearly adjacenting chimneys streaked like black tears. (487)

Despite its imagistic quality, Faulkner's prose in this passage reveals much about the facility where Joe is housed. Though darkened and blurred by "tears," the eyes/windows of the orphanage cast a constant unwavering gaze on the orphans below, an impression furthered by the suggestion of animals looked at by spectators in a zoo or inmates guarded in a prison. It seems hardly necessary to point out that at the earliest point in his childhood that the novel gives us, Christmas is placed within an institution and social machinery that serves a normalizing function of discipline. The orphans' "identical and uniform blue denim" and their enclosure within a prison-like environment is only the outward manifestation of a circumstance that, as subsequent events in the orphanage prove, is concerned with establishing a homogenized social order.[39] Hines's appearance in the narrative a short time later only confirms the role of the orphanage in maintaining a disciplining, monitory action.

Readers as well, through an elaborate device on Faulkner's part, are drawn into the orphanage's invisible and monitoring center. In a textual operation that occurs in the paragraph following the orphanage's description, we are secured in a position within both the constructed space of the building and, I would argue, the interiorized "space" of the narrative. In addition to the ongoing surveilling position that we come to occupy as readers of the novel's mystery, it is this constructed space of internal surveilling that deepens the novel's work of making readers into monitors. Following his impressionistic but external description of the orphanage, Faulkner moves immediately (and rather effortlessly) to its inside and to an account of a very young Joe. "In the quiet and empty corridor, during the quiet hour of early afternoon, he was like a shadow, small even for five years, sober and quiet as a shadow" (487). Again we find Joe's presence rendered in the vague, phantom-like language that characterizes him generally. Yet unlike other passages depicting Joe as an adult, Christmas here is ultimately detectable: "Another in the corridor could not have said just when and where he vanished, into what door, what room. But there was no else in the corridor at this hour" (487). No one, that is, besides the narrator—and the reader. Vacating the space of the orphanage and the corridor of other characters, Faulkner nevertheless "fills" it with the narrator's presence and gaze. Doing so effects the reader's ability, along with the omniscient narrator's, to know to where Joe has vanished, "into what door, what room." Following him from this furtive glimpse in the abandoned hallway, the reader is taken into the dietician's closet, a space constructed as private but to which we have privileged access. As the episode with the dietician ensues,

Faulkner furnishes several details that complete the sense of Joe occupying a hidden, yet secretly accessible space. Crouching among her shoes and "suspended soft womangarments," Joe overhears the sounds of scuffling feet, the dietician's hurried warnings, and, importantly, "the turn of the key in the door" (488).

Granted access to the locked bedroom, as we were to the abandoned corridor, the reader is ushered into the orphanage's innermost reaches. Aligned with the centralized, panoptic power of the institution, readers are thus able to watch Joe even, or especially, when he thinks he is not being seen. Faulkner makes this breakdown of Joe's presumed "invisible" position explicit, of course, in the next pages, when the dietician discovers him. Following her discovery of Joe, she solicits help from Hines, the novel's supreme figure of violent and watchful disciplining. As she says, " 'You've been watching him too,' " (492), a statement that only hints at the extent and malevolence of Hines's gaze (evident most unsettlingly in his return to the narrative in Mottstown to witness Christmas's execution). Readers too, however, have already been structured into the activity of monitoring Joe by the alignment between the gazes of the narrator, the dietician, and Hines. We are also positioned with what has been called the "institutional gaze," that is, one maintained by carceral institutions such as the orphanage, factory, or prison and that, like the panoptic view Faulkner here describes, turns inward.[40] As the dietician says to Hines, " 'You never sit here [in his chair] except when the children are outdoors. But as soon as they come out, you bring this chair here to the door and sit in it where you can watch them' " (493). When Hines is "inside," in the orphanage's private spaces, we may assume he performs his normalizing and fanatical vigil. As the dietician indicates, Hines follows the children outside only to maintain it. Institutions like the orphanage and its embodiment in Hines, then, perform an action that is repeated in the narrator's acts of monitoring events that take place within its walls—an activity that Faulkner's text, in turn, requires of its readers.

That the description of the orphanage in *Light in August* resembles that of the Court of Chancery in *Bleak House* seems hardly incidental.[41] For the orphanage sections of Faulkner's novel introduce a range of issues about Joe's childhood and about his "place" both in the novel and in the society it depicts that share many of the concerns of Dickens's fiction.[42] Key to this aspect of *Light in August* is the question of Joe's social place, represented by his difficulty belonging to any family. In his analyses of *Bleak House* and of *Oliver Twist*,

D. A. Miller points to the relationship between the establishment of carceral institutions and the breakdown of traditional family norms. "After all, what brought carceral institutions into being in the first place were lapses in proper management of the family: in its failure to constitute itself (the problem of illegitimate or orphaned children and the institutional solution of foundling hospitals and baby farms)" (*The Novel and the Police*, 59). Readers of Dickens come to sense (falsely, Miller argues) a feeling of their own freedom from carceral and normative constraints, a feeling structured into the experience of reading him. "The often ferocious architecture that immured the inmates of a carceral institution seemed to immure the operations practiced on them there as well, and the thick, spiked walls, the multiple gateways, the attendants and the administrators that assured the confinement of those within seemed equally to provide for the protectedness of those without, including most pertinently the novelist and his readers" (58).

It is a similar "protection" for its readers that, ultimately, *Light in August*'s regulating and panoptic operations will ensure. In Miller's view, the protectedness that privileges the family's workings and associates the subject's freedom with it merely switched the agency of surveillance and control from carceral physical institutions to families: "The topic of the carceral in Dickens . . . works to secure the effect of difference between, on the one hand, a confined, institutional space in which power is violently exercised on collectivized subjects, and on the other, a space of 'liberal society,' generally determined as a free, private, and individual domain and practically specified as the family" (59). That semblance of freedom and privacy, Miller indicates, nevertheless requires the subject's submission.[43]

It is in such familial and domestic efforts to contain Joe that *Light in August* shows the continuity of the carceral work of the institution begun at the orphanage. Joe Christmas is a character who, as all of *Light in August* testifies, cannot belong to any definition of the "family." As the sections of the novel set in the orphanage as well as the history of his adoption by McEachern and the story of the Hineses at the end of the novel make clear, Joe's plight is, above all, solitary. Questions of belonging and social identity vex him throughout his life, a problematic struggle for family that is initiated by his rejection by Hines. As such, Joe's story illustrates the way the failure to belong to the family, identified in the novel as both the nuclear Christian family (and epitomized, if ironically, by Byron, Lena, and her child) and the social community represented by Jefferson (or even by the African-American community that Christmas also fails to join), results in ever more strenuous and violent efforts to discipline the subject. The preoccupation in *Light in August* with watching or surveilling Christmas begins with practices put into play when he is quite young and in the orphanage, but it extends to social pressures exerted outside of the carceral institution—by families and social ordering—that are just as coercive as those within it.

The Limits of Observation: Christmas's Aestheticizing

The outcome of the efforts at disciplining Joe is made pointedly clear at the novel's end. Having run away from his adopted family, the McEacherns, and refusing what he sees as another institutional form of subjugation (Joanna Burden's efforts to educate him at the Negro college), in the final chapters Joe seems to give up resisting. He allows himself to be captured on the street in Mottstown, and though he flees the law again, it is clear that Christmas is resigned to his fate. Giving himself over to the state apparatus and its representative in another policing eye, Christmas experiences the full weight of his society's disciplining practices. Disturbingly, the text's manner of depicting that discipline—as with the orphanage—places readers in the same position as those exercising it.

One of the novel's final invocations of the gaze involves Christmas's executioner, Percy Grimm. On the day before Christmas escapes and on which Grimm mounts his vigil—organized, ostensibly, in order to maintain civic order—a rumor spreads through Jefferson about a pending decision on Christmas's case by a special Grand Jury. Though until this point Grimm's squad has lacked conviction about their role in the affair, the evoking of an unseen but watchful authority helps assure them. "About the square it was already known that the special Grand Jury would meet tomorrow. Somehow the very sound of the two words with their evocation secret and irrevocable and something of a hidden and unsleeping and omnipotent eye watching the doings of men, began to reassure Grimm's men in their own makebelieve" (736). The notion of an invisible authority "watching the doings of men" here is consoling, reassuring the men that their "makebelieve" martial and policing games are supported by a larger state power. (As the day goes on and Grimm's notoriety grows, people in town assume that he is a "[s]pecial officer sent by the governor" [737].) In the light of my earlier discussion of the ways in which the town's collective fantasy resembles the experience of cinema, it is significant that Grimm mounts his vigil at the same time of night "as the picture show emptied" (736). Without the movies to organize and direct the townspeople's gaze, Grimm and his civilian patrol serve as a substitute. The alliance here is troubling. For as I have suggested, readers too have been involved in several sustained acts of "watching." In particular, as we have noted, they engage in a protracted politial surveillance of Joe as well as in a popular cultural habit of vision. Our activity of looking, then, shares something with that of the policing eyes of Grimm or of the townspeople, as they displace their own acts of gazing (at Christmas and at the picture show) to him.

In addition, our own act of "looking," not only at only Christmas but at the novel generally, resembles the omnipotent eye of the Grand Jury. Its way of overseeing all "the doings of men" is similar, that is, to our overseeing the novel's events. For the narrative and scopic reach of *Light in August*, incorporating multiple story lines, perspectives, and temporal registers, is among the broadest and most encompassing of Faulkner's novels. In its constant ability to shift focus, to move back in time through often extensive flashbacks (as with Joe's childhood and upbringing) or to begin a new narrative line (as with Hightower's training at the seminary, Joanna's family history, or even Grimm's and the furniture salesman's backgrounds), the novel gives the impression of a narrative reach that is seemingly inexhaustible. Anything and everything can be covered by the narrative's constantly alternating and active modernist "gaze." Searching for Christmas as the novel's mystery format encourages, and anticipating his punishment or tragedy as the novel's opening prescribes, readers perform an act of looking at and integrating events that resembles Faulkner's reference at the novel's end to a punishing, encompassing, all-seeing law, "watching the doings of men." As such, our perspective is aligned with the law's or with its manifestation in Percy Grimm and the novel's other representatives of policing.

As Faulkner's reference to the picture show suggests, however, Grimm's and the town's treatment of Christmas also recalls cinematic acts of looking and the fantasies sustaining them. We have already seen the way the crowd at Joanna's fire demonstrates a fantastic, spectatorial habit of thought about race and sexual violence. Like the townspeople's attitudes about black rape, Grimm's final act of castrating Christmas similarly reveals a white racist hysteria and follows a popular cultural model. Faulkner's treatment of Percy Grimm suggests a specific filmic and historical allusion. Like the ending of *Light in August*, the original version of *Birth of a Nation* included a scene of the purported rapist Gus being castrated by one of the Klansmen. Though excised in later versions of the film, this scene epitomized the fear of black sexuality that the film both pandered to and produced.[44] Although this scene was cut from later versions of the movie, Faulkner's novel explicitly includes the act of castrating Christmas, as well as Grimm's pathological belief in the racist myth of black potency that we've seen subtended popular models. Declaring "Now you'll let white women alone, even in hell," (742), Grimm voices the belief that Griffith's film both drew on and promulgated.[45]

Unlike *Birth of a Nation,* Faulkner's novel attempts to critique the racist hysteria evident in acts of vigilantism through its depiction of Grimm and the Jefferson crowd. The force of this critique inheres in Faulkner's willingness to implicate his text and his readers in its several acts of objectification and aestheticizing as well as to reveal to readers those attitudes and habits of thought. At the same time, however, Faulkner's effort at critique is compromised. This is one reason why the ending of the novel is so particularly unsettling. Having participated in the textual formation of Joe as an object of observation, we have, by the point at which Grimm pursues him, also participated in the imagining of him as a menacing threat. Effectively, then, our own attitudes are bound into Grimm's chase and the book's outcome. Judith Wittenberg refers to the novel's willingness to expose its own and the reader's use of received notions of blackness in a way that speaks to this point about the reader and Grimm: "[W]hile the novel clearly exposes (in order to indict) the pernicious (though virtually inevitable) effects of the prevailing codes, its structure and other aspects of the narrative method to some degree subtly participate in the process of 'framing' [Christmas]" ("Race in *Light in August,*" 153). These "pernicious" and "inevitable" effects of the prevailing code include the racist hysteria that drives Grimm, and they pertain to the social terms with which the novel's community struggles to define Joe. They also, however, as Wittenberg suggests, apply to readers' efforts to understand or to "know" who Christmas is: what she refers to as "the process of framing."

I would argue that the process of framing and fixing, manifested in the reader's desire to know Christmas, is produced by the narrative as well as by what readers bring to their experience with it. Because Christmas remains stubbornly resistant to efforts to place him, including his own, he prompts the impulse to label and identify him all the more. As a result, readers too participate in the categorizing effort.[46] James Snead also remarks on this tendency, indicating that "like Jefferson, readers seem compelled to supply anything that makes Christmas significant, even what is not in the text. It is as revealing as it is embarrassing to consider how many readers fall into the same racist mentality as Jefferson" (*Figures of Division*, 88). Drawing on some, but by no means all of the sources for racial typing by evoking images from popular culture, Faulkner encourages readers to fashion their own (stereotypical) definition for who Joe is.

Moreover, our own desire to follow the story, even without our knowing it, produces a coercive impulse that exercises itself over Christmas's body. Snead claims that "the town wishes to capture and confine Joe's meaning more than his actual body" (89). Though Snead separates the recoverable "meaning" of Joe as a person in Jefferson, or as a character in a novel, from his carceral, disciplined body, I would submit that they are in fact more closely connected. For by the end of the novel, the homologies between the reader and the town and between Joe's "meaning" and his body are, effectively, complete. Considered in light of what we see in Joe's death and the position of the reader in regard to it, as well as in the short span of text that follows, questions about what "coercion effects" the novel produces seem applicable to both Joe's body and to his meaning.

This is nowhere clearer than at the moment of Christmas's dying. Looking down on his bleeding and disfigured body, we are positioned with the men who stand above Christmas and for whom, as for us, Christmas's death is "apotheosized."[47] Reading of the way the "black blood seemed to rush like a released breath. It seemed to rush out of his pale body like the rush of sparks from a rising rocket," we see an image of Christmas dying that is supposed to "rise soaring into their memories forever and ever. They are not to lose it, in whatever peaceful valleys, beside whatever placid and reassuring streams of old age . . . they will contemplate old disasters and newer hopes" (743). Faulkner's language gives the impression of Christmas dying as a highly wrought, vividly striking image—an impression that, while attributed to the onlookers in the scene, clearly registers for readers as well. Despite this vividness, however—or in a way, because of it—we, along with the "they" of this passage, see Christmas's death as an aestheticized, and therefore distanced, event. It is this distancing that provides the passage with its crucial aspect of affect, or more importantly, its lack thereof. In their position vis-à-vis Christmas's death, readers experience something of its (perhaps unintended) effect of calmness or soothing; we are not shocked or viscerally affected by the violence because we are separated from it by a particularly imagistic prose. Unlike a more graphic depiction of Christmas's wounding, one that might inscribe visceral, nerve-stimulating (and thus threatening) shocks to the reader's body, novelistic practices such as those Faulkner uses here inculcate in readers a sense of security and even perverse comfort in the face of a violent act.

D. A. Miller's discussion of what he calls the "sensation novel" helps clarify my point about the "non-affect" of Faulkner's depiction of Christmas dying. Unlike the distancing effects we see with Christmas's death, "the sensation novel . . . produces repeated and undeniable evidence—'on the nerves'—that we are perturbed by what we are watching. We remain unseen, of course, but not untouched: our bodies are rocked by the same 'positive personal shocks' as the characters' are said to be" (*The Novel and the Police,* 162–63). Because none of the characters in Christmas's death scene are described as experiencing "shocks," including and especially Christmas himself (despite his mutilation), the scene produces what I see as a decidedly unphysical response on the part of both characters and readers. Even Christmas's inexplicable silence, which envelops the entire scene, including the sound of the siren that "pass[es] out of the realm of hearing," contributes to the passage's abstract and unreal quality.[48] Readers may well remember "it," the image of Christmas dying, along with the characters in the scene. Yet they will not identify with it or register it as an experience of pain. As with other events in the narrative, we as subjects "see" the novel perform the act of Joe's murder; unlike Joe, we never feel ourselves to be those events' violated, objectified victims.

This effect of aestheticizing and "sealing off" readers from Christmas in his death scene does much to distance them from an otherwise shattering event. It also reveals a more general aspect of Faulkner's novel. The conclusion of the narrative and its "search" for Joe, like that of other novels that depict an exercise of social ordering, fashions a supposedly comfortable and thereby powerful place for readers. Positioned outside of several acts of violence committed on social subjects who, like Joe, are deemed "different" by the Jefferson community, readers are protected from feeling the full weight of those violations. Miller's argument about this aspect of novels has particular relevance in light of Faulkner's active soliciting of readers' involvement in the plot, as well as that plot's various acts of physical and social violence. Though we take part in the narrative's ongoing activity of watching and detecting Joe, the tendency of *Light in August* to conceal its own panoptic power, like that of other novels, results in the readers' comfort in feeling that they are not involved in such aggressive acts of correction and policing. More importantly, because of our position constructed as "external" to these events, we are not vulnerable to their being visited upon us. In an extended passage, Miller describes novelistic actions that are uncomfortably close to those Faulkner's text performs repeatedly, in particular those that extend the initially violating act of looking:

> Novel reading takes for granted the existence of a space in which the reading subject remains safe from the surveillance, suspicion, reading, and rape of others. Yet this privacy is always specified as the freedom to read about characters who oversee, suspect, read, and rape one another. It is not just that, strictly private subjects, we read about violated, objectified subjects but that, in the very act of reading about them, we contribute largely to constituting them as such. We enjoy our privacy in the act of watching privacy being violated, in the act of watching that is already itself a violation of privacy. Our most intense identification with characters never blinds us to our ontological privilege over them: they will never be reading about *us*. It is built into the structure of the Novel that every reader must realize the fantasy of the liberal subject, who imagines himself free from the surveillance that he nonetheless sees operating everywhere around him. (162)

In its willingness to point to characters' acts of watching Joe or of Joe watching himself, as well as moments such as the town's reassurance at the thought of the overseeing state apparatus, Faulkner's novel foregrounds the activity of looking. In so doing, it also implies that activity's violent or suppressive nature. Readers' acts of looking upon violated subjects, particularly upon characters who, like Joe, are defined as marginal and therefore in need of "discipline," occur throughout the novel. Punctuating its action are suggestions and instances of beating, rape, murder, and mutilation. Joanna may not have been raped before she was killed (we cannot know), but the townspeople imagine that she was; Hightower, early in his life in Jefferson, is beaten unconscious and tied to a tree in the woods because of a perception that he is gay; the "nigger" whom Kennedy interrogates at the fire scene is whipped; Joe beats and kicks the black woman whom his friends have already assaulted sexually; he nearly beats to death the prostitute who fails to respond to his announcement that he is black. Finally, and most obviously, Joe himself is repeatedly and viciously attacked (by the white and black men he challenges on his fifteen-year journey), whipped (by McEachern), beaten (by Max), and lastly, murdered and mutilated by Percy Grimm. Though we are witness to all of these acts, we are maintained in a position of "innocence" outside of them and from which we are, so we imagine, safe from a role in their perpetrating. As Miller suggests in the above quotation, performing the act of watching allows us the liberal fantasy that we ourselves are not violated or surveilled.

Most importantly for my consideration, Faulkner racializes this situation. Following Miller's account of the creation by novelists of the reader's "liberal subject position," it is crucial to indicate the way in which, in the case of *Light in August*, the reader of the novel is effectively coded as white in a world in which whites watch bad things happen to various "others." This is one of the determining properties and—alarmingly—"pleasures" of Faulkner's novel. Witness to repeated acts of brutality, all of which move ineluctably toward Joe's execution, we are made secure in the knowledge that such acts will never be performed upon us. Possessed of an all-encompassing knowledge and, additionally, of a clearly defined subject position from which to integrate the novel's disparate elements, we remain at a safe remove from them. We know or are encouraged to believe we will never be haunted by the existential anxiety that damns Joe and that contributes to his confusion and his crime. We know, furthermore, that we enjoy a freedom from the effects and violations that the novel exercises on its several victims, each of which are "outsiders" to the community of Jefferson.[49] Though Faulkner's text is critical of that community, it nevertheless places readers on the "inside" of the circle the community forms, "looking" with them at Christmas, Joanna, Hightower, and the novel's African Americans.

There is one other outsider to the community of Jefferson. In her very immunity from violence and violation, however, and in her apparent mobility and freedom, Lena Grove offers a final reflection on the novel's treatment of Joe. For in Lena's and Byron's open-ended traveling at the novel's end, we find a clear contrast to the violent "fixing" to which Christmas, throughout the novel, is subjected. Roaming the countryside and aided by people they encounter like the furniture salesman, Lena and Byron are allowed to wander freely. Even Lena's socially transgressive circumstances as a single mother traveling with a man who is not her husband do not, in the end, prohibit her mobility. Faulkner ends *Light in August*, that is, on a particularly optimistic note, as well as through the comic framing of the furniture dealer's narrative. And he does so with a scenario that, unlike the ending of Joe's narrative, clearly invites readers' identification. After disappearing from the carriage on which he and Lena have been traveling, Byron doggedly tells Lena when he rejoins her, " 'I done come too far to quit now' "—to which she amiably responds,

" 'Aint nobody never said for you to quit' " (774). Encouraged in this way by Lena to continue with her in her journeying, Byron, we understand, will never quit. Nor, as the salesman indicates, will Lena. " '[S]he had got along all right this far, with folks taking good care of her. And so I think she had just made up her mind to travel a little further and see as much as she could' " (774).

As will, by implication, the novel's readers. Setting off to an unknown future, Lena will continue to enjoy the kindness of strangers and Byron's solicitude. Gesturing toward an open and potentially limitless road for his couple, Faulkner's ending also proffers readers an enticing prospect. " 'My, my. A body does get around,' " concludes Lena serenely in the book's last line. In the case of Lena and Byron, a body does get around. She will be free to move and, to a surprising degree, to define herself as she wishes. Readers too, especially the novel's white-coded, liberal subjects, are manifestly able to "get around," free of both textual operations and socializing stigmas that seek to situate, objectify, or define them. Through the book's open-ended conclusion especially, they are encouraged to share Lena's liberating sense of motion.

Other bodies in the novel's world, however, particularly Christmas's, do not get around. Despite his fifteen-year wandering and generic, mysterious elusiveness, Christmas is rigorously fixed from the start of the novel within a collective social gaze that includes all the characters he encounters and, through various textual strategies, the reader as well. Faulkner's text indicates this frankly in a number of instances, a fact that Lena's coda serves to emphasize. In addition, Joe evokes the mass-cultural image of "Negro" that he resembles and that is also "watched" by the anonymous spectators, readers, and consumers outside of the novel. Black bodies, mulatto bodies—suspected or distrusted bodies like Joe's—fall, for the other characters in the novel and for its readers, under the rigid classifying systems of a racially obsessed southern society or bear the weight of expectations generated by a pervasive and stereotyping mass culture. Scrutinized, surveyed, violated, and entered—yet at the same time spectralized, imaged, de-realized, and aestheticized—Joe Christmas's body, throughout the novel but especially and inevitably at his death, remains frighteningly still.

CHAPTER THREE

"Some Trashy Myth of Reality's Escape"

Romance, History, and Film Viewing in *Absalom, Absalom!*

"I must be in the story (verisimilitude needs me), but I must also be *elsewhere:* an imaginary slightly detached, this is what I demand of the film."
— ROLAND BARTHES, "Upon Leaving the Movie Theatre"

In the middle of narrating her chapter of *Absalom, Absalom!* Rosa Coldfield describes herself watching the "*miragy antics of men and women*" (134). Throughout her life, she claims, she has watched and seen the world as something dream-like or unreal, a "mirage" or a projection of her own longing, not a place inhabited by living people or concrete matter. "*I displaced no air,*" she declares, "*and so acquired all I knew of that light and space in which people moved and breathed as I . . . might have gained conception of the sun from seeing it through a piece of smoky glass*" (120). The filter through which Rosa observes events in which she does not participate, figured here as a piece of "smoky glass," is also her romantic and sentimentalizing sensibility. Rosa asserts her belief in the "*might-have-been which is more true than truth*" (118) and refers to herself as "*I the dreamer*" (116) and as "*I [who] dwelt in the dream*" (122).

In the illusory, dream-like world that enthralls Rosa, Confederate soldiers possess the stature of larger-than-life heroes, and Thomas Sutpen is a "demoniac," fantastic figure. She particularly romanticizes Charles Bon, whom she admits never having seen and who may be a product of her imagination. "*I never saw [his body],*" she tells us, describing Bon's burial. "*Why did I not invent, create it?*" (122). In her treatment of Bon as an exotic paramour and of Sutpen as the fateful "curse" on her family, Jefferson, and the South, Rosa reveals a pattern of thought that personalizes and romanticizes southern history rather than considering it critically. She reveals a similar perspective in her attitude toward Quentin as a southern gentleman, demanding that he escort her out to Sutpen's Hundred and expecting him to carry a pistol with which to defend her, and toward Judith as a southern lady. Judith, Rosa asserts, could not have been expected to work and take care of herself when Rosa lived with her and Clytie because she had been "*handicapped by . . . [that] which in her was ten generations of iron prohibition*" (129)—a reference to the Old South myth of gentility that prohibited work and self-sufficiency for a class of southern women to which, she believed, Judith belonged.

In chapter 5, Faulkner combines Rosa's romantic attitudes toward the South with a uniquely abstract and hypnotic voice. Rendered almost entirely in italics, Rosa's chapter presents problems concerning both its audience (to whom is Rosa speaking?) and its "source" (when does Rosa deliver this speech and under what circumstances?). Ostensibly free-floating and seemingly disembodied, Rosa's voice is attached to no clearly situated, "physical" narrator as are the voices of the novel's other character-narrators (Shreve and Quentin in the dorm room, Mr. Compson on his porch, Sutpen sitting on a log with Quentin's grandfather). As such, Rosa's voice exists in a particularly murky and ill-defined narrational "space." This shadowy ground for Rosa's narration is mirrored in her voice itself. At turns obscure, rhapsodic, and dense, Rosa's speech makes it difficult to "see" the object of her narration; we are often more aware of the difficulties of her language than we are of what exactly she is describing. This difficulty is related to Rosa's romanticizing attitude. Her monologue, like other manifestations of romantic thought, idealizes and modifies the world she sees: the confederate soldiers are not the crusading, chivalrous knights she admires (and whom she lionizes in hundreds of odes); Thomas Sutpen is not an agent of Satan (she says of him "*that only through the blood of our men and the tears of our women could [God] stay this demon*" [8]). Similarly, the language Rosa uses to narrate her portion of the Sutpen story never fully conveys what occurred, but rather gives a highly wrought impression of Rosa's state of mind. And this high style has a particular impact. What we experience with Faulkner's prose (throughout the novel, but especially with Rosa) is a narcotic, abstract, or surreal effect, such that the world of the novel appears exotic or strange and resists "objective" representation. Language and a romanticizing tendency, then, come together in Rosa's section, demonstrating a habit of mind and a commensurate form of expression that similarly give reality the lie.

Rosa's language and her romanticizing narrative have much in common with another representational system of which Faulkner was aware and that he sought, in much of his 1930s writing, to critique: film. References in Faulkner's fiction to film and Hollywood abound, and several critics have traced Faulkner's problematic relationship to cinema as both a commercial and artistic medium.[1] I propose a reading of Faulkner's relationship to the movie industry that shows the way that several aspects of film practice and viewing, above all the relationship to the South's past that historical film produced, inform his strategies in *Absalom, Absalom!* In short, this understanding allowed Faulkner to use his novel to critique the reified, commodified relationship to history that he saw early film encourage.

The novels *Pylon* and *If I Forget Thee, Jerusalem,* for instance, each contain pejorative references to the influence, infection, or "contagion" of the film industry.[2] In addition to the stories discussed in my introduction, "Dry September" and "Golden Land," other short stories from the 1930s, such as "Turnabout" (1932) and "All the Dead Pilots," (1932) suggest Faulkner's critical awareness of the film medium and industry.[3] In a letter from this period that was typical of Faulkner's correspondence about his film work, he lamented to one of his agents: "The trouble with the movies is not so much the time I waste [in Hollywood] but the time it takes me to recover" from the city and, supposedly, its products' excesses (*SL,* 90).

Perhaps most significantly for my consideration of *Absalom,* in the period in which he first indicated having conceived the story for this novel, Faulkner's disdain for the film industry was also evident in his description of a project that amounted to a critique of Hollywood practices and materials. In a letter sent from Oxford, Mississippi, to the editor, Harrison Smith, dated in February of 1934, Faulkner mentions a novel he intends to call *Dark House* that would be about "the violent breakup of a family from 1860 to about 1910" and that uses Quentin Compson as a narrator (*SL* 78). The next extant letter shows Faulkner writing about an idea for another new project:

> I am going to work on something else right away, though I don't know what yet. I have a plan, a series to be called
> A Child's Garden of Motion Picture Scripts

They will be a burlesque of the sure-fire movies and plays, or say a burlesque of
how the movies would treat standard plays and classic plays and novels, written
in the modified form of a movie script. (*SL*, 79)

Blotner indicates that Faulkner never completed his idea for a "burlesque of
sure-fire movies and plays." And Bruce Kawin asserts that Faulkner "abandoned" this project in the process of writing *Pylon*, a novel that, in Kawin's
words, "bled off some of the incoherent and frenzied energy that might have
ruined *Absalom*" ("Faulkner's Film Career," 175).

Film's Immanence

Bloodletting notwithstanding, I disagree with Kawin that Faulkner got the
idea for a critique of cinema out of his system as he prepared to finish *Absalom*.
Rather, I contend, Faulkner's ideas about the film industry were sharpening
throughout the period in which he worked on *Absalom*, which included the
completion of *Pylon*. Though *Absalom* is not written in the form of a movie
script, as Faulkner describes his project above, it is nevertheless a "burlesque"
of standard film treatments of the South. One clue to this aspect of the novel
is a highly suggestive mention in it of film and narrative. The episodic, violent nature of Charles Etienne Saint-Valery Bon's life after leaving Sutpen's
Hundred—corresponding to periods of stasis and recovery following his ritual
beatings—are compared by the narrator to a "succession of periods of utter
immobility like a broken cinema film" (170). Years later, Faulkner would again
invoke film to describe a narrative effect when, referring to *The Sound and the
Fury*, he wrote in a letter to Malcolm Cowley that the reasons for the novel's
delayed reception was that it resembled "the homemade, the experimental, the
first moving picture projector—warped lens, poor light, clumsy gears, and
even a bad screen—which had to wait eighteen years for the lens to clear, the
light to steady, the gears to mesh and smooth" (quoted in Blotner 1974, 2:1216).

Faulkner's use of a broken cinema as a metaphor in these instances is
revealing, for it suggests a relationship between his self-consciousness about
his literary experiment—his fractured, disjointed narrative structures—and his
understanding of the apparatus of film. It also demonstrates that Faulkner's
sense of his modernism, or the terms he used to describe it, were connected to
his awareness of other new cultural forms. In the decade in which he spent
several extended periods as a screenwriter in Hollywood (including positions

at MGM, Universal Studios, and Twentieth-Century Fox), Faulkner gained a familiarity with the Hollywood product from working within the industry. In *Absalom, Absalom!*, a novel that occupied him throughout the period of his scriptwriting, he found a means to engage his cultural criticism and his literary practice concurrently.

In addition to the understanding of Hollywood he gained working as a screenwriter, Faulkner's view of film was informed by the silent movies he had seen as a child.[4] Among the earliest film narratives, cinematic representations of the South from the period in which Faulkner grew up demonstrated a manner of representing its materials which, like Rosa's account of the Sutpen narrative, was highly romanticized and unreal. The earliest film narratives about the South presented an idealized plantation-era period that was a product of the filmmakers' imagination but that audiences embraced as real. This tradition began with films like Edwin Porter's adaptation of *Uncle Tom's Cabin* in 1903, which glossed over the novel's more severe message about slavery, or David Ward Griffith's "His Trust" (1911) and "His Trust Fulfilled" (1911)—films that depicted doting blacks faithful to their masters throughout the Civil War, repelling Union troops or forging their own Confederate regiments. Later movies such as *The Fighting Coward* (1924) or *Hearts in Dixie* (1929) similarly offered an image of benevolent race relations in which slaves labored in the fields while singing happily and without the presence of an overseer.[5]

Towering above these pictures in its historical revisionism as well as its impact on cinema, however, was D. W. Griffith's *Birth of a Nation*. Monumentally influential, it was a film that Faulkner almost certainly saw and one that not only provided a basis for commercial cinema's approach to southern history but also furnished the semiology and "grammatical" systems of narrative film.[6] *Birth* had an impact on the development of film history and thus on American cultural history that it would be difficult to overstate. In its depiction of the end of Reconstruction and the South's redemption by the White Knights of Christ coming "to the rescue of the downtrodden South,"[7] *Birth* evinced a habit of thought about the region that later films emulated and that provided one of the earliest and most pervasive examples of film's capacity to alter southern history. Griffith's opus demonstrated a range of forward-looking, innovative techniques in storytelling that enthralled audiences but that contrasted with the film's regressive ideology, an irony that helped it accomplish its more backward-looking goal: the seducing of audiences to the film's sympathetic and nostalgic vision of the South.

Marshalling developments in visual narrative that he had gathered from earlier films—such as varied camera angles and distances, camera movement, location shooting, depth of field, the juxtaposition of events separated in space (through parallel editing), the "subjectivizing" of time (slowing or accelerating real time to dramatic ends), the eyeline match or 180° rule, cutting to movement, variations in shot duration, split-screen, and masking—Griffith produced a film of unparalleled expressiveness and impact. Several of these techniques are now standard practices of narrative cinema and generally go unrecognized by audiences long used to seeing them. Griffith, however, discovered these uses in the first years of learning how to effectively communicate with an audience and tell a story on film. Shooting outdoors and on location was for Griffith, as it would become for directors ever since, a key element of *Birth*'s efforts at realism.[8] Keeping the camera on one side of an axis while shooting (the 180° rule) allowed a consistent background across different shots and thus a more uniform context for dramatic events. Likewise, maintaining the direction of action from right to left of the screen, or left to right, keeps viewers oriented spatially within a narrative sequence. (Avant-garde or experimental films revel in violating these sorts of "natural" visual strategies.) Varying the distance of the camera from the action, as in the close-up, to allow more intimate expression or a focus on only a portion of the action in a scene, was uncommon before Griffith's exploration. Perhaps the innovation that *Birth* exemplifies and for which Griffith is most well known is the variation in shot duration. In the famous climax of the film, he juxtaposes a more and more rapid cutting of shorter and shorter shots of the Klan with shots of the Old Colonel and other white characters defending themselves in the cabin. An example as well of parallel editing, this section of the film galvanized audiences by the sheer force of its accelerating visual rhythm, drawing otherwise neutral viewers into the drama of the "ride to the rescue" by the Klan.

One particular sequence demonstrates the new "language" Griffith used to create film narrative—as well as his efforts to instruct audiences in how to read it. Early in the picture Griffith masks, or darkens, a portion of the frame, revealing in its corner only the image of a grieving mother and her children. As the camera's iris opens, letting in more of the image, audiences discover the source of the family's grief: on a hillside opposite, Confederate troops are revealed, marching off to the battle in which many of them will die. Directing audiences, next, in how to read the film, Griffith edits between the shot of the troops and of the young mother—a montage that repeats the connection of events produced earlier in the sequence through masking. In organizing the whole sequence this way, Griffith shows readers how to understand the principles of parallel editing while he applies them. Later in the film we see another of Griffith's formal and visual flourishes, one that further draws viewers into the mind-set and experience of its characters (and into the film's revisionist ideology). Using split screen to psychological as well as dramatic ends, in one shot Griffith superimposes the image of Atlanta burning over footage of retreating Southern troops. Positioned above the image of the retreating Confederate army, the picture of Atlanta in flames connects events that take place in different locations. More suggestively, this technique creates a psychological connection between the characters in the foreground (the defeated Confederates) and the kind of nightmare image of the South they might be harboring— a scenario that in fact occurred, as this shot reveals, but that Griffith's new cinematic method made all the more forceful and haunting by connecting it to individual characters' psychology.

This use of split screen to ally viewers with characters' feelings or imagination also occurs in the film's closing shot, in which Griffith produces an effect for his characters that is analogous to the process viewers go through in watching the film. As Ben Cameron and Elsie Stoneman sit together on a hillside overlooking the ocean, an image of the City of God appears in the left half of the frame—a paean to the Confederate dead and to southerners like Ben Cameron's sister Flora (who dies fleeing a would-be black rapist) who have ascended there. Positioned within the frame, the image appears as a projection of the characters' thoughts, a reminder of the losses they have experienced as a result of Reconstruction and the war. In closing the movie as he does, Griffith encodes its final image of union between a northern woman and a southern man with the ideological message that the new "nation" that will follow the film's events (and that includes the suppression and re-disenfranchisement of blacks) will be built on the sacrifices of a region that has been terribly, tragically wronged.

As it is with the characters, who are depicted projecting their own understandings of the war onto imagery of death and sacrifice, so it was with audiences watching the film. For Griffith's formal and ideological methods offered a similar projection of the story for viewers—a similar "meaning" of southern history that many of them, initially at least, believed. With *Birth*, Griffith told a history of the South in a manner that proved too compelling for audiences to resist, despite its interpretive extravagances.[9] In shaping narrative so forcefully, Griffith revealed the capacity for film to captivate viewers and to sustain both an extended, complex plotline and audiences' collective imagination. In so doing, he created not only the "birth" of a new, imaginary "nation" from the tenets of southern racist ideology, but a veritable new nation organized around the cultural activity of film viewing.

The reasons for the success of Griffith's and others' films of the South were historical as well as aesthetic. During a period of national reconciliation, when northern and southern audiences alike were eager to find reasons to forget the Civil War, nostalgic depictions of Old South life were readily accepted as an alternative to the ravages of both contemporary and historical truth. At the time of the movie's release, northern cities had experienced a burst of civil strife following the social and economic dislocations created by waves of immigration from Europe and the Great Migration. Between 1898 and 1908, race riots occurred in New York, New Orleans, Wilmington, Atlanta, and in Springfield, Illinois.

The film's racial conflicts were also not contrary to those experienced by blacks in the period in which *Birth* appeared. They had been denied the ballot in several states, and many whites in the South saw in the 1912 election of Woodrow Wilson to the White House (the first southern president since the Civil War) an opportunity to expand Jim Crow.[10] Lynchings in the period before Griffith made the film were at their highest point in history.[11] The year the film was released, 1915, also saw the founding of "the second Ku Klux Klan." Its growth was stimulated by Griffith's movie and Dixon's novel as well as by the fervid patriotism inspired by American military action in the Philippines, Mexico, and, later, involvement in World War I.

Perhaps most significant to the film's reception were northern white attitudes toward immigration. Following the waves of European immigration at the end of the nineteenth century as well as the northern immigration of freed slaves, negative attitudes toward blacks and other ethnic minorities increased tremendously. At the time of the film's release, nativist sentiment and rhetoric were raging. The growing audience for movies, which by the teens was increasingly middle-class, took *Birth*'s message about racial conflict as an earlier, regional manifestation of the contemporary and national "problem" they saw themselves confronting.[12] In this they were provoked by several public and "official" statements prior to the appearance of Griffith's film. A 1910 report to Congress by a federal commission detailed the impact on the supposed displacement of white labor by a younger, less-skilled European workforce and its effect on American wage earning.[13] By the time of *Birth*'s release in 1915 social dissent had peaked, epitomized in 1916 by the publication of an immensely popular, virulently anti-immigration tract by Madison Grant of the American Museum of Natural History in New York. Grant's polemic, nearly as extreme as that of Griffith or even Dixon, traced the breakdown in white power and "purity" to the Civil War: "The agitation over slavery [in the North] was inimical to the Nordic race, because it thrust aside all national opposition to the intrusion of the hordes of immigrants of inferior racial value and prevented the fixing of a definite American type. . . . The Civil War, however, put a severe, perhaps fatal check, to the development and expansion of this splendid type, by destroying great numbers of the best breeding stock on both sides, and by breaking up the home ties of many more" (*The Passing of the Great Race,* 79).

Faced with an influx of immigrants from Southern and Eastern Europe that was concentrated in the cities, white Americans saw in the immigrant populace a threat to what was already a fragile hold on an "American" national identity. As the historian Oscar Handlin describes it, this response found an outlet in the imaginative pastoral vision of the country's past: "The injunction that the newcomers must conform to an American style of life took for granted that such a style of life with a distinctive American character actually existed. . . . Perhaps it was because they themselves bore so little resemblance to this image of America, that many Americans insisted on ascribing the blame to the Outsiders, insisted on hoping that if only those others conformed, all might revert to a purer, pleasanter state" (*The American People in the Twentieth Century,* 98). The idea of a preindustrial, pastoral history as well as the longing for its supposedly "pure" life led by a white, nonimmigrant population informed cultural thought of the period; this vision was also central to the ideology (and hence the success) of Griffith's film.

In addition to a destabilized social climate in the teens, members of the country's increasingly dominant middle class felt threatened economically in ways that contributed to *Birth*'s potency and relevance. The film represents two main sources of insecurity to the middle class in the early decades of the century: the rise of big business, and the prospect of organized labor. In a period of trusts and monopoly growth, the middle class feared the overwhelming power and concentration of capital in the conglomerates; as a representative of both northern liberalism and industry, Austin Stoneman offered an image of the threat to small businesses and farmers by the interests of monopolized ownership. Stoneman's opposition in the film to the class of small, independent farmers like the Camerons could have embodied middle-class fears of big business.[14]

At the same time and in the period in which the film appeared, the middle class was also threatened by opposition to its economic well-being from "below." Though hostile to big business, the country's emerging middle class was distrustful of organized labor. The vision of a violent—and successful— overthrow of government in the Russian Revolution in 1917 and the spread of bolshevism abroad contributed to the idea of an American workforce infiltrated from without. In Stoneman's decision in *Birth* to empower blacks and strip landholding southerners of their property, he could also have put contemporary viewers in mind of the threat posed by organized labor and "outside agitators," a threat to many Americans that was quite real. The "red scare" about domestic Communism eventually took hold in the federal government, epitomized in Attorney General A. Mitchell Palmer's arrest and deportation of hundreds of alleged subversives between 1919 and 1921 during the so-called Palmer Raids.

Against this contemporary scene, audiences found visions of the antebellum South both relevant and appealing. Cinematic depictions of the South of the sort *Birth* offered were compelling because of their vision of an idyllic past that had overcome its own disorder, as well as a corresponding populist ideology that galvanized northern and southern audiences alike. Film was the perfect medium for this national reconciliation for several reasons. Centrally produced and widely distributed, it provided a singular consensus narrative for the entire country. And, beginning as an inexpensive form of popular entertainment, film—especially the early short subjects—relied on stock characters and simplified melodramatic plot lines that lent themselves to ready mass consumption and reification. The screen and the artificial settings presented there became the site of a collective national projecting of the southern "idea."[15]

Other films that followed *Birth* brought about this response through a nostalgic, artificial image of history. Two highly visible and widely viewed films of the period immediately following *Birth* suggest the Hollywood pattern of transforming the nettlesome details of southern history to a more palatable and comforting ideology. Both films, in particular, traded on distorted images of slavery. *Hearts in Dixie* (1929), directed by Paul Sloane for Fox Studios, and King Vidor's *Hallelujah!* (1930) for MGM, like earlier Griffith films, presented blacks embracing their subjugation. One of the first Hollywood movies to employ an all-black cast, *Hearts in Dixie* was also a musical, and it relied on several stereotypical set pieces such as the African-American spiritual or workers singing while picking cotton. As in *Birth* and Griffith's two short films, "His Trust" and "His Trust Fulfilled," *Hearts in Dixie* presented an image of black contentedness in subservience, epitomized by the introduction of Clarence Muse as Stepin' Fetchit. Despite Vidor's reputation as an accomplished, serious artist, *Hallelujah!*, like other features, mocked African Americans and made use of what were already conventions of black screen behavior, including a docile temperament, mirthful work songs, and superstitious religious beliefs. In particular, the scene of a crowd of white-clad African Americans preparing for baptism (but fearful of the water) struck audiences variously as comic and condescending.[16] White viewers considered the film and this scene as evidence of Vidor's "sincerity" in depicting blacks. Paul Robeson, writing in *Film Weekly*, demonstrated a greater sensitivity to the movie's ideological strain when he pointed out that to British audiences "the burlesquing of religious matters appeared sheer blasphemy" (quoted in Noble, *The Negro in Films*, 54).[17] The depictions of plantation life in particular, like that of the faithful slaves and house servants in Griffith's films, relied on an ideological construction of the "natural" and peaceful condition of black servitude.[18]

Rosa and the Mesmeric

It is this "natural" image and its accompanying ideology, evident in *Birth* and in other films that appeared in the period before *Absalom, Absalom!*, that Faulkner's novel reproduces and, in turn, critiques. One of the clearest ways Faulkner does this is through Rosa, for through her language and her romanticizing sensibility, Rosa represents a "filmic" consciousness, particularly as it regarded the Civil War. Rosa Coldfield offers a specific example of a consciousness in the throes of a fascination with the Old South myth. While not a character in a movie, or herself a film viewer, Rosa reveals tendencies of thought that resemble those encouraged by early southern film narratives. Moreover, her language reproduces the effect I have been attributing to the cinema—the capacity to mesmerize, captivate, or enthrall viewers confronted with a sensuous spectacle.

Rosa draws attention to this aspect of her narration herself in a manner that reflects on her style of speaking. Twice, in telling her version of the Sutpen story, she refers to herself as "*I, self-mesmered fool*" (114, 116). It is as if Rosa recognizes that she has mesmerized or hypnotized herself in her gauzy, hazy vision of Sutpen—quite possibly through the "notlanguage" Quentin attributes to her in the novel's opening (6). "Notlanguage" becomes, then, a useful way to consider the way Rosa's chapter works differently than ordinary language, functioning "extra-verbally" or even visually. I suggest a connection between Faulkner's critique of film and his use of language with Rosa that produces an effect of cinema, not as a realist medium, but as something unreal or mystifying.[19] While Rosa's language is not as overwhelming as the film image, it is nevertheless notable both for its material density and for Faulkner's presentation of it as a sensuous object to be marveled at or even "seen."[20]

One passage stands as a clear example of this tendency in Rosa's section, and it is of particular interest because it also draws attention to Rosa's romanticizing habit of mind. At this point Rosa is speaking about the moment when she returns to Sutpen's Hundred after Bon's death and the moment of discovering Judith on the mansion's stairs. In a passage typical of Rosa's stylistic "excess," she speculates about her willingness to face "facts" and reality:

> *Or perhaps it is no lack of courage either: not cowardice which will not face that sickness somewhere at the prime foundation of this factual scheme from which the prisoner soul, miasmal-distillant, wroils ever upward sunward, tugs its tenuous prisoner arteries and veins and prisoning in its turn that spark, that dream which, as the globy and complete instant of its freedom mirrors and repeats (repeats? creates, reduces to a fragile, evanescent iridescent sphere) all of space and time and massy earth, relicts the seething and anonymous miasmal mass which in all the years of time has taught itself no boon of death but only how to recreate, renew; and dies, is gone, vanished, nothing: nothing—but is that true wisdom which can comprehend that there is a might-have-been which is more true than truth, from which the dreamer, waking, says not "Did I but dream?" but rather says, indicts high heaven's very self with: "Why did I wake since waking I shall never sleep again?"* (118)

To begin, in describing the abstract quality of Faulkner's style we need to note the strain produced by the length of the sentence. In reality, what Faulkner offers here is not a sentence at all, but rather a continuous sequence that (like the film image) commands rapt, unbroken attention. Stretching syntax to such a point that it "breaks," Faulkner produces a cluster of words whose syntactic relation to each other is difficult to follow and that offers a flow of imagery that evokes a vague and shifting pattern. In so doing, he also fashions a prose in which the sensuous or material properties of language overtake its referential function.[21] This quality also echoes certain properties or effects of film. Although the full meaning of Rosa's language is not immediately clear, it is present in the language—or more precisely, that meaning is immanent through the forward movement of the prose. In this way the passage above (like others in Rosa's section) produces the vivid and yet ephemeral, ongoing impressions characteristic of film.[22] Faulkner's prose with Rosa is particularly associative in its process of articulation; meaning or linguistic sense is spectral or vague, "haunting" readers' minds after one sentence ends and they move forward to another. As a verbal approximation of film, meaning is carried over in the form of ongoing hints, images, and traces of what we've only just read or "seen" and which blur with new references and images.

Other features of the passage produce this break in verbal signification. Words or phrases such as "relicts" or "miasmal-distillant," materially present with the sound of hard, sharp consonants, are also archaisms or inventions of language that deliberately fail to produce meaning in a conventional way. These moments show Faulkner's language at its most inventive and charged, forging uses that compel a kind of awestruck, uncomprehending response. Because the abstract quality of Faulkner's language causes the reader to be more aware of the language itself than of its referent, we do not engage fully with the objects of description or reference but rather "watch" that language perform or experience it in passing, like the shifting imagery on the film screen. It is in this respect that Faulkner's prose with Rosa resembles the sensory, material aspect of cinema.[23]

Other references of Rosa's to her own escapism—she describes her memory elsewhere, revealingly, as "some trashy myth of reality's escape" (119)—are significant in that they place Rosa's romanticism in a historical context and show the way in which it operates in a manner similar to film. In the middle of her chapter, at the moment of Rosa's discovery of Bon's murder and Henry's flight, she describes imagining Henry remaining at Sutpen's Hundred and emerging from a room to greet her. It is an important point in Rosa's narrative and memory, for the death of Bon and her subsequent confrontation with Clytie mark for Rosa a sharp distinction between an old and a new time: the past and the future of the South. In her imagined encounter with Henry, Rosa sees him endeavoring to wake her:

What did I expect? . . . Henry to emerge and say, 'Why it's Rosa, Aunt Rosa. Wake
up, Aunt Rosa; wake up'?—I the dreamer, clinging yet to the dream . . . waking into
the reality, the more than reality, not to the unaltered and unchanged old time but
into a time altered to fit the dream which, conjunctive with the dreamer, becomes
immolated and apotheosized. (116)

Like historical film, Rosa's dreaming shows a time that has become "immolated and apotheosized." Rosa knows that she cannot awaken to the "unaltered
and unchanged old time." The South as she has known it before the war is
gone, a fact that is driven home for her by Bon's death and Clytie's bold
assertion of physical contact on the stairs. Her statement, however, shows
Rosa's inclination to cling still to the past imaginatively, as she describes awak-
ening to a time "altered to fit the dream." Rosa's dream, we know, is of a
romantic, mythical world that defines itself less by the actual events of southern history than by her (and other southerners') idealized conceptions of
gender, class, and race relations. That dream, however, "conjunctive with the
dreamer," also performs an act of violence or negation. Time and history that
have been "immolated" have been sacrificed or destroyed. To change or immo-
late the "old time" into a dream or something other than it actually was, as
Rosa does, is to perform an act of historical revision and erasure. Similarly,
time or events "apotheosized" have been abstracted or made into an ideal.

What Rosa describes herself doing in relation to the "old time" of southern
history is a way of considering it that was common among southerners resistant to the forces of historical change—an attitude and approach to history
that was also evident in films like *Birth of a Nation*. Film representations of
history and the South also "immolated and apotheosized" the "old time,"
turning history into something other than it was and thereby "sacrificing" it
(as in *Birth of a Nation*), or idealizing it (as in films like *Hearts in Dixie* or
Hallelujah!). Faulkner's interest was with putting that attitude—evident in
both Rosa's dreaming and in southern film narratives—on display for readers'
critical recognition.[24]

In addition to the "film effect" produced by Rosa's voice and her treatment of
the past, other passages from her chapter use a language that specifically connotes the processes of film production and film viewing. We have seen her
describe the way she sees the world "through smoky glass," a description that
sounds like the image of reality viewed or presented through the projector or
camera lens. Rosa's treatment of Charles Bon, in particular, manifests attitudes

and perspectives we might most readily describe as "cinematic." To Rosa, Bon is always a romantic, "shadowy" figure, an object of projected desire or a "reflection" (121). Describing her feelings about Bon, she reveals the extent to which her longing is not for a real person but rather a projection of her own fantasy or desire. Having only seen his photograph in her niece's bedroom, Rosa claims that *"even before I saw the photograph I could have recognized, nay, described the very face"* (122). Elsewhere, continuing her rapturous account of her feelings for Bon—or for her romantic conception of him—Rosa suggests the specifically pictorial and technological dimensions of film. In a passage that stunningly relays her (and other young women's) longing for a means to retain an image of desire, Rosa invokes a mechanical instrument that sounds strikingly like a camera: *"And I know this: if I were God I would invent something out of this seething turmoil we call progress something (a machine perhaps) which would adorn the barren mirror altars of every plain girl who breathes with . . . this pictured face"* (122). Expressing a reverence for the transcendent, near-sacral powers of the technical image, Rosa voices a longing and perspective that was one of the hallmarks of her Victorian period as well as of modernity.

Part of the cinematic quality of Rosa's as well as other characters' attitudes toward Bon is the aspect of motion; he is depicted not only as a portrait or still photo but as a shadowy, impalpable presence that moves through the Sutpen narrative silently and over time. Narrating the Sutpen story to Quentin, Mr. Compson describes Bon and Judith walking in Sutpen's garden and uses a language that invokes both motion and the process of film presentation: "You can not even imagine him and Judith alone together. Try to do it and the nearest you can come is a projection of them while the two actual people were doubtless separate and elsewhere—two shades pacing, serene and untroubled by flesh" (80). The notion of an image—and, significantly, a moving image—of two people walking "serene and untroubled by flesh" offers a clear approximation of the ontological status of film.

These accounts of Bon's presence in the mind's eye of various characters, especially Rosa's, also suggests another optical property of film. The impression of a continuous, unbroken motion in the film image is really an effect on the retina, which itself "projects" complete images after they have been perceived as individual, discrete frames. Through the phenomenon of persistence of vision, audiences themselves "project" the phantom-like image of figures in film, analogous to the act of projecting an image of Bon that Rosa and Mr. Compson describe.

The most striking passage in Rosa's section that offers this cinematic rendering of the past, however, occurs in her description of Sutpen: "*Because he was not articulated in this world,*" she says of him. "*He was a walking shadow. He was the light-blinded bat-like image of his own torment cast by the fierce demoniac lantern up from beneath the earth's crust and hence in retrograde, reverse*" (142). In this passage we see a figuring of the process I have been attributing to Rosa's section generally and its "cinematic" quality: an acceding of speech to the visual, as she points out that Sutpen was not "articulated" (or spoken) in this world, but was rather "a walking shadow," a visual or silent (film) image of moving light. In addition, Sutpen's image is cast "in retrograde, reverse"—in the same fashion as photographic images were cast onto the receiving plate of a camera obscura. The "film account" that Rosa and Mr. Compson offer of Bon and of Sutpen is of characters cast as visual images or as shadows endowed with motion—dreamy and romantic (as Rosa views Bon), or phantasmagoric (as Rosa here describes Sutpen). As a demonic figure cast in light, one who reveals the overwrought terms of Rosa's imagination, Sutpen stands as the most forceful and potent influence on Rosa's sensibility—as well as another example of her section's cinematic method.

Southern History, Film, and Melancholia

In my account of Rosa's "filmic" narrative, she stands as an example of what Richard Moreland, in his reading of *Absalom*, calls the "melancholic." Like Rosa, early film narratives of southern history appear as melancholy "nostalgizers" of a dead past, a state or condition that can only be endlessly, mechanically repeated or reproduced. Pointing to Rosa and the novel's other narrators, Moreland suggests that "if . . . the South is 'dead,' one potentially useful question to ask is whether the South's 'survivors' have undertaken the work of mourning and understanding that death, or whether they are melancholically stuck repeating the traumatic scene of loss" (28).[25] Film versions of the Old South, like Rosa's narrating, are rooted in an idealized and therefore nostalgic and moribund time. My interest is in the way Moreland's characterization of Rosa's narrating, which he calls melancholic, resembles the practices of commercial cinema. Both share an obsessive, nostalgic relationship with the past, one that for different reasons but no less assiduously, avoids the "work of mourning and understanding that death" and remains fixated on a repeated image of purity, innocence, and utopia. The film industry did this by capitalizing on an emerging film market's escapist fantasies, ideas that allowed audiences to consume wholly the screen version of an Edenic, southern agrarian life; Rosa's mythopoeic narrative maintains her version of Sutpen and his impact on her family and Jefferson. Both approaches avoid coming to terms with the real causes and developments in southern history that led to the war.[26]

With Rosa and, as we will see, with Shreve and Quentin (though to a lesser degree), we find a relationship to the South that epitomizes what was true for the country generally during the modern period: a willingness to be entranced by a romantic vision of southern history. In particular, Rosa's ahistoricism and romanticizing resembled that of other Americans, including northerners, when it came to considerations of the Civil War. This process had in fact begun earlier, in attitudes toward the Civil War that sought in it a heroic, noble memory on which to project, paradoxically, an image of national unity. It may not be incidental, then, that the dates of the present-tense events of the novel occur at a time when, as Alan Trachtenberg has suggested, the public taste for war nostalgia was at a peak: "Interest in the war and its images culminated in 1911 in a ten-volume *Photographic History of the Civil War,* assembled by Francis Trevelyn Miller, editor of the *Journal of American History,* on the fiftieth anniversary of the firing on Fort Sumter" (*Reading American Photographs,* 78–79). Like the films that followed it, Miller's "explanation" of the war in his introduction described it as a romantic period of high adventure, one in which both sides of the cause were "just" and that demonstrated above all a common American spirit of nobility: "This [the Civil War] is the American epic that is told in these time-stained photographs—an epic which in romance and chivalry is more inspiring than that of the olden knighthood. . . . No Grecian phalanx or Roman legion ever knew truer manhood than in those days on the American continent when the Anglo-Saxon met the Anglo-Saxon in the decision of a constitutional principle that beset their beloved nation."[27] Far from a violent, bloody, and bitter conflict, the war in Miller's treatment was a test of the honor of each side, equally devoted to their "beloved nation" in defending an abstract "constitutional principle." In the rarefied atmosphere of nostalgia, the war took on an edifying or even aesthetic dimension that contributed to the country's inevitable reconciliation.[28]

Though public taste for images of the war may have peaked in 1911 as evidenced by Miller's book, it surfaced in the reactions to Griffith's epic—and again in the period when Faulkner worked on *Absalom.* The crisis of national identity that in the teens gave rise to a nativist emphasis on an American "type," as well as nostalgia for the Old South, also troubled the popular consciousness in the thirties due to anxiety brought on by the Depression. Trachtenberg points to this reappearance of cultural anxiety in the thirties and to a repetition of a longing for a unified American heritage: "As the Depression deepened, the very meaning and identity of the nation were questioned, and a concerted search began in scholarship as well as in popular culture for American traditions."[29] As a cultural effect, narrative film of the South extended the role played by still photography in shaping popular conceptions of the war. By the time they found their way into the films, romantic notions of the war had been present for some time and through different historical periods. *Absalom, Absalom!* itself may have included its own mythified approach to southern history, as is clear in several of its characters' perspectives. But in its treatment of Rosa's romanticizing and, as we will see, Quentin's spectatorship, it seems far more aware of the need for exposing those perspectives as an object of critique.

Quentin, like Rosa, is another of the novel's characters who evinces a cinematic relationship to the South. In the novel's depiction of Quentin's act of hearing and later "telling" the Sutpen narrative, Faulkner further suggests a connection between his characters' experience of southern narrative and those of the audience for film. Throughout *Absalom,* Quentin occupies a position of passive, voyeuristic spectatorship. Immediately clear in the novel's opening is the way Quentin "watches" imaginary, visualized projections of the Sutpen narrative. In its insistence on Quentin's looking at silent moving images of the historical past as well as, significantly, the story's introduction of Sutpen, the novel evokes the atmosphere, apparatus, and aesthetic dimension of the cinema. "Abrupting" onto the past in Jefferson, into a scene "as decorous and peaceful as a schoolprize watercolor" (6), Sutpen's appearance in the novel—and into Quentin's mode of apprehending it—makes use of the aestheticizing and pictorializing of narrative on which early silent film depended. As Rosa's captive audience in her "dim hot airless" parlor (5), Quentin occupies a position similar to that of the film viewer. In this darkened space, Sutpen emerges into the silence of the "dim coffin-smelling gloom sweet and oversweet with the twice-bloomed wistaria against the outer wall" (6). Redolent of coffins, time past, and death, the gloom in Rosa's parlor is nevertheless "sweet and oversweet" with a reanimated southern aura—like the screen images of historical figures. And those figures are, quite literally, projected. Contrasting with this dark of the room, the "latticed . . . yellow slashes full of dust motes" from the "savage quiet September sun impacted distilled and hyperdistilled" are filled with the density and saturation—again, like the film image—of myth (5). Finally, as a response to this staging of the scene, Quentin demonstrates a spellbound state like that of the viewer before the film spectacle: "Then in the long unamaze Quentin seemed to watch them overrun suddenly the hundred square miles of tranquil and astonished earth and drag house and formal gardens violently out of the soundless Nothing" (6).[30]

Immediately following this vivid and aestheticized depiction of both Sutpen and the scene of Quentin watching him, Faulkner injects a direct reference to the popular cultural market for such images of the South. Initiating the Sutpen narrative, Rosa offers an invitation to Quentin (and to the reader) to recognize the commercial appeal of the kind of story he is about to "witness": "So maybe you will enter the literary profession as so many Southern gentlemen and gentlewomen too are doing now and maybe some day you will remember this and write about it. You will be married then I expect and perhaps your wife will want a new gown or a new chair for the house and you can write this and submit it to the magazines" (7).[31] Preparatory for hearing the Sutpen narrative, Quentin is both alerted to the story's marketability and positioned, along with the reader, as a spectator or "viewer" of its events.

From this point until nearly the end of the novel, Quentin maintains this position regarding the Sutpen narrative. Throughout the book Quentin is described "seeing," "watching," or "seeming to see" the Sutpen story as it is rendered to him by Rosa (10, 17), the narrator (109), his father (157), and even himself (308). His detached, voyeuristic position is sustained until the novel's conclusion when Quentin, with Shreve, narrates a portion of the Sutpen story that brings them into "direct" contact with the objects of their imaginative gaze—the highly celebrated passage in chapter VIII in which the boys appear to merge with their story of Henry, Sutpen, and Bon. As often noted, Faulkner's interest in this scene is with the peculiarly immediate relation Quentin and Shreve experience with their subject: southern history and a narrated episode from the Civil War. Faulkner's interest in this immediacy and this scene, however, also concerns its aftermath, his understanding of the painful and difficult transition Quentin goes on to experience when he is forced to give up his closeness to or involvement in the Sutpen narrative—to "come away," as Shreve puts it (180), from their film-like experience of watching.[32] In the novel's final chapters Quentin occupies a position that, through Faulkner's narrative machinations, resembles that of both Rosa and what film theory has described as that of the cinematic "subject." Yet unlike other characters or the viewers of film, Quentin's struggle to cope with a stance both within and outside of southern history prove, as we will see, overwhelming.

Historians' comments about the need for American "audiences" of the war to see in it a cause for national unity and reconciliation point up that response's contradiction to the very real fissure that the war produced. Efforts at joining the populace or "healing" the country through a consensus, revisionist narrative also appear in Quentin and Shreve's section of *Absalom*. At the heart of a version of the Sutpen story fashioned mutually by a northerner and a southerner is a detail that tellingly invokes the violent fact of the war's effect. Figured in Quentin and Shreve's version of the story in which it is Henry, and not Bon, who is wounded in battle (283-84), we also find a suggestion of the psychic and political wounding that the war produced on another body—the body politic. That Faulkner was acutely, painfully aware of this wounding is unquestionable. In the boys' narrating of events from the war, however, its meaning and its violence are couched in a romantic treatment similar to that we've seen in Rosa. The closing sections of the novel, in their approximations of cinema and in their tragic treatment of Quentin, offer Faulkner's critical commentary on the way that southern film narrative falsely endeavored to heal or "suture" the national consciousness of its wounding from the war.

Viewing History: Modernism's Suture

In a manner similar to viewers' relation to the imaginative space produced by the film frame, the end of the novel offers a crucial passage in which Quentin and Shreve are both drawn into the imaginative and exegetical space of the Sutpen narrative. The moment in question involves Quentin and Shreve merging with Henry Sutpen and Charles Bon in an extended italicized passage that has been described by critics alternately as supremely "compelling," "audacious," and even, by one critic, as "cinematic."[33]

My own reason for relating this section of the book to film is that the workings and effect of this passage involve a narrative process similar to that described by film theory as *suture*. As conceived by theorists such as Jean-Pierre Oudart and Daniel Dayan, suture refers to techniques that manage the relationship of spaces outside and inside a film's frame. In their account, the off-screen space of film narrative requires a viewer's sustained imagination of an image or shot that is located beyond the frame, such as the object of a character's look. "Entering" this space in the following shot, through an image of what the character had been regarding, viewers are "sutured" back into the space of the film's narrative. Stephen Heath describes the way the frame in cinema produces this palpable sense of loss and recovery:

> The narrative elision of the image-flow, the screening of point of view as the ground of the image, the totalizing of image and space in the form of field/reverse field—these are some of the procedures that have been described in terms of *suture*, a stitching or tying as in the surgical joining of the lips of a wound. In its process, its framings, its cuts, its intermittences, the film ceaselessly poses an absence, a lack, which is ceaselessly bound up in and into the relation of the subject, is, as it were, ceaselessly recaptured *for* the film. (*Questions of Cinema*, 12–13)

In an earlier article and using the classic shot/reverse shot sequence in narrative film, Oudart initiated the discussion of suture by describing the way most film narrative relies on an absence (or signified content), suggested by a shot's presence (or signifier), such as a character's look off-screen.[34]

In a similar fashion, Quentin and Shreve furnish an imagined "presence," the narrative of Henry and Bon, into which they will insert themselves through a crucial and extended passage of shared narrating. As narrating subjects in the present of 1910, Quentin and Shreve occupy a position outside of the history they tell. In this light, the Sutpen narrative can be seen as the "absence," or signified, implied by their narration—and the novel's efforts to inhabit the past with the present as a kind of suturing device. The gunshot to Henry's body, like the narrative "wound" in film that suture endeavors to close, also binds the two Harvard freshmen together in their colorful and dramatic rendering of the events that surround it. We learn of this wound to Henry at a high point of narrative tension, both between Henry and Bon and between Shreve and Quentin as they vie for the privilege of "telling." At this particular point in the narrative, the novel breaks into one of its several italicized sections. The passage is crucial to setting up the novel's conclusion, leading, as it does, to Bon's murder, and including the exchange between Henry and Bon about Bon's intentions to marry Judith as well as Henry's intention to prevent him from doing so. It also depicts what might be considered the novel's emotional climax: Sutpen's final denial of Bon as his son.

This climactic, italicized break, occurring when it does and sustained for several pages, signals a move back in time and to a different historical register—a move Faulkner makes several times in the novel but that here functions ostensibly without the mediating presence of the novel's character-narrators. In a passage in which Quentin and Shreve "become" Henry and Bon and lose their own identities, Faulkner's narration moves, through a reference to the smell of wood smoke, out of the dorm room and to the scene of the campfire forty-six years before. "[N]ow neither one of them were there. They were both in Carolina and the time was forty-six years ago, and it was not even four now but compounded still further, since now both of them were Henry Sutpen and both of them were Bon, compounded each of both yet either neither, smelling the very smoke which had blown and faded away forty-six years ago from the *bivouac fires burning in a pine grove*" (289). In the move to italics and to the campfire in Carolina, Faulkner's narration attempts the novel's most radical fusing of identities and historical periods, extending beyond the present-tense scene in the dorm room into a sustained narration of events from the past. As he does so, Faulkner leaves his narrators behind in an effort to represent these past events "directly." These events, although separate in time from the present-tense act of narrating occurring in 1910, are notable for a certain immediacy or fullness of presence, a vivacity or heightened visual power that brings the reader, along with Quentin and Shreve, into an immediate apprehension of past events. Interestingly, and of a piece with the novel's earlier accounts of Quentin watching (and with my overture to cinema), this passage makes use of both readers' and characters' imaginative acts of looking. The section's first detail notes the strong visual contrast of firelight seen at night, as well as the

> *gaunt and ragged men sitting or lying about [the fires], talking not about the war yet all curiously enough (or perhaps not curiously at all) facing the South where further on in the darkness the pickets stood—the pickets who, watching to the South, could see the flicker and gleam of the Federal bivouac fires myriad and faint and encircling half the horizon and counting ten fires for every Confederate one, and between whom and which . . . the Yankee outposts watched the darkness also.* (289)

Drawn into this scene of characters on "watch" and with an emphasis on the flickering play of light, tracing the direction of the Yankee and Confederate soldiers' scanning gazes, the reader is positioned to follow a particularly cinematic operation: the fashioning of narrative through the activity of the look.[35] Into this highly visualized passage, as the section continues, will appear the orderly who searches out Henry (290), as well as another exchange of glances—between Sutpen and Henry in the officer's tent.[36] Colleen E. Donnelly points to Faulkner's move to the present progressive tense in this section to argue her view that it "becomes the most compelling and insistent found in the novel" and that "[b]y writing this passage in the historical present, Faulkner is also claiming that the 'true' historical experience is being enacted in the present" ("Compelled to Believe," 118). The switch to the present-tense narration, epitomized in constructions such as Faulkner's description of the orderly who *"passes from fire to fire, asking for* [Henry]" (290), is indeed key to this section's visualized or heightened impact. (The present tense aspect is also clear at the end of the passage when the narrator states that Henry is *"not as heavy by thirty pounds as he probably will be a few years after he has outlived the four years* [of the war], *if he do outlive them"* [290].) Yet despite Donnelly's assessment, the rhetoric of the entire novel argues against notions such as "true historical experience." If Faulkner represents the past here more immediately or "compellingly," in either an emotional or historical sense, he does so in an effort to examine the effects of doing so. For these effects, as we shall see, can be quite damaging—even fatal.

It is the joining of past and present registers in this chapter that contributes to the novel's formal resemblance here to cinema. That movement or identification, precisely because of the historical conditions of the act of narrating, produces an effect in this scene that is analogous to that of suture. The characters in this scene are drawn back into a "space" from which the narrative action of telling history has excluded them. Here, that absence is the space of history; in film practice, it is the off-screen space (or "signified") articulated by the frame. Quentin and Shreve are effectively sutured back into the historical narrative they have been both watching and telling; historical distance, like the distance between the viewer and the screen, is elided in this action of narrative conjoining. Both classical film practice and Faulkner's particular method in this scene rely on a process of making what was present absent, of reversing the position of subject and object or looker and seen. And as with suture, that process occurs repeatedly in Faulkner's narrative, accelerating as the chapter nears its formal climax in the bivouac campfires scene. Faulkner's narrator refers several times to the linking of the narrating subjects, Quentin and Shreve, with the "objects" of their narration, Henry and Bon. Like suture, the process occurs as a constant movement *back and forth* between the two periods and positions. "[N]ow it was not two but four of them riding the two horses through the dark . . . ; four of them and then just two—Charles-Shreve and Quentin-Henry" (275); "the two of them (the four of them) held in that probation . . . by Henry" (276); "Four of them there, in that room in New

Orleans in 1860, just as in a sense there were four of them here in this tomblike room in Massachusetts in 1910" (276); "two, four, now two again, according to Quentin and Shreve, the two the four the two still talking" (285).

It is important to note that following this scene, Shreve will provide one of the novel's most sentimental perspectives on the Sutpen story. Describing Charles Bon's decision to keep a photograph of his mistress in a locket he knows Judith will find, Shreve reveals a romanticizing ideology and turn of mind about southern history that resembles that of the early silent cinema. Correcting Mr. Compson's earlier account (he thinks) Shreve says, " 'And your old man wouldn't have known about that too: why the black son of a bitch should have taken [Judith's] picture out and put the octoroon's picture in . . . But I know. And you know too. Don't you? Don't you, huh?' " (295). As the culmination of his act of narrating, Shreve's belligerence and vituperation give over in the next moment, and he offers one of the most patently romantic interpretations of the novel. As such, this moment reveals the true character of Shreve's imagining. Sounding faintly like Rosa Coldfield, he offers, " 'It was because he said to himself, "If Henry dont mean what he said, it will be all right; I can take it out and destroy it. But if he does mean what he said, it will be the only way I will have to say to her, *I was no good; do not grieve for me*" ' " (295).

Significantly, Quentin concurs. At the end of a chapter that "returns" the boys to an earlier moment of history and that purportedly corrects earlier versions of the story, we find a clear indication of the romantic turn of mind that the Sutpen story engenders. What I mean to suggest is the connection between the *manner* of Shreve's and Quentin's narrating, what I have described as similar to suture in film, and the *content* or *quality* of their narration. In depicting Shreve and Quentin in the thrall of a narrative that subsumes and contains them, as the film frame does its viewer through the effect of suture, and by showing the romantic shading of their narration, Faulkner points to a manner of conceiving history similar to that encouraged by early film. Quentin and Shreve participate in a production of narrative and a reproduction of romantic myth, processes that find a structural and ideological paradigm in the historical cinema.

In particular, Shreve offers a version of personalizing events of the Civil War, a habit of thought Rosa demonstrates and that, like her thinking, also relies on the conventions of melodrama. (It is worth noting that Shreve's section as narrator begins with the simple declarative: " 'And now we're going to talk about love' " [260]). The determinant generic mode of early film, melodrama and its characteristic narratives, imagery, and structures of thought appear as the boys' final "answer" to the conflicts of the Sutpen narrative. As such, they offer Shreve and Quentin, as they had Rosa, what seems a satisfying way to reduce and contain the historical, social, and economic complications surrounding the war into a personalized (and melodramatic) plot.[37] All of the boys' earlier efforts to understand Sutpen, and thereby a period of southern history, collapse at their narrative's end into a tragic image of failed romance. As with most of the films of Griffith's career, and in particular with *Birth of a Nation*, Shreve's and Quentin's version of southern history evinces a Victorian and melodramatic preoccupation with the family and an attitude that denies history's broader outlines by personalizing and domesticating it.

In the pages that follow, however, and in his treatment of Quentin in the novel's close, Faulkner pointedly critiques the effects of that ideology and of its (cinematic) reproduction. The problem with romanticizing southern history as Shreve does becomes evident when he and Quentin return to their dorm room and to their position outside of the historical past as subjects in their contemporary reality. At least, this is a problem for Quentin; Shreve, for reasons that will become clear, is able to maintain a certain comfort and distance from the effects of Sutpen's story. It may not be necessary to recall here the fate that awaits Quentin following the close of the novel. Returning to Quentin's freshman year at Harvard, which he had described seven years earlier in *The Sound and the Fury*, Faulkner leaves Quentin at the end of *Absalom* in a state of mind that will lead to his undoing. "Coming away" from his relationship to the South and its history, as Shreve describes it earlier—leaving the movie theatre, as it were—becomes for Quentin the problem. Lying in his bed in the dark after he and Shreve finish talking, Quentin begins to shake violently, and though the narrator confirms that physically "he felt fine," Quentin's anxiety and tension do not subside. Prompted by Shreve's ironic, prospective vision of a mixed-race "conquering" of western civilization, and by his pointed query, "Why do you hate the South?" (311), Quentin gives over to his shrill, interior denial, *"I dont hate it. . . . I dont. I dont! I dont hate it!"*(311). Faulkner does not depict Quentin's death in either *Absalom* or *The Sound and the Fury*. Yet as the earlier novel makes clear, Quentin is rent asunder by his confrontation with his family, modernity, and the southern past. Though Quentin's suicide is more central to the earlier novel, we can see here, at the end of *Absalom*, a manifestation of the conflict and self-division that hasten it. Asked a deceptively simple question by Shreve, Quentin reveals the pressure and self-hatred that Faulkner understood haunted many southerners and that in Quentin's case approaches hysteria.

As we know well and can see at the novel's close, Quentin does hate the South, or the part of him that identifies with it, and he will die in part because of this fissure and shame. Contributing to that state of mind at the end of *Absalom* is the pain of having to deal with the reality of the present following the roommates' act of narrating, or in Shreve's account, "playing" with the past (231). The suture-like process that Quentin and Shreve go through allows them to forget, temporarily—like the viewer of historical film—their place in the present and their remove from southern history.

By bringing the country imaginatively, if falsely, together through the image of a bucolic, pacific past, early cinema about the South had attempted its own act of "healing" or suture, contributing to a national reconciliation and recovery from the wounding of the war. To a large extent, as the career of a film like *Birth* suggested, that effort succeeded. Through *Absalom*'s treatment of Rosa's monologue and its intimations of the cinematic experience, however, Faulkner's novel suggests the effects of that success: a broadly defined, cultural melancholia encouraged by film and its reproducible, technological images. Captivated and gratified, audiences gave over to the pleasant distractions of the new medium and, like the nostalgic market for photography, "forgot" the reality of violence, slavery, and the Civil War.

Unlike the viewer of historical film, however, Quentin finds matters more difficult. "Unsutured" by his return to reality and the dorm room, ripped open as it were, Quentin fails to undergo the healing, restorative process that historical amnesia and cinematic narrative effected. For Shreve, that process is simple, even pleasant. It involves an act like creative play, and he manages, unlike Quentin, to retain some distance from the objects of his narration because they seem to him unreal or even faintly absurd. He even compares talking about the South to watching *Ben Hur* (180), a 1925 release that performs its own romanticizing of history. For Quentin, however, the stakes of historical remembrance and of manufacturing nostalgia are much higher. Unlike Shreve he cannot "come away" from his contact with an historical past that marks him, as a southerner, as complicit with its violent events and its wounding of both the "body" of the South and of the country's political past. As long as Quentin, with Shreve, maintains a film-like identification with the images of his past narration and an unbroken reverie in their visual play, he is comfortable. Giving up that sense of aesthetic, imaginative pleasure, however, and returning to the reality of his position both in history and in the North is painful. And the psychological effects of being forced to forgo his detached, cinematic position prove, indeed, extreme.

Screening Readerly Pleasures

Modernism, Melodrama, and Mass Markets in
If I Forget Thee, Jerusalem

The opening chapter of *If I Forget Thee, Jerusalem* contains a reference to the prefabricated tastes of the provincial doctor and his wife that introduces one of the novel's principal concerns. Describing the wife's gumbo, the narrator points to their dislike of fresh fish: "And when he (the doctor) came home at noon she had the gumbo made, an enormous quantity of it . . . to be warmed and rewarmed and then rewarmed until consumed by two people who did not even like it, who born and bred in sight of the sea had for taste in fish a predilection for the tuna, the salmon, the sardines bought in cans, immolated and embalmed three thousand miles away in the oil of machinery and commerce" (499–500). Although only a passing reference, this mention at the novel's outset of industry and commerce, of the large-scale production of "consumable" goods and the manufacture of mass-market commodities at a distant (coastal) location, suggests a key point of reference for the narrative that follows. The doctor and his wife epitomize for Faulkner a kind of consumer and a kind of taste. Prefabricated, mass-produced consumer items, packaged in industrial fashion and distributed as part of a centralized national economy are for these characters preferable to home-spun, freshly cooked recipes with a local or regional flavor. They even "can" the gumbo, after a fashion—letting it grow stale and consuming its monotony serially. The doctor and his wife also represent the kind of people and sensibility against which Charlotte and Harry define themselves: the conservative, "respectable" couple who live in the passionless, sterile confines of marriage. As such, the older couple appears in the frame portions of "Wild Palms" as an index of the sort of people who live narrowly and for whom the stimulations of genuine experience, whether it be in art, love, or food, are distasteful.

Such is the case, this novel will assert, for many of its readers. Although Faulkner had already, with the publications of *As I Lay Dying, The Sound and the Fury, Light in August,* and *Absalom, Absalom!,* established himself as a practitioner of a rarefied, regional modernism, in *If I Forget Thee, Jerusalem* he returns to a subject and a method he had taken up in one of his earliest novels. As in *Sanctuary,* though more ironically and obliquely, Faulkner here addresses the reading tastes and pleasure of the commercial market. Commenting as he does on the tastes of the doctor and his wife in the novel's opening, Faulkner makes clear his disdain for people who prefer bland, ready-made industrial products to something with a more personal or idiosyncratic stamp. Yet as Faulkner's potential audience, those people or their tastes prompted the stories and formal devices of both "Wild Palms" and "Old Man." With each section, Faulkner shows his readers a distinct but different kind of reading experience. Through both sections' formal and generic aspects, and through the way Faulkner manipulates their relationship, "Old Man" and "Wild Palms" refer to one other as well as to popular cultural models outside of themselves. In particular, "Old Man," the more recognizably modernist section, works to undermine the kind of generic or mainstream pleasure afforded by "Wild Palms."[1] As with *Sanctuary,* which drew on pulp fiction for setting its terms and method, or *Absalom, Absalom!,* which mounted an immanent critique of historical film, *If I Forget Thee, Jerusalem* shows readers their own "canned" tastes for certain forms of narrative. In particular, its strategies of representation and the nature of its stories suggest another immensely popular and influential genre: the domestic tragedy or melodrama.

Referring as he does to the mass-produced cans of preserved fish (the salmon, sardines, and tuna favored by the doctor and his wife), Faulkner also suggests the predilection of readers for commercial, mass-marketed cultural forms. The analogy between the two is clear, and it follows from more than the novel's several references to film and popular fiction.[2] "Wild Palms" derives from the conventions of domestic melodrama, both cinematic and theatrical, a genre that Faulkner rightly understood to be prefabricated in terms of its plots and characterizations. Presenting his story's melodramatic elements self-consciously, Faulkner includes several ways for readers to recognize how the narrative of Wilbourne and Charlotte functions parodically and as a critique of these generic figures and modes.

Faulkner's critique of the commercial market and popular taste manifests itself in other ways as well. Part of his immanent critique of melodrama in "Wild Palms" includes positioning Wilbourne as a typical spectator for melodrama and as an audience for his own love story with Charlotte. Faulkner also includes, through the section at the Utah mine, references to the effect on audiences of silent film that contribute to his interrogation of popular culture's political impact, even suggesting specific melodramas. Later Faulkner uses the setting of the cell in Parchman Prison and Wilbourne's "viewing" of Charlotte's memory as a way to extend his critique of consumer culture and of film genre. In the close of "Wild Palms," and in a culminating critical move for this novel—as well as for his decade-long exploration of popular culture—Faulkner considers commercial film's inherent affinity with pornography, in particular the way both work to simultaneously stimulate and frustrate desire. Before arriving at these conclusions, Faulkner establishes a critical backdrop in the opening sections of "Old Man." Here Faulkner uses a central trope—the repeated descriptions of the broad, flat surface of the Mississippi—both as a reflexive device for readers and as a figure for a pervasive and influential popular cultural object: the movie screen. These various aspects of the novel provide a means for readers to reflect on the kinds of mass-market pleasure that "Old Man" and "Wild Palms" both draw on and expose.

"Old Man"

The River, Empathy, and Description

The overriding image of *If I Forget Thee, Jerusalem* is the vast, broad surface of the River. Repeatedly in the "Old Man" section, Faulkner's narrator describes the floodwater as it flows from the Mississippi, continuous and smooth.[3] In the second section of "Old Man," we encounter the River directly for the first time. Faulkner presents it in a series of descriptions that function ostensibly to set the "scene" for the flood but that in fact do little to provide a realistic account of the setting. Rather, these passages undermine processes of both description and characterization. At the outset of the novel, that is, Faulkner uses a descriptive strategy that is unreal or abstract in order to counter conventions of realism that are associated with earlier American literature and with generic models for fiction, both of which provide the novel's backdrop.[4]

In his descriptions of the River, Faulkner fashions an object that corresponds less to a natural presence or location than to a broad, flat, reflexive surface that forces readers' confrontation with their own act of reading. Doing so allows Faulkner to use "Old Man" as a means to reflect on the methods and content of the novel, including those of "Wild Palms" as well as other examples of popular narrative such as pulp fiction, film, and melodrama. The larger project of *If I Forget Thee, Jerusalem* is a critique of those popular models that Faulkner incorporates into his text. The flood, as we shall see, is one specific, material means of doing so.[5]

Presenting readers with a reflexive, unbroken expanse, the descriptions of the River subvert a common aspect of reading experience. Performing figuratively, even abstractly, rather than offering an element of setting or description, the River takes on the properties of a mirror which, by showing readers themselves reading, breaks the process of imaginative identification and empathy. Being "blocked," as it were, from imaginatively entering the narrative space of these sections, the reader is effectively not "absorbed" into the story or into an identification with character.[6] In addition, certain descriptions suggest another two-dimensional, flat plane that suggests Faulkner's concerns with the culture industry. These passages about the River evoke both the movie screen and the mirror, and they function similarly: to show readers something about their own tastes and pleasure. The motives for this are clear. Writing, in "Wild Palms," what amounts to a romance story or a family melodrama, Faulkner sought with "Old Man" a narrative strategy that would deny readers the mode of reading to which they were accustomed and that they would experience in the novel's other story.[7] We will see how "Wild Palms" includes its own way of subverting or parodying readers' generic expectations. In its story of run-away lovers and its use of a conventional narrative method, however, "Wild Palms" nevertheless resembles cultural practices and standards. From its opening, "Old Man" functions differently, operating formally in a manner that actively frustrates readers' expectations.

This element of "Old Man" is clear in key passages of description. One of the distinctive features of the landscape and the River in "Old Man," for instance, is, paradoxically, its featurelessness. Rather than a variegated vista, this portion of the novel offers a flat, monochromatic surface, evident in Faulkner's first depictions of it. Looking at the River, the convicts note its stillness and apparent two-dimensionality: "[T]hey now looked at a single perfectly flat and motionless steel-colored sheet. . . . It was perfectly motionless, perfectly flat. It looked, not innocent, but bland. It looked almost demure. It looked as if you could walk on it. It looked so still that they did not realize it possessed motion until they came to the first bridge" (536). Faulkner's language here both emphasizes the act of looking and takes on the flat, recurring aspect of the image the convicts see. In its near-incantatory repetition of the phrase 'it looked' moreover, this description conveys the trance-like state of abstraction that the convict enters upon contemplating his scene. Later, the tall convict "looked at the rigid steel-colored surface not broken into waves but merely slightly undulant" (544). The very first description of the River's appearance includes language that stresses its flat, still, and—importantly—reflexive qualities: "[N]ow they saw that the pit on either side of the road had vanished and instead there lay a flat still sheet of brown water which . . . ravelled out into long motionless shreds in the bottom of the plow furrows . . . gleaming faintly in the gray light" (536). This "gleaming" gray or colorless sheet provides an object for the Tall Convict's hypnotic act of reflection, not a marker of location or orientation (indeed, the convict never finds his bearings while on the water). That the River provides the occasion for this reflection is clear when, upon seeing it for the first time, the convict finds himself musing on his own appearance. Facing the open expanse of the water and seeing the faint, thin line of the other levee, he realizes, "*That's what we look like from there. That's what I am standing on looks like from there*" (544). Prodded out of his reverie by the guard, the convict has to leave off a moment of specular identity forming.[8] Like the convict, readers too are thrown back on themselves as they confront this static, shapeless surface. For what they "see" in such descriptions is not an illusory, realistic space of depth or an imaginary setting but a singular, flat monolith possessed of a gray-colored, reflective sheen.

That the surface of the River provides no element of spatial illusion, no realist account of the landscape in which readers can place themselves also contributes to the "Old Man" section's odd, abstract quality. Without the creation of illusionist narrative space through which to enter the story, readers are thwarted in their ability to fully identify with that story's central character.

Undermining identification in this way, Faulkner offers readers an experience at variance with many of the standards for adventure plots and romance narrative, especially of the type that readers knew from nineteenth-century realism or from popular fiction. In this light, the convict's own reading experience is instructive. In our introduction to the convict, when we learn the impact of his over-identifying with the characters in adventure stories, we are given an object lesson in the dangers Faulkner associates with a naïve or too-direct involvement with characters in fiction: "[F]ollow[ing] his printed (and false) authority to the letter [,] he had saved the paper-backs for two years, reading and rereading them, memorizing them, comparing and weighing story and method against story and method" (509–10). Using a gun he purchases by selling subscriptions to the *Detective's Gazette,* the convict's attempted robbery is a complete fabrication from popular cultural materials. Basing his failed plans for a train robbery on the popular and sensationalized stories he reads in pulp fiction, the convict makes a painful discovery about the limits of readerly identification. For after the robbery's failure, all it gains him is a fifteen-year prison sentence.

In "Old Man" Faulkner means to avoid the fault that the convict later attributes to the dime-novel writers. This is clear when the narrator indicates that the convict blames, not himself for the crime, but those "whom [the convict] believed had led him into his present predicament through their own ignorance and gullibility regarding the medium in which they dealt and took money for, in accepting information on which they had placed the stamp of verisimilitude and authenticity" (509). Here Faulkner associates mimetic or realist practice with taking money for writing. For this reason and others, Faulkner's practice with "Old Man" avoids the harbingers of novelistic "verisimilitude and authenticity" such as realist description. In an extension of Faulkner's nonrealist account of setting, the convict (despite his centrality in "Old Man"), possesses little interior life, depth, or psychology whereby readers are encouraged to (falsely) identify with him.[9]

Description and the Movie Screen

Faulkner's treatment of the flood scene includes other indications that, as a narrative space, it operates differently from other sections of the novel, particularly the realist "dimensions" and account of setting in "Wild Palms." Passing into the area of the flood in the second chapter of "Old Man," the convicts enter a space that is less a recognizable landscape or location than a uniquely surreal, imaginary realm. From the time the convicts, riding the truck, leave the marker of their trail back to the penitentiary and what they know of reality—the main road, which, we're told, has "vanished" (538)—they enter a space denoted as unreal. Making their way into the waters and area of the flood, the convicts cross out of the clearly defined and plotted geography of their rural setting into the unplotted, formless topography of dream: "They crossed another bridge—two delicate and paradoxical iron railings slanting out of the water, travelling parallel to it for a distance, then slanting down into it again with an outrageous quality almost significant yet apparently meaningless like something in a dream not quite nightmare. The truck crawled on" (538).

Leaving the area of the farms and the extension of the penitentiary, an institution that structures itself physically like a plantation or a penal colony, the convicts enter into a new kind of reality, connoted by a description of a new kind of space. Upon confronting the vast, boundaryless body of water that the truck (and the narrative) is entering, one of the convicts, fearful of drowning in the truck bed, succumbs to hysteria and begins screaming. Described as "a middle-aged man with a wild thatch of iron-gray hair and a slightly mad face" (538), this convict and his madness herald a departure from the normative or ordinary in this section of the novel. Entering into the dream-like, watery space of the flood, the novel foregrounds its interest in evoking a narrative system and visionary space that functions as oneiric, hallucinatory, or unreal.

At this point Faulkner's other figure for the River may have become clear. The other model for experiencing narrative that interested Faulkner in this novel was film, in particular the silent cinema that he knew and that he viewed so assiduously when he was young.[10] In addition to resembling a mirror (or to performing like one), the descriptions of the flood recall the movie screen— another flat, two-dimensional surface Faulkner had in mind in the period he wrote this novel and that, he understood well, encouraged audiences' collective acts of dreaming. As we have observed, Faulkner cast the scene of the convict's crossing into the flood in language that specifically recalls the dream-state and that, in so doing, demonstrates an affinity with cinema.[11]

In the opening chapters of "Old Man," film figures in several other ways in addition to Faulkner's invocations of dreaming (each of which I discuss in turn). One includes a reference to an image associated with the South and its history that was peculiar to popular narratives, both literary and cinematic, and with which Faulkner was undoubtedly aware: the image of the plantation.

Another is that, like the film screen, the descriptions of the River provide an innocuous, blank surface onto which the convict projects his own imagination or longing. Like the film screen, the River later offers a surface for the play of color and light that produces a captivating, mesmerizing "spell." Through all of these passages and discursive moves we can see the way Faulkner's treatment of the River as a figure for cinema serves his critique of popular commercial cultural practices and forms.

In the middle of the second chapter of "Old Man," Faulkner's convicts witness a plantation burning. Seen from the moving train that takes the inmates to the levee in the midst of the flood, the image of the flaming plantation house appears as a surprise, mirage-like and surreal:

> Two hours later in the twilight they saw through the streaming windows a
> burning plantation house. Juxtaposed to nowhere and neighbored by nothing it
> stood, a clear steady pyre-like flame rigidly fleeing its own reflection, burning in
> the dusk above the watery desolation with a quality paradoxical, outrageous, and
> bizarre. (542)

Isolated and remote, the house appears in the narrative as it does in the landscape—unexpectedly and seemingly without motivation. Anachronistic, it is out of place physically as well as historically, and its contrast to the watery landscape is emphasized visually. Or rather, it would be, were its visual aspect (or at least its realist illusion) not undercut by the lack of background or relief (juxtaposed "to nowhere," surrounded "by nothing"). The description of the plantation suggests a simultaneous presence and absence, as the fire denies its own image or connection to its surroundings, "fleeing" its reflection and flaunting its contradictory, "paradoxical" state of being.

What are we to make of this odd, substanceless image in the middle of Faulkner's novel? Clearly, Faulkner means to evoke an image of the southern past—but he does so in order to render its (re)disappearance. Though plantation houses remained in Mississippi in 1927 when the events of "Old Man" take place, they did not function in the region's social and economic life then as they had historically. Where and how they existed more predominantly in 1939, however, when *If I Forget Thee, Jerusalem* appeared, was in representations of Old South living, particularly in that supremely visual medium, the Hollywood cinema. What I suggest that Faulkner offers with this image is a "screening," on the River's surface, of the image of the burning plantation. Reflected on the surface of the water, the house appears to the convicts as an image or a representation, not as an actual material presence in itself. In the same year that the novel was published, David O. Selznick's International Pictures offered another spectacular and sustained image of a burning plantation—"Twelve Oaks," along with much of the city of Atlanta, in the film version of Margaret Mitchell's *Gone With the Wind*. While not a direct reference to Selznick's film (though it may have been to Mitchell's novel), Faulkner here refers to the act of preserving or evoking the plantation, which Hollywood had already performed in other southern movies—evoking it to raze it, burning in the eye and in the public imagination.[12]

Later in "Old Man," happening on the pregnant woman in the tree whom he's been sent to retrieve, the convict reveals a habit of thought produced, Faulkner makes clear, through his film viewing, and in particular from the kind of romanticizing practiced by Hollywood.[13] Despite the fact that he blames the dime novels for his imprisonment, the convict has maintained his habit of reading them in jail. We are told that "[H]e had continued (and even with the old avidity, even though they had caused his downfall) to consume the impossible pulp-printed fables carefully censored and as carefully smuggled into the penitentiary" (596). An eager consumer of the dime novels, the convict reveals a similar susceptibility to the "impossible" stories of the movies. Seeing the pregnant woman lower herself into the skiff, the convict is shocked at how much his real charge is at odds with a popular-cultural or Hollywood version of the female in distress. He also reveals that the movies, like his reading, contribute to his manner of seeing himself and his world: "and now he watched her move, gather herself heavily and carefully to descend . . . and who to say what Helen, what living Garbo, he had not dreamed of rescuing from what craggy pinnacle or dragoned keep, when he and his companion embarked in the skiff" (596). The significance of this mention of Greta Garbo, occurring when it does, is not only that it furnishes a specific reference to popular culture and to film. More importantly, it indicates the convict's mental operation of projecting himself into an imaginary or fantasized role, a process experienced by film viewers and facilitated by the presence of an innocuous blank surface onto which those imaginings can be projected. As he sees himself here, the convict plays a role like one he has seen in the movies. This moment of projecting his self into an idealized role occurs soon after the convict encounters the River and, with the reader, confronts its still, gray two-dimensionality, an image that, as we've seen, provides the occasion for identity forming.

In a signal passage that occurs later in this section, this act of dreaming or of projecting effected by the River (and the screen) extends from the convict, through his listeners in the prison barracks, to the novel's readers. For the description of the convict's act of telling his story in the prison barracks specifically evokes the apparatus of cinema and its projective surface, the screen. Inserted into the middle of the novel, this reference to the convict's act of telling his story after he has been returned to prison suggests the dream-like, hazy quality of the images his story evokes—as well as the shadowy figures that appear on the movie screen. As the convict relates the sequence of being shot at by the National Guardsmen when he attempted to surrender, his story affects his listeners in a singularly captivating way:

> And now when he told this, despite the fury of element which climaxed it, it (the telling) became quite simple . . . as though he had passed from the machine-gun's barrage into a bourne beyond any more amazement: so that the subsequent part of his narrative seemed to reach his listeners from beyond a sheet of slightly milky though still transparent glass, as something not heard but seen—a series of shadows, edgeless yet distinct, and smoothly flowing, logical and unfrantic and making no sound. (613)

The "bourne" from beyond which the convict tells his story implies a remote, shadowy realm or dreamy space—like that of film—of either extreme, hyper-clarity or of bewilderment. The images depicted there, moreover, strikingly resemble figures from film—"a series of shadows, edgeless" that are fluid and moving, "yet distinct" in that they depict realistically the human form. As a further connection to the earlier reference to Greta Garbo, the 1920s icon of the silent cinema, the images from the convict's narrative are "not heard but seen." Here, in other words, is Faulkner's overt interest in the terms and manner of the convict's narrative: its roots in, and similarity to, the fantasy world of film, both of which are supported by the framings and articulations of the screen. It is the mental processes produced by those articulations that Faulkner critiques throughout the novel, and in its following section.

"Old Man"'s Immanent Critique: Pictorialism, Narrative, and Melodrama

Another similarity between silent film's manner of representation and the early sections of "Old Man" has to do with the specific role played in these sections by silence and pictorialism. Throughout "Old Man" appear descriptions that, in their emphasis on the image, offer readers a momentary visual simulation or picture whose effect, in part, is to arrest the movement of the convict and his story. Occurring in the middle of an ongoing narrative, these moments provide a form of spectacle that operates in many ways like the film image, especially as it is used in a particular genre: melodrama. To historians and theorists of the genre, and in both its theatrical and cinematic versions, melodrama demonstrates an emphasis on *mise-en-scène*. Frequently offering an elaborately composed spectacle, melodrama made use of what Robert Lang calls "speaking pictures."

In his history of American film melodrama, Lang elaborates the role in the genre of silence and the image. The section "Spectacle and Narrative," especially, establishes several elements of early film that, as we shall see, figure in Faulkner's descriptive method in the opening sections of "Old Man." Stressing the role in melodrama of *mise-en-scène*, Lang refers to the origin of melodrama's "image-emphasis" in the late-seventeenth-century theatrical ban on the spoken word in France and England. As a result of Louis XIV's prohibition of spoken performance by any theatrical company other than the Theatre-Français, the rest of the theatrical community devised an aesthetic that was oriented toward spectacle, pageant, and silence—but that was especially stylish and expressive visually. Defining this aspect of melodrama, Martin Meisal writes, "In the new dramaturgy, the [theatrical] unit is intransitive; it is, in fact, an achieved moment of stasis, a picture" (quoted in Lang, *American Film Melodrama*, 23). Lang connects the emergence of the tableau or the stage-image to the origin of the cinema, and of silent film melodrama in particular:

> The silence of the early movies thus imitated the popular theater of this earlier time and grew out of the peculiar relationship between narrative and spectacle. . . . What is being described here [as the new dramaturgy], of course, is not the cinema—not quite, not yet—but what found its logical culmination in the tableau of the theatre and tableau vivant of the nineteenth-century parlor. The cinema—its spectacular component, at any rate, sprang from the impulses that produced the tableau vivant, but successfully sought a dialectic between stasis and movement, between spectacle and narrative. (23)

Moving from the notion of the "speaking" picture furnished by stage melodrama, Lang describes a similar speaking image in film. "Because the first films were made and screened without the benefit of recorded dialogue, and because their first audiences were vast and heterogeneous . . . the cinema drew heavily on melodrama's investment in *mise-en-scène*. The movies were made to 'speak' without dialogue" (24).

Because of inherent properties of the film medium, evident particularly in its early short subjects, film was effective at summoning up dramatic, suggestive images that efficiently communicated a great deal of narrative information. Well-composed, striking, and offered for audience's visual pleasure, these images produced a tension between a static spectacle and a narrative unfolding over time. "Old Man," as we shall see, generates a similar tension in its own use of the "speaking picture." In its emphasis on description, often at the expense of dramatic or narrative event, "Old Man" produces an element of what has been referred to as melodramatic "excess" (Lang, 25). Faulkner's use of spectacle or description in "Old Man," however, makes productive use of that tension between stasis and motion, offering it as a corrective to the utopian, escapist ideology of the lovers' constant travel in "Wild Palms."

Much of Faulkner's modernism emphasizes the image frozen in time, the famous "Faulknerian tableau" (epitomized in moments such as Caddy climbing the pear tree in *The Sound and the Fury;* Jewel and his horse at the beginning of *As I Lay Dying;* Rosa Coldfield's feet dangling from her chair in the opening of *Absalom, Absalom!;* or Lena Grove, waiting and watching the approaching wagon from the top of a hill in *Light in August*). In "Old Man," we find a similar presentation of the silent, frozen image or tableau in many passages of description. These moments, however, possess a significant difference: they show as well a new self-consciousness on Faulkner's part about this strategy. The first page of the third section includes a description of the skiff as it drifts away on the current "like a tableau snatched offstage intact" (592). Later in this chapter another reference to the theater highlights the timeless, static quality of the stage image. In the passing from night to day, the convict sees dawn break like "another of those dreamlike alterations day to dark then back to day again with that quality truncated, *anachronic* and unreal as the waxing and waning of lights in a theatre scene" (610–11; emphasis added). Faulkner invokes another silent theatrical model in an earlier description of a flooded town, one that includes a striking, tableau-like image:

> While the two guards talked with the sentry before the tent the convicts sat in a line along the edge of the platform like buzzards on a fence, their shackled feet dangling above the brown motionless flood out of which the railroad embank-

ment rose, pristine and intact, in a kind of paradoxical denial and repudiation of change and portent, not talking, just looking quietly across the track to where the other half of the amputated town seemed to float, house shrub and tree, ordered and pageant-like and without motion, upon the limitless liquid plain beneath the thick gray sky. (539–40)

In the terms provided by Lang and others, this account of the convicts and the flood epitomizes melodramatic and silent film expression. The nontemporal aspect of the melodrama—its emphasis on spectacle over event—is evoked in the scene's "denial of change" and by the use of the image of the men's dangling feet. Its silent, speaking picture is also created by the floating town—an image that "says" volumes about the violence and devastation of the flood. Moments such as these suggest that Faulkner's account of a natural disaster or crisis is expressed through filmic modes of representation, strategies he likely absorbed through his own exposure to the medium.[14] Significantly, for a consideration of Faulkner's filmic imagination, this passage presents an image of description spread out (or "projected") against the backdrop of the flat, gray River, a moment in which the River operates again like the cinema screen. Finally, the function of the tableau (the cultural form Lang cites in his "pre-history" of cinema) is emphasized in the passage's reference to that orderly, silent form, the pageant. Even Faulkner's prose in this passage takes on a feeling of "silence." Ending with a short, clipped, monosyllable, as he does nearly every paragraph in this section, Faulkner puts an abrupt stop to his otherwise long and flowing sentence, a move that seems to cut the rhythm of the sentence off and enforce a closing up or silencing of narrating, speech, or sound. The impression of the melodrama and the early cinema, in particular its formal compositions and, obviously, its use of silence, are here evoked by Faulkner's strategy.

In addition to fashioning "cinematic" silent pictures or theatrical tableaux, Faulkner's descriptions in "Old Man" include an emphasis on stasis that further suggests the atmosphere and aesthetics of melodrama. In its tumultuous third chapter, when the convict tries to control the skiff on the River, all time appears to him to stop. Struggling with the current, the convict finds that "he was not exhausted and he was not particularly without hope and he did not especially dread getting up. It merely seemed to him that he had accidentally been caught in a situation in which time and environment, not himself, was mesmerized; he was being toyed with by a current of water going nowhere, beneath a day which would wane toward no evening" (594). This aspect of time arrested, described by Faulkner's narrator as "mesmerized," corresponds to the state of mind effected by film generally, as well as by early cinematic melodrama in particular.[15] "Time and environment," are here arrested, captured photographically or "mesmerized," as in film. Another description of the flood and of the movement of the convict on the water produces this feeling of the mesmeric. Referring to the convict's continual rowing, the narrator states, "[A]fter a while it no longer seemed to him that he was trying to put space and distance behind him or shorten space and distance ahead but that both he and the wave were now hanging suspended in pure time, upon a dreamy desolation" (610). Like other passages in this section, the convict's "dreamy desolation," partakes of the qualities of silent film, its "suspending" of action through spectacle or stasis "in pure time."

Faulkner's distortion of time in key sections of "Old Man" are important, as they can be seen as an instrument of his effort to critique melodramatic and cinematic strategies of representation. In addition to reproducing many of those strategies in his narrative method, Faulkner references silent film icons and, we have seen, demonstrates the influence of film on the convict's imagination. Viewed in this light, the temporal distensions and the at points grinding inactivity of the "Old Man" narrative, its seemingly excessive emphasis on description, function to put certain formal properties of the section—and of its corollary in silent film—on display. Faulkner's immanent critique in "Old Man" can thus be seen to produce a certain kind of "unpleasurable" effect, one in which stasis and inactivity emerge as definitive aspects of the narrative. We can also see how Faulkner's intimations of silent film melodrama serve his broader interests in the novel. Putting these qualities of the "Old Man" on display, however, he draws them to readers' critical attention. This approach can also be read as a deliberate counter to a different, contradictory aspect of melodrama—one that is also a crucial element of "Wild Palms."

If "Old Man" epitomizes stasis, the ongoing, forward-rushing movement of a story like "Wild Palms" manifests another element of melodramatic "excess." As a romance narrative of lovers on the run, "Wild Palms" stands in direct opposition to the static, description-laden method of "Old Man." In the "Wild Palms" section, Faulkner is interested in demonstrating the effects of such a concern with travel and escape, showing his lovers in the thrall of what amounts to a utopian ideology. Richard Godden refers directly to this aspect of "Wild Palms": "By showing how his couple confuse mobility with freedom,

Faulkner demonstrates an infinite regress that allows no exit and no future; his is a precise representation of the prison of liberal utopianism that elects flight from the bourgeois relations rather than their transformation" (*Fictions of Labor*, 207). As a result of the characters' preoccupation with motion and their constant travel, the "Wild Palms" section reads like a fluid, escapist narrative—at least in comparison to several aspects and sections of "Old Man." That is to say, the story of Harry and Charlotte "moves." Because of the emphasis in "Old Man" on stasis, produced often, as we have seen, by its emphasis on the image, the convict's story offers a deliberate counter to Harry and Charlotte's. Such a contrast reveals Faulkner's awareness of his own strategies and effects, suggesting a willingness to use those effects in opposition. This, of course, was Faulkner's own assessment of the novel when he used a musical metaphor to refer to its use of "counterpoint." The two sections were written alternately, he said, so as to "sharpen" or bring into relief the difference in affect or tone of each.[16]

My point here is simply that Faulkner's means of creating contrast also includes a difference in a visual aspect of either story, with "Old Man" making greater use of a static pictorial method than the more "flowing" realist narrative of "Wild Palms." Initiated as it is by the "projector" of the doctor's light on the stairs, "Wild Palms" appears in its own right to take on properties of a motion picture.[17] What follows its opening is the kind of escape story that movies favored (and continue to produce) but that "Old Man," in its insistence on description and stasis, arrests and offers readers a way to see critically.[18]

Key to distinguishing Faulkner's immanent method in *Jerusalem* is his self-consciousness about his narrative practice. A description of the flood appears in the second chapter of "Old Man," for example, that establishes the section's mode of presenting static, imagistic renderings of the scene—but it does so in an acutely self-referential fashion, showing Faulkner working the novel's two sections off of each other to rhetorical effect. The narrator describes the way the convicts' truck, moving along the flooded road, "slipped abruptly beneath the brown surface with no ripple, no ridgy demarcation, like a flat thin blade slipped obliquely into flesh by a delicate hand, annealed into the water without disturbance, as if it had existed so for years, had been built that way" (538). This description draws attention to its own image (or what Lang refers to as melodramatic "effect"—the predominance of scenic and visual elements [23]), emphasizing its static quality. In addition, it prefigures the pivotal action Wilbourne is to perform in "Wild Palms" and thus refers to the rest of the novel's narrative. Such self-referential moves on Faulkner's part at this early point in the novel reveal him emphasizing his own materials and strategies as well as the way they are directed at readers.

A final "summoning" of film practice confirms the immanent critique Faulkner mounted throughout the "Old Man" section. Significantly, it indicates Faulkner's self-consciousness about the ways "Wild Palms" will be keyed to melodramatic strategies, and it reveals Faulkner's deliberate ironizing in "Old Man" of materials and language that will appear in "Wild Palms." At the end of his first day on the River, as darkness falls, the convict's sensory experience of the light misleads him, a fact that further enables the play of his imagination. As a result of the change in light, he continues to believe himself to be somewhere—as well as someone—he is not. In a passage that focuses on the convict's ocular experience, Faulkner provides a description of the River's surface that suggests the play of light on the screen:

> It was full dark now. That is, night had completely come, the gray dissolving sky had vanished, yet as though in perverse ratio surface visibility had sharpened, as though the light which the rain of the afternoon had washed out of the air had gathered upon the water as the rain itself had done, so that the yellow flood spread on before him now with a quality almost phosphorescent, right up to the instant where vision ceased. The darkness in fact had its advantages. (600)

Relying on what he doesn't see, or more properly on what the "phosphorescent" light on the water's surface allows him to think he sees, the convict negotiates his way through this part of the story by way of an optical illusion. The convict's experience of the River is similar to that of the viewer in the cinema: each observes an image in which "darkness has its advantages" because it allows a greater clarity to the light as it plays on its different surface (River or screen). Elsewhere, this light is described in terms that anticipate moments of the narrative in "Wild Palms" and that also invoke the sentimental patterns of melodrama—but that do so ironically. At the end of the convict's first afternoon on the water, the narrator points to that fact that "[i]t was raining steadily now though still not hard, still without passion, the sky, the day itself dissolving without grief" (599). "Passion" and "grief"—these are the currency of the romance narrative and the melodrama, not of naturalist descriptions of nature. Falsely animating the rain and twilight, Faulkner invokes terms that are specific to melodrama and that, moreover, appear in key moments of the story of Harry and Charlotte. Unlike the melodramatic narrative of "Wild Palms," especially its conclusion, passion and grief are here denied: the rain falls "without passion," the day dissolves "without grief."

Although these terms as they are used in either section of the novel appear in different contexts, it is difficult not to consider that Faulkner's effort here in "Old Man" is to flatten or empty out the sentimental modes that are melodrama's stock in trade. He will use these modes in "Wild Palms," specifically on the section's final page when Harry declares, *"Between grief and nothing I will take grief"* (715). Here "Old Man" anticipates Harry's statement, demonstrating the way that, as I have been arguing, Faulkner uses the convict's story to reflect or to comment critically on the lovers' melodramatic escape narrative. As doomed lovers on the run, Harry and Charlotte epitomize a romance genre that Faulkner seeks, with "Old Man," to ironize and subvert. In the "Old Man" section, Faulkner comments obliquely on narrative elements common to film and popular romance that had appeared in cinematic melodrama and that also go on to inform "Wild Palms." He also, however, seeks to deny the emotional effect of those elements and to expose their limitations. Portions of "Old Man" serve to deny empathy, to flatten out the depictions of illusionist narrative space, and to parody the Hollywood hero. With his self-conscious references to the language of melodrama and to Harry's self-pitying closing statement in "Wild Palms," Faulkner further points up the hollowness of that language and of sentimentalizing narrative. In "Old Man," through a range of strategies, he forecloses the possibility of their use.

"Wild Palms"

Harry's Melodramatic Imagination and Movie House

Having detailed some of the ways in which "Old Man" simultaneously invokes and subverts melodramatic method, it is crucial to see how "Wild Palms" offers a particular version of a melodramatic narrative—and the ways Faulkner also subverts it. One of the clearest and most immediate differences between the novel's two sections is the general use in "Wild Palms" of conventional novelistic method. Like other popular forms, melodrama relies on readerly and audience empathy, an identification that is facilitated by realism. The narrative of Charlotte and Harry has its descriptive flourishes, such as the descent into the Utah mine, or its flights of metaphysical speculation, such as Wilbourne's monologue to McCord at the train station. Yet overall it presents its characters and their story straightforwardly, with realist versions of setting, character, and dialogue. The "Wild Palms" section, for all its meditations on the cultural market (including Charlotte's artworks' devolving status to commodities and Wilbourne's writing pulp pornography), presents a generic, commercial version of narrative. Though they mean to escape bourgeois convention, the couple's adultery and flight from conventionality is itself a hallmark of popular, generic narrative: it is a melodrama, and a scandalous, sensational one at that. As the story of a "fallen" woman who leaves a bourgeois marriage and her children to pursue passion, only to die a painful and graphically depicted death, "Wild Palms" takes up a classically melodramatic plot of misguided love.

With the movement between the novel's sections, Faulkner provides an alternation not only between two narratives but also between two kinds of reading experience. We have seen how "Old Man" negates or denies the kind of reading experience that "Wild Palms" furnishes. This is not to say that "Wild Palms" is merely a "cheap," escapist entertainment; it too, as we shall see, provides its own reflexive, self-critical elements and turns. But it does function, like much realist narrative, to draw readers into the world or space of its characters' lives. In addition, like "Old Man," it reflexively "shows" readers their own experience of reading and their expectations for a particular kind of narrative pleasure.

One of the clearest ways the novel does this is through the character of Harry. For in his own tastes and proclivities, Harry stands as a surrogate for the reader and the popular culture consumer. Several sections of the novel demonstrate Harry's taste for melodrama, including the melodramatic story in which he himself takes part. In the scene in Audubon Park in New Orleans in which Harry watches a type of "mental home movies,"[19] he demonstrates this narrative preference. In this scene and others, Wilbourne shows readers their own taste for melodrama and for what Faulkner considered hackneyed forms of narrative. In order to see this, it is important to note that in the Audubon Park sequence Faulkner does not show Charlotte and Rittenmeyer directly. As in other novels, he reveals a scene "filtered" through the subjective, watchful consciousness of one of his characters. Wilbourne's imagined scene of Rittenmeyer and Charlotte includes a characteristically Faulknerian introduction:

And now, sitting on his bench in Audubon Park . . . he watched against his eyelids the cab (it had been told to wait) stopping before the neat and unremarkable though absolutely unimpugnable door and she getting out of the cab . . . and mounting the steps. . . . He could see them, the two of them, Rittenmeyer in the double-breasted suit . . . ; the four of them, Charlotte here and the three others yonder, the two children which were unremarkable, the daughters . . . the younger sitting perhaps on the father's knee, the other, the older, leaning against him; . . . he could see them, he could hear them. (645)

Like Quentin Compson "watching" scenes of the Sutpen narrative or imagining them with Shreve, Wilbourne here produces a version of events that pleases him. And as with Quentin, we find an emphasis on seeing narrative action ("He could see them . . . he could see them"). "Projecting" their story in his head, using his eyelids as a kind of screen, Wilbourne casts Charlotte and Rittenmeyer in the standard roles of wanton woman and scorned husband and watches a scene of family tragedy. What is pleasing to Harry about this is that it conforms to the kind of plot he would expect of Charlotte—or of any married woman with her husband. Rittenmeyer's behavior especially, his rectitude and moral forbearance, accords with Wilbourne's misplaced sense of honor. While Rittenmeyer's behavior may be reasonable, it nevertheless appears here as part of a narrative construction of Wilbourne's (not as a reproduction of a past event). Faulkner positions Wilbourne on the bench so as to consume created images of Charlotte and her husband as viewers do the images of commercial and generic film.

For what is this scene with Charlotte and Rittenmeyer but a set piece from a melodrama?[20] As Harry plays it out, the scene includes several elements of classical film melodrama, portraying in its brevity the entire moral universe that early film scenarists favored and evoked so economically—like D. W. Griffith in films such as *The Voice of the Violin* (1909), *Home Sweet Home* (1914), and *Broken Blossoms* (1919). Over all, there is the sanctity of the nuclear family (with the father kneeling, his daughters sitting and leaning against him, forming a triangle, Christian symbol of divinity and the holy Trinity). There is also the image of the scorned husband bearing, tragically and stoically, the loss of his children's mother. Finally, this scene offers a "blessing" of the world Rittenmeyer and his family represents. Following the couple's stoic goodbye, in a passage that confers "rightness," we find a literal benediction:

and they will both know they will never see each other again and neither of them will say it. 'Good-bye, Rat,' she says. And he will not answer, [Wilbourne] thought *No. He will not answer, this man of ultimatums, upon whom for the rest of his life*

> *will yearly devolve the necessity for decrees which he knows beforehand he cannot*
> *support, who would have denied the promise she did not ask yet would perform the*
> *act and she to know this well, too well, too well;—this face impeccable and invincible*
> *upon which all existing light in the room will have seemed to gather as though in*
> *benediction, affirmation not of righteousness but rightness, having been consistently*
> *and incontrovertibly right; and withal tragic too since in the being right there was*
> *nothing of consolation nor of peace.* (648)

In a description that uses a piece of photographic key-lighting, Rittenmeyer appears as though bearing the light of grace. Yet whereas the scene recalls cinematic melodrama in its formal details and its tone, its use of melodramatic method is ironic. Faulkner's irony in this description comes from the fact that it is Harry, not the authorial narrator, who is positioned as having produced it. For it is his imagination, as well as his interests, moral sense, or longing, that the passage points up. Harry conjures and embraces the Victorian, domestic worldview evinced in film melodrama, evident in his invoking of sacrifice and paternal "decrees." But this is a vision that Faulkner's self-conscious staging of the scene subverts. Even its phrasing is suggestive of the sentimental excesses of melodrama and romance—the fallen heroine knowing "*too well, too well*" of her lover's forgiveness and the contrition such knowledge implies; the strong husband's "*impeccable and invincible*" face; and above all, the husband/hero's "*incontrovertible,*" "*tragic*" rightness. This is the phraseology and value system of melodrama, writ large for the purposes of Faulkner's critique of what this scene, generically, represents.

It is important in this respect that Harry's imagination repeatedly stresses the two-dimensional or surface elements of Rittenmeyer's character, a quality that contributes to his function as a plot device. As Thomas Elsaesser points out, melodrama works in stock types and surfaces, not psychologically motivated behavior or individualized experience. Rittenmeyer, simply put, is a type. (As such he departs radically from standard modernist treatments of character, particularly Faulkner's own in his famous explorations of interiority in all of his early modernist novels.) This quality in Wilbourne's conception of him is evident the first time he encounters Rittenmeyer on the train, when he and Charlotte initiate their journey. Describing Wilbourne waiting for Charlotte at the Carrolton Avenue station, the narrator registers her arrival through Wilbourne's perspective: "They were both there, the husband and the wife, he in the conservative, spuriously unassertive dark suit, the face of a college senior revealing nothing, lending an air of impeccable and formal rightness to the paradoxical act of handing the wife to the lover" (530). "Wife," "husband," "lover"—these are the stock theatrical and melodramatic movie roles to which Wilbourne consigns Rittenmeyer, Charlotte, and, ultimately, himself. And they all function as purveyors of Wilbourne's vaguely defined but recognizably Victorian conception of "rightness." Wilbourne's limiting of the "players," especially Rittenmeyer, to a conventional, flat role is complemented by his description of Rittenmeyer's appearance: his conservative dark suit, we are told, "revealing nothing" of his interior life or psychology.

Even more clearly than through Rittenmeyer's appearance, Wilbourne's thoughts about Rittenmeyer's role in his and Charlotte's story reveal the melo-dramatic conception he has of their narrative. Walking behind Rittenmeyer down the aisle of the train as it leaves the station, Wilbourne reflects: "*He is suffering; even circumstance, a trivial railroad time table, is making comedy of that tragedy which he must play to the bitter end*" (532). As the scene continues, its contrived, theatrical nature becomes clear, particularly Wilbourne's act of constraining Rittenmeyer to the role of the wronged but virtuous husband. "He was trembling" to control himself, Wilbourne observes of Rittenmeyer, "the impeccable face suffused beneath the impeccable hair which resembled a wig" (532). Eventually Wilbourne himself becomes a part of the spectacle or performance. Responding to Rittenmeyer's threat to punch him when the two men face each other alone, he appears to watch and to hear himself speak from a position outside his own body: "Then suddenly Wilbourne heard his own voice speaking out of an amazed and quiet incredulity; it seemed to him that they both stood now, aligned, embattled and doomed and lost, before the entire female principle" (533). No longer a subject in his own life, a life he renders to himself passively and as a (film) spectator, Wilbourne too becomes a stock figure in a tragic, tortured love story. Charlotte herself is no longer his lover but an emblem, a symbol for a set of assumptions about the "entire female principle" with which Wilbourne constantly struggles and that Char-lotte represents in her role as bourgeois wife.

Represents, that is, to Harry—for it is important to note that the scene of Charlotte and Rittenmeyer is played out entirely through Harry's speculation. He is not there to see it, and therefore he only imagines what would take place between Charlotte and her husband. Sentimentalist that he is, Harry imagines this scene as it would have been depicted in melodrama, as a confession of repentance on the part of the wanton woman. Met with her daughters' coldness, Charlotte, in Harry's "scenario," utters a string of remarks that are demonstrably out of character for her (in Faulkner's conception) but entirely fitting for the heroine of melodrama. She came home "*[t]o see the children,*" she tells Rittenmeyer (despite showing little interest in them throughout the rest of the novel); she reacts with uncharacteristic bitterness and self-pity when the girls scorn her, remarking to her husband, "*So that's what you have taught them*" (646). This scene of high drama and moral conflict conforms to standards of melodramatic content, affirming the Victorian sanctity of the family and punishing the reprobate mother. That this scene conforms to Harry's and not to the rest of the novel's sensibilities is entirely to the point. For with this demonstration of Harry's fantasy and spectatorial pleasure, Faulkner shows readers the tragic world of melodrama they had seen in film and drama and that they (unwittingly) expect from the "Wild Palms" story.

And, consequently, are denied. Not only in the novel proper, but in the immediate aftermath to this scene, which clearly shows Faulkner ironizing it. Finishing his "screening," Harry leaves the park and joins Charlotte in the cab to the train station.[21] Maintaining his reverie, he asks, "They were both well?"—to which Charlotte responds by jolting him back to reality and to her harsh, unromantic sensibility. Promising that he "will hold [her]" if something goes wrong with her abortion, he is cut off by Charlotte's admonition that he not "be a fool" and that he "[g]et to hell out" (649) if in fact it does. Charlotte's voice here speaks in the tone of the novel's ending (epitomized in the convict's expletive in the book's last line, "Women, shit"), and against Harry's longing for a romantic, tragic conclusion to his escapist fantasy. Here again, we see the dangling of a romantic plot only to subvert or frustrate it, an example of what I have been arguing is central to the method of the novel.

Silent Film Screening and the Proletarian Audience

Melodramatic plots and narrative strategies appear elsewhere in "Wild Palms" and are similarly offered up to readers for their recognition of the novel's critical use of cinematic content and method. At the dramatic "climax" of Charlotte and Wilbourne's stay in Utah, Charlotte confronts the angry mob of immigrant workers from the mine. What is significant about this scene, immediately, are the similarities between Charlotte's method of placating the workers—her charcoal drawings—and the formal elements of silent film, as well as the way her drawings depict characters and content particular to cinematic melodrama. Of interest too is the way Faulkner's rendering of this scene shows Charlotte communicating with the "audience" of the miners, as well as that communication's effect. Coming toward the end of the couple's stay, this scene addresses the exploitation of the workers that Wilbourne knows of and in which he has been, at least passively, complicit. Simultaneously, it registers a political effect of early cinema toward maintaining that exploitation. In a perhaps unwitting outcome, Faulkner's treatment of the melodrama and the commercial cinema, evident elsewhere in the novel as a form of critique or protest, here replicates its socially conservative function.

To begin, the miners are positioned in the passage as spectators. Following Charlotte and Wilbourne from the mine into the commissary, they are described as though they have entered the cinema and are reduced to watchful, expectant eyes: "In the gloom after the snow-glare the faces vanished and only the eyes watched [Wilbourne] out of nothing, subdued, patient, obedient, trusting and wild" (630). Like the audience for silent film watching from the darkened space of the cinema ("the eyes watched . . . out of nothing"), the miners are spellbound before a mysterious and novel spectacle. And also like the audience for the early silent cinema, they are immigrant laborers.[22] Displacing the workers from the urban industrial centers where many of them lived, Faulkner nonetheless shows the miners in circumstances similar to those of the audience for the earliest movies: exploited, overworked, and susceptible to the sensory stimulations of the new medium.[23] Important to this resemblance is the motive for Charlotte's drawing, as well as her staging of it. She and Wilbourne feel uneasy, recognizing the miners' pent-up energy over months of not getting paid and sensing that their frustration may soon be directed at them. For Charlotte's actions ultimately function in the same way as much of silent film: to quell or re-contain an outburst of proletarian energy.

Typically, throughout this scene Wilbourne fails to act. Seeing the miners watching him and Charlotte, he asks her impotently, "Now what?" (630). Charlotte's response strikingly calls forth both the cinematic apparatus and the subjects of the silent film: "[A]nd now they all watched [Charlotte], the five women pushing forward also to see, as she fastened with four tacks produced from somewhere a sheet of wrapping paper to the end of a section of shelves where the light from the single window fell on it" (630). Setting up her "screen" on which falls the projection light, Charlotte proceeds

to draw swiftly with one of the scraps of charcoal she had brought from Chicago—the elevation of a wall in cross section with a grilled window in it unmistakably a pay window and as unmistakably shut, on one side of the window a number of people unmistakably miners (she had even included the woman with the baby); on the other side of the window an enormous man (she had never seen Callaghan, [Wilbourne] had merely described him to her, yet the man was Callaghan) sitting behind a table heaped with glittering coins which the man was shoveling into a sack with a huge hand on which glittered a diamond the size of a ping-pong ball. Then she stepped aside. (630–31)

There are several details to note about this description. In the first place, Charlotte's drawing recalls a scene from a classic melodrama: the New York section of D. W. Griffith's *Intolerance,* with its labor dispute modeled on an actual strike at Lawrence, Massachusetts. Important to this similarity is the role in Charlotte's drawing, as earlier in Wilbourne's imaginary film, of the stock type. The image of Callaghan is recognizable to Charlotte (she's never seen him "yet the man was Callaghan") as well as to Wilbourne and the miners—because as in most melodrama, the figure she depicts is a generic one: the corporate owner as villain. This image of Callaghan itself suggests a specific moment from Griffith's film: the industrialist boss in the deep-focus shot of him sitting alone and isolated at his desk (intercut with shots of his workers being gunned down by the police).

Before returning to the political meanings of Charlotte's drawing, it is useful to note its other formal similarities to early film. Significantly, the picture Charlotte draws is in charcoal, rendering it, like the photography of silent movies, in black and white. Also, Charlotte's drawing, like film, depicts motion: the man "was shoveling" money into a sack. The use of the past progressive tense here is key. For by way of it, Faulkner connotes an image of ongoing, sustained action.[24] Lastly, the description suggests one of film's principal technical properties: its capture and manipulation of light. The passage twice uses the word "glittering" to depict its details (the coins and the boss's ring). Unusual for a charcoal drawing, which is more often used to depict volume, shading, and depth, Charlotte's "filmic" image remains lingeringly on hard, shimmering surfaces—planes and lighting elements suited to the camera.

The depiction of Charlotte's drawing goes on in ways that further enforce the political overtones of its cinematic model and that, in so doing, reveal something of Faulkner's position on labor in this section of the novel. Upon recognizing the import of the scene Charlotte draws, the miners are enraged and are on the verge of seizing Wilbourne. Working fast in order to save him,

Charlotte again takes up the drawing. She draws an image of an immediately recognizable physician-figure (Wilbourne), who is being pickpocketed by the owner—thus who is himself being exploited, like the workers her drawing addresses. Charlotte then elicits help from one of the miners; drawing images in succession, she produces individual, separate "frames." The "movie" she makes suggests the vision of cinema that D. W. Griffith, one of its originators as well as one of its most committed melodramatists, harbored. Watching Charlotte draw, Wilbourne muses:

> This time [the figure Charlotte drew] was himself, indubitably himself and indubitably a doctor, anyone would have known it—the horn glasses, the hospital tunic every charity patient, every hunky gutted by flying rock or steel or premature dynamite and coming to in company emergency stations, has seen, a bottle which was indubitably medicine in one hand, a spoonful of which he was offering to a man who was compositely all of them, every man who has ever labored in the bowels of the earth. (631)

Charlotte's drawing here is an example of Griffith's "universal language," the utopia that he envisioned cinema to be. Imagined as a liberating tool for the masses, for a man "who was compositely all of them," cinema spoke in an idiom "beyond words" and communicated in a manner and a spirit Griffith hoped would cut across national, class, and ethnic lines. As Griffith said in his famous pronouncement to his actors, "We've gone beyond Babel, beyond words. We've found a universal language—a power that can make men brothers and end wars. Remember that, remember that when you go before the camera" (quoted in May, "Apocalyptic Cinema," 25).

The effects of Charlotte's drawing, however, like those of Griffith's and other early filmmakers, are less clearly allied with the worker. Specifically oriented toward the proletarian masses, both Griffith's cinema and Charlotte's drawing appear to function progressively. As Griffith conceived it, his great vision for film was that it inspire, edify, or enlighten viewers. Offering images that were immediately recognizable to non-English-speaking or even illiterate workers, Griffith's cinema hoped to empower laborers and working class audiences—or at the least, offer them a way to bond collectively without the benefit of a shared language or education. By the same token, the melodramatic mode of a film like *Intolerance* and the strike portion clearly sought to illicit sympathy for the worker.

Yet though conceived as a way to reach out to immigrant working classes, much of silent film served mainly as a way to distract workers from their economic circumstances. Charlotte's actions ultimately function in the same way: to diffuse workers' revolutionary energy. Charlotte intervenes in a near riot on the part of the miners, and her production of a silent, moving image serves to siphon off the threat the disgruntled men are posing. Although she makes the drawings to establish an identification between Wilbourne's and the miners' shared exploitation, Charlotte's actions nevertheless serve the interests of the mine's owning company. Like the early nickelodeons, Charlotte's silent, moving pictures distract workers from their economic discontent and working conditions and thus preempt their act of violently resisting them.

This, finally, is what also distinguishes Faulkner's scene. In this section of "Wild Palms," Faulkner reproduces not only the content or the form of silent film melodrama, the moving black-and-white images of exploited workers. In depicting the miners as Charlotte's spectators, this scene also includes a reference to the (largely) urban, immigrant labor market that attended early film. In this way, it places his readers outside of the scenario of film viewing. Structuring the passage with the miners as he does, Faulkner allows readers to "watch" a silent melodrama in Charlotte's drawings, but also to recognize her drawings' generic qualities and their effect on her audience. The importance of this layering is that it affords readers an opportunity to see the way melodrama functioned, both formally and politically. The drawing's main resemblance to film is that it helps to maintain a social and economic order that is disadvantageous to labor. Though Faulkner's own politics may be not be immediately discernible in the effect of Charlotte's "screening," it is worth noting that his reproduction of a filmic process in this scene demonstrates the more conservative effects of early silent movies.[25]

This seemingly conservative bent may help explain a paradox in one of Faulkner's revisions of the novel. In the published version of *Jerusalem*, Faulkner's narrator compares the visual impression of the Utah mine as Wilbourne first sees it to an "Eisenstein Dante" (621). This appearance in "Wild Palms" of the Marxist ideologue and Soviet filmmaker is, ultimately, ironic, appearing as it does in the context of a setting and circumstance (the exploitation of labor) that Eisenstein wanted film to redress. The montage strategies that Eisenstein employed in classical proletarian films such as *Strike!* and *Potemkin* served, he hoped, to spur exactly the kind of revolutionary energy that the miners in "Old Man" manifest but that we see Charlotte's drawing disarm. Revealingly, in the original and typescript versions of "Wild Palms," Faulkner's description of the interior of the mine—its calamitous visual impression, or, as others have described, its *mise-en-scène*[26]—refers, not to Eisenstein, a radical leftist visionary, but to a giant of Hollywood spectacle filmmaking, Cecil B. DeMille. Later, in final revisions, Faulkner deleted "DeMille" and wrote in "Eisenstein" instead.[27] The irony of this change is that Charlotte's silent film may correspond better to both the political function of DeMille's filmmaking (providing escapist entertainment for the middle and the working classes) than it would to Eisenstein's Marxist-informed, revolution-inspiring dialectical editing.

Harry's Peep Show

The seemingly irreconcilable tensions generated by this reading of the mine and Charlotte's drawing may find a resolution, or at least a clearer indication of Faulkner's position on film, if we turn to the novel's close. For in the prison sequence and the last pages of "Wild Palms," we find a final suggestion of film that, unlike the conservative implications of the Utah scene, shows Faulkner making a more pointed criticism of the movie industry. Most specifically, the scenes of Wilbourne in the prison cell suggest Faulkner's sense of the confinement or imprisoning of spectators in the trap of consumer culture. The prison setting offers a model of the way commercial film, like all commodity culture, stimulates consumers' desire, only to frustrate (but then sustain) it by refusing satisfaction. In his construction of that model, Faulkner evokes the generic form whose function is, above all, to organize and manage viewers' desire: pornography.

In my discussion of a widespread cultural melancholy in the last chapter, I described viewers' nostalgia for an unattainable image of the Old South myth promulgated by historical film. In his depiction of Wilbourne's nostalgic longing for Charlotte in his prison cell and his masturbatory, visual recollection of her naked body, Faulkner suggests that the workings of a genre like pornography make similar use of viewers' longing. Generic, commodified forms of pleasure, he implies, whether in historical film or pornography, are underpinned by a common motive: to manipulate audience's desires for the sake of profit. Faulkner's larger concern in much of his thirties fiction, which he addresses directly at the end of "Wild Palms," is that generic forms such as melodrama, the historical film, pulp fiction, and pornography all rely on a pleasure that is produced by the culture industry and whose nature is, finally, the same: projective, solipsistic, and melancholy.

The ending of *Jerusalem* offers a culmination of the critical dialogue in which Faulkner's thirties fiction had engaged, its examination of a range of popular cultural strategies and effects. In specific, the close of "Wild Palms" sharpens Faulkner's commentary on the relation between this novel and the commercial market. At the same time, it also provides a final model for considering modern consumer art. Ending this section as he does in a prison cell, with Harry providing a focalizing consciousness, Faulkner offers readers another way to witness Wilbourne's treatment of his affair with Charlotte as a consumable narrative. Like the mass market and its repeated acts of cultural consumption, Wilbourne's eroticizing of Charlotte's memory furnishes him a way to endlessly re-view his encounter with her.[28] Wilbourne's nostalgic treatment of Charlotte's memory while he is in prison amounts to a form of narrative autoeroticism, providing a pseudo-pornographic object for his mental gaze that will provide him both titillation and, he believes, a means to retain Charlotte's memory.

In order to remember her this way, Wilbourne first needs to "record" his time with Charlotte and, in particular, his images of her body. In the final pages of "Wild Palms," as he realizes she is dying and what her death will mean, Wilbourne reacts to Charlotte's struggle and his trip to the hospital in a routinely detached, passive manner. Standing apart from his and Charlotte's last hours together, resigning himself, it seems, to her dying, Wilbourne watches from a distance the playing out of Charlotte's "death scene." His muted response to the end of his story with Charlotte is, for Wilbourne, hardly unique. But in his passivity at this point in the novel we see the deadening of affect and responsiveness that the novel attributes to consumers of commodity culture, an effect that was signaled at the start of the novel in the figure of the doctor and his wife—their stale marriage, stale gumbo, and taste for the ready-made. Here, at the novel's end, we see a similar characterization of Wilbourne, after he has demonstrated his own removed, voyeuristic preferences for consumer forms.[29] Wilbourne's impassiveness at the hospital is important for another reason as well. Anticipating his imminent prison sentence, Wilbourne's demeanor during the novel's final events provides him with the detached, "objective" position necessary for a mental "recording" of them, a process Faulkner evokes in his use of several cinematic details in the pages depicting Charlotte's death.

Waiting in the hall of the hospital during Charlotte's surgery, Wilbourne remarks to himself that the lighting inside the operating room resembles Kleig lights—high-powered floodlights used in Hollywood film production (697, 701). For Wilbourne, Charlotte's death occurs under the circumstances of a film shoot, allowing it to become another source of replayable visual pleasure for him, like the scene of Charlotte and Rittenmeyer in New Orleans. Once the operation is finished, the Klieg lights are turned off and Wilbourne notices a ventilator blowing—like the cooling fan for the projector. And the projector is suggested elsewhere in the sound of the palm trees clashing outside, similar to the whir of the movie projector's gears.[30] After Charlotte dies, Wilbourne is permitted to enter the operating room, where the recording process continues. Although the "Kleigs were off" (702), another "single dome light burned" above the operating table, lighting Charlotte's body, which appeared "arrested for the moment for him to look at" (702). Earlier in the chapter is another more explicit reference to Charlotte's nudity artificially "lit" for Wilbourne's consumption and gaze. This description of Charlotte is rendered from Wilbourne's perspective, and it provides him with an eroticized image that he will take with him to prison. Waiting in the coastal shack for the doctor to return, Wilbourne sees Charlotte on the bed

> on her back, her eyes closed, the nightgown . . . twisted about her just under the arms, the body not sprawled, not abandoned, but on the contrary even a little tense . . . [I]t began to seem to him that the sound [of the wind] was rather the murmur of the lamp itself sitting on an upended packing case beside the bed, the rustle and murmur of faint dingy light itself on her flesh—the waist ever narrower than he had believed, anticipated, the thighs merely broad since they were flat too, the swell and neat nip of belly between the navel's flattened crease and the neat close cupping of female hair. (687)

The erotic elements of this image hardly need enumerating. "Sprawled" on the bed with the nightgown "twisted" around and binding her, her eyes closed, and naked, Charlotte appears in the throes of a vaguely masochistic ecstasy. As in the operating room, the light here is trained on Charlotte's body in ways that facilitate Wilbourne's clear view of it as well as his technical remembering. Even the light itself has become "dingy," suggesting the tawdry quality of Wilbourne's imagination and the potentially shocking, but also standard pornographic image it offers him.

The artificial or synthetic "preservation" of Charlotte is suggested as well in a conversation between Wilbourne and the police officer who is guarding him at the hospital. Seeing Wilbourne's worry, the officer offers an anecdote about the surgeon's work on another patient that relays the doctor's ability to remake human bodies.

> "Just take it easy. They'll fix her up. That was Doc Richardson himself. They brought a sawmill nigger in here couple three years ago where somebody cut him across the guts with a razor in a crap game. Well, what does Doc Richardson do, opens him up, cuts out the bad guts, sticks the two ends together like you'd vulcanise an inner tube, and the nigger's back at work right now." (699)

The "vulcanizing" of the black man's intestines performed by Doc Richardson allows him to continue living, but only by supplementing his damaged body synthetically. That his body is diminished is clear: " 'Of course he aint got but one gut and it aint but two feet long so he has to run for the bushes almost before he quits chewing. But he's all right. Doc'll fix her up the same way' " (699). Doc Richardson does not "fix Charlotte up" the same way—that is, his efforts, synthetic or otherwise, to preserve Charlotte fail, as she dies on the operating table. Wilbourne's own efforts at preservation, however, are more successful. And they rely on techniques, like Richardson's, that make use of synthetic materials and technology.

Later, in several passages from Harry's cell, Faulkner conflates Wilbourne's acts of memory, masturbation, and what may be seen as a kind of film viewing. Charlotte's memory, we are told, cannot exist for Wilbourne completely apart from her body; there must be "flesh to titillate" (714), or at least the palpable, material reminder of flesh. In the absence of Charlotte's actual body, Wilbourne's filmic memory of her in a reproducible, visualized narrative provides this "titillation." Masturbating over the quasi-pornographic image of Charlotte, "thinking of, remembering, the body, the broad thighs and the hands that liked bitching" (715), Wilbourne is able to re-view scenes from their erotic life together in ways that allow her to live on. "*But memory. Surely memory exists independent of the flesh,*" he reasons. "But this was wrong too," the narrator corrects—to which Harry responds *Because it wouldn't know it was memory,* he thought. *It wouldn't know what it was it remembered. So there's got to be the old meat, the old frail eradicable meat for memory to titillate*" (709). The "old meat" Harry needs to stimulate himself and his memory is Charlotte's eroticized body. In the absence of her body, then, he uses his stored-up images of it. In the "grief" that Harry accepts in place of "nothing," he reanimates the scenes of Charlotte he has chosen to record. Doing so provides him with solace; it also stimulates his arousal as, we are told, "it did stand to his hand, incontrovertible and plain" (715) once he remembers Charlotte's body.

Preparing himself for a fifty-year prison sentence, Wilbourne gives himself ample material to both inspire and sustain his nostalgic longing. This nostalgia, however, does not function, finally, to help Wilbourne overcome Charlotte's loss. Rather, it takes the form of a sustained, faintly pleasurable suffering. In this way Wilbourne's "grief," his memorializing of Charlotte through the storehouse of her images, is also a form of indulgence. And this indulgent aspect of Wilbourne's serial, repeated grieving returns us to a broader consideration of commercial culture. The masturbatory pleasure Wilbourne experiences stands, for Faulkner, as the kind of sensation and experience prompted by many popular cultural forms. Commercial film, particularly in genres such as pornography or the silent film melodrama, may—like the memory of Charlotte for Harry—"titillate the senses" or even provide temporary satisfactions. It does not, however, fulfill the longings it stimulates. Thus it leaves consumers in a state something like Harry's at the end of the novel: a melancholy condition of being repeatedly drawn back to the source of an unfulfilled loss or longing.[31]

Seeing Harry in his prison cell at the end of the novel, readers may recognize the similarity between his position of entrapment and passive spectatorship and that of the consumer of commercial fare such as film. Like the viewers of silent films of history discussed in the previous chapter, the film viewers of melodrama or pornography, both of whom Faulkner suggests through Harry, also experienced what in the modern period became a widespread cultural melancholy. Consumer art, whether it seizes on narratives of history, images of the female body, or depictions of the bourgeois family, produces in its audience an appetite that is constantly stimulated but constantly frustrated. It is this unsatisfied longing inherent in commercial forms that Faulkner recognized and that I refer to as a kind of Freudian melancholy.

Earlier in this discussion I argued that the nostalgic longing for the southern past prompted by early film narratives derived from and effected a generalized American melancholia, an incapacity for many Americans in the modern period to understand meaningfully the historical lessons of the Civil War. With the ending of "Wild Palms," and with *If I Forget Thee, Jerusalem* generally, Faulkner demonstrates the ways in which other forms of popular culture produced a similarly morbid, debilitating effect. Melancholy thus defined describes a compulsively repeated action and an accompanying cast of thought that attaches to a nostalgia-rich and neurotically charged object of longing. Watching his memories of Charlotte as though they were a movie, standing in his private screening room and masturbating, Wilbourne shows readers what Faulkner wanted them to see about their own experience: the deadening, narcissistic prison of popular culture that refers consumers only to projections of their own desire.

The ending of "Wild Palms," however, like Faulkner's other novels from this period, provides something more for readers than the films and popular cultural models Faulkner critiques through so much of his thirties writing. Harry's story in "Wild Palms" may not itself provide the kind of satisfaction I am here suggesting that popular culture denies. Yet through the novel's workings—its references to the culture industry that Faulkner deplored, its ironic representation of its generic materials, and the undermining of "Wild Palms" by the strategies of "Old Man"—it provides readers with something unavailable to Harry in his prison cell, namely, a critical reflection on the nature of consumerist pleasure. And in doing so, it furnishes something else unavailable to Harry: a way out of the metaphoric prison of consumer culture and its transient pleasures—artificial, "melancholy," and profit-serving.

Modernism, Jail Cells, and the Senses

Caddy smelled like trees.

— B E N J Y in *The Sound and the Fury*

Vision, mass culture, imprisonment: my discussion has identified these as the pervasive tropes and dominating subtexts of Faulkner's writing of the thirties. Beginning with the Negro murderer in the original version of *Sanctuary* in 1929 and ending with both Wilbourne and the Tall Convict in Parchman Prison in *If I Forget Thee, Jerusalem* in 1939, Faulkner uses the figure of the jail cell to communicate something specific about the circumstances of writing in this decade. Within this frame and through a range of strategies, including parody, imitation, and critique, he also makes use of materials from popular art and what he saw as its dominant mode of sense perception: vision and the attending social and psychological impact of the look.

That vision became a dominant element in Faulkner's novels of this decade is hardly surprising if we consider its role in the cultural life of the period as well as what this emphasis on visual experience signified. As Faulkner understood, and as several theorists contend, a central component of modernity was a diminishing of authentic experience and understanding due to the influence of the new technology media. My discussion has endeavored to detail Faulkner's response to these developments in texts often considered distinct from the realm of popular culture—above all, the high-modernist novels he pro-duced in his mature period. Immediately prior to Faulkner's sustained involve-ment with popular art in the thirties, however, are moments in Faulkner's writing that differ meaningfully from it. A glance at those moments, as well as another question about the motives for his figurative approach to mass culture—in particular his recurring image of the prison cell—suggests a final way to understand the historical quality of Faulkner's modernism.

In assessments of Faulkner's career, critics have often noted the singular importance of *The Sound and the Fury* as well as of Faulkner's own account of this novel in his development as a writer. As Eric Sundquist has pointed out, it is perhaps Faulkner's famous celebration of the novel and its "lost" figure, Caddy Compson, more than the book itself that has compelled consideration of it in this way. Retrospective efforts to understand the relationship of Faulk-ner's novels after *The Sound and the Fury* frequently make use of Faulkner's emphasis on his experience of writing around and from the story's originating point of loss and yearning.[1]

The idea that *The Sound and the Fury* possesses signal importance for understanding Faulkner's writing after it—that there are issues "latent" in it that Faulkner would later confront in greater depth—obtains in considering the novels I have treated in this study. In particular, aspects of Benjy's experi-ence and Faulkner's manner of depicting it suggest another area of loss that, like Faulkner's statements about the "beautiful and tragic" Caddy, appear significant in light of his later work. Benjy helps close my argument about the thirties, mass culture, and vision because of the role in his section of *The Sound and the Fury* of sensory perceptions other than vision, as well as the meaning of Faulkner's emphasizing them.

The importance of sensory experience in this context is what it signifies historically, both in terms of the cultural history I have been detailing and in a broader, materialist understanding of consciousness and identity. As media that emphasized vision in new and unexpected ways, photography and film had a demonstrable effect on people's experience of the world around them through its representation—including and especially representations of gen-der, race, and the historical past. If modern subjectivity was influenced by visual experience of the sort emphasized by film, as cultural historians and theorists of modernity have argued, as well as by advertising, commodity fetishism, or acts of social organizing, we may also note that, historically speaking, this has not always been so. Benjy and his place both in *The Sound and the Fury* and in Faulkner's modernism show the meaningful differences between a fullness and range of sense perception, and the singular emphasis we see in the thirties novels on sight and on vision's political and economic uses. Benjy helps to see how sensory perception, as theoretical accounts of it have argued and as it has been affected by shifts in technology, culture, and social experience, may itself be historicized.

Like many characters in Faulkner's fiction, Benjy is irretrievably focused on his past. Though this longing is ultimately narcissistic, referring him to his possessive longing for his sister, it nevertheless removes Benjy from an attachment to his contemporary circumstances in Mississippi in 1928. This temporal "displacement" combines in *The Sound and the Fury*'s first section with a uniquely vivid rendering of Benjy's sense perception, a combination that implies Faulkner's recognition of historical change. As a purely sensory character, Benjy is at odds with a modern social reality and, we might add, with an economic system that placed greater and greater emphasis on processes of abstract, rational calculation.

Unlike the characters of Faulkner's later novels, Benjy demonstrates an extraordinary depth, as well as range, of sense perceptions. As opposed to characters like Quentin, Horace, or Harry Wilbourne (or in different ways the anonymous Jefferson crowd or various agencies of surveilling power), he is not defined by the exercise of sight. Benjy also repeatedly evokes a remembered and, for him, a more fulfilled period from his childhood. Kevin Railey sees *The Sound and the Fury,* and the novel's first section in particular, as the mark of Faulkner's "birth into history." His motives for doing so reveal Railey's explicitly materialist reasoning: "In Benjy, Faulkner creates a character who closely relates to an earlier time period. In tune with sensory experience, Benjy does not possess any of the qualities and abilities so definitely valued—too valued Faulkner would say—in this twentieth-century capitalist world—those of calculation, classification, and prediction. Faulkner seems to be completely in unison with Marxist critiques of capitalist society, implying that the need to own things and the skills necessary to obtain them in this society diminish the ability to perceive through the senses" (*Natural Aristocracy,* 52).

The move from Benjy to Marx is, admittedly, extreme. But Railey's attention to Benjy's status as "an 'idiot' in touch only with his sensory experiences" (51) suggests something important about Faulkner's understanding of the historical quality of the senses. Specifically, Benjy represents an alternative to the increasing diminishment in modernity of individuals' sensory capacity and emotional life. As such, he suggests the problems posed to a human, affective sensibility by changes in economic and social reality.[2] Modern capitalistic values do not produce a complete disavowal of sensory activity; vision, as we will see, functions effectively as those values' correlative. And Benjy's life and chapter are themselves also informed to a degree by his acts of looking.[3] Yet Faulkner's rendering of Benjy ultimately emphasizes his greater fullness of sensory activity and what that fullness reveals about the limitations of modern capitalistic abstraction.

Benjy's sensory capacity, his simple, repeated assertion that "Caddy smelled like trees," as well as other poetic utterances in his section—"I could smell the bright cold" (4); "the flowers rasped and rattled against us" (3); "The ground was hard, churned and knotted" (3)—register an immediacy of experience and quality of sense perception that for Faulkner's characters of the thirties becomes harder and harder to find. Even a cursory gloss on Faulkner's characteristic manner of conveying Benjy's world reveals his affective wholeness: "*The bed smelled like T.P. I liked it*" (19). "The bowl steamed up to my face, and Versh's hand dipped the spoon in it and the steam tickled into my mouth" (17). "Then they all stopped and it was dark, and when I stopped to start again I could hear Mother, and feet walking fast away, and I could smell it" (22). "A door opened and I could smell it more than ever" (22). "The trees were buzzing, and the grass" (24). "I fell off the hill into the bright, whirling shapes" (34). "Then the dark began to go in smooth, bright shapes, like it always does, even when Caddy says that I have been asleep" (48). Without the capacity to name things or identify his experience, as in this last example of dreaming, Benjy nevertheless powerfully communicates that experience's felt quality. Though this particular example makes use of a visual impression, many of Benjy's most vivid assertions about his world rely on other sensory apprehensions, often and particularly the sense of smell. (Vision, in this last example, is qualified too by touch, as Benjy refers to the "bright *smooth* shapes.") Like Benjy, characters such as Horace or Quentin feel alienated from their present and helplessly cut off from their past. Unlike Benjy, however, they have little compensatory experience to make up for it, nor do they have his ability to so fully and powerfully *feel*.[4]

The stunted affective and sensory potential of Horace, Quentin, or Wilbourne that I am contrasting with Benjy is not limited to Faulkner's characters. I suggest that Benjy's section is forceful not only because of how immediately his inner life and sensory capacity are drawn, but because he is a reminder of a quality of experience that for many people was lost—or was in the process of being lost—in the period in which Faulkner was writing. After *The Sound and the Fury*, Faulkner emphasizes not touch, smell, or hearing, but sight. The results of that shift are clear in Faulkner's writing of the thirties, as I hope my analysis demonstrates. Viewed in this way, Benjy offers perhaps a last glimpse of a culture or world that organized itself differently than does that of characters like Horace, Popeye, Quentin in *Absalom, Absalom!* and Harry Wilbourne. As such, he stands as one of a very few examples in Faulkner's fiction of what we might call a "premodern," nonreified consciousness. In light of the almost exclusive emphasis on vision that we find in the thirties and of what it connotes about modernity, Benjy's richer and better-integrated sensory life is instructive.

I am not proposing here that Benjy stands as a fully realized historical subject. Far from it. As noted, his consciousness, however linked to the past, is not productively, actively so. Benjy clearly does not offer a model or a project for historical awareness or change. Yet I think that we may nonetheless allow Benjy and even his more limited cognitive capacity to express something, if only suggestively and by way of contrast, about the impoverished nature of a modern, rationalistic subjectivity. Particularly as that subjectivity is manifested in Faulkner's thirties novels—both in their characters, and in the consciousness and operations of the novels themselves, as it were—we may find in Benjy an alternative position that informs our understanding of Faulkner's later treatment of sensory life. Benjy's mental limitations prevent reading him nostalgically and as part of an impulse for an earlier, "purer" time or mode of being. If he offers a positive alternative to the affective, sensory, and emotional shortcomings of Horace, Quentin, Sutpen, or Wilbourne, he does not exactly represent a state to which Faulkner urges us to return. He does, however, mark the orienting point of a concern Faulkner increasingly voiced in the novels that followed, as well as an example of a character who lacks the particular afflictions we see in so many of Faulkner's thirties protagonists.

Elsewhere, and in a more general manner, Fredric Jameson has strenuously asserted the need in cultural criticism for a historicizing of sensory life. In *The Political Unconscious*, he describes the way sense perception has altered in different historical epochs and in response to various modes of production, especially cultural production and expression. In doing so, Jameson refers to Marx's statements about the historical disconnection between human sensory life and the status of objects or commodities: "'The *senses* have therefore become *theoreticians* in their immediate praxis. They relate to the *thing* for its own sake, but the thing itself is an *objective human* relation to itself and to man, and vice-versa' " (Marx quoted from *Economic and Philosophical Manuscripts* in *The Political Unconscious*, 62). Though in this discussion Jameson treats the shifts between the romance novel and realism, his thinking is useful for a consideration of Faulkner's historical modernism. In a statement that might apply to the "primitive" or affective aspect of Benjy that I am here raising, Jameson goes on to claim, "The scandalous idea that the senses have a history is . . . one of the touchstones of our historicity; if, in spite of our thoughts about history, we still feel that . . . primitive peoples, were very much like ourselves and in particular lived their bodies and their senses in the same way, then we have surely not made much progress in thinking historically" (229). As rendered by Faulkner's novelistic experiment, Benjy's experience offers a version of a different, and perhaps *historically* different way of living the senses.

As other theorists of the novel form and of modernism point out, sense perception and the way we "live our bodies" had been undergoing changes well before Faulkner imagined Benjy or wrote *The Sound and the Fury*. In advance of Jameson's consideration of the senses and the transformations of the novel, Georg Lukács described this historical and affective shift in his early meditation on the genre, *Theory of the Novel*. Referring to the advent of the lyric voice in prose (for him the origins of the novel genre), Lukács wrote,

> In lyric poetry, only the great moment exists, the moment at which the meaningful unity of nature and soul or their meaningful divorce, the necessary and affirmed loneliness of the soul becomes eternal. At the lyrical moment the purest interiority of the soul . . . solidifies into substance; whilst alien, unknowable nature is driven from within. (63)

Benjy's section may be said to express in several moments this "meaningful unity of nature and soul," particularly in references to his natural surroundings and their profound effect on him. His awareness of his sister's presence and her affinity with trees; the smell of rain or of the cold outside; his intense responsiveness to the sound of insects in the grass or the flapping of birds' wings—all of these suggest Benjy's powerful connection to his physical environment. Following Benjy, and throughout the thirties, we find a sustained treatment of the "divorce" of the unity of nature and the soul and its historical causes as well as the attendant effects on characters of a newly "unknowable" nature.[5]

The close of *The Sound and the Fury*'s last section perhaps shows an indication of the direction Faulkner was to turn after it, the "divorce from nature" and from perceiving it directly that begins with Horace and Popeye (in their mechanical, detached scene in the forest clearing) and reaches its apogee in a color-blind Harry Wilbourne. Having maintained something of Benjy's affective vivacity in *The Sound and the Fury* with Quentin (in the smell of honeysuckle and in the focus on Quentin's interiority), with Jason we arrive at a more fully exteriorized experience as well as the beginnings of an emphasis on sight. In addition to highlighting Jason's relentless and controlling observation of Miss Quentin, the novel's account of him includes its famous double "cue" to the act of looking that is associated with Jason and his overly cerebral experience: the graphic depiction of the eye in the sign at the Mottson gas station, "Keep your 👁 on Mottson" (193). Throughout Jason's monologue we find an emphasis on calculation, commerce, and profit, concerns that would reappear obsessively in thirties characters such as Thomas Sutpen and Harry Wilbourne (and to a degree during this period, as his correspondence reveals, in Faulkner himself).

In the fourth section and with the arrival of Dilsey and her family at church, we find some of the earliest intimations of the turn that Faulkner's perspective in the thirties was to take not only to an emphasis on vision but also to its related effects. Referring to the country setting, at the end of Dilsey, Frony, and Benjy's walk the narrator offers a description that hints strongly at a diminished perceptual ability:

> The road rose again, to a scene like a painted backdrop. Notched into a cut of red clay crowned with oaks the road appeared to stop short off, like a cut ribbon. Beside it a weathered church lifted its crazy steeple like a painted church, and the whole scene was as flat and without perspective as a painted cardboard set upon the ultimate edge of the flat earth, against the windy sunlight of space and April and a midmorning filled with bells. (292)

Throughout this passage are references to vision, but in particular, to a notably shallow perspective. In addition to the repetitions ("as flat," "flat earth"), there are indirect suggestions of two-dimensionality and foreshortening in the "painted backdrop," "painted church," and "cut ribbon." Sense perception is almost entirely reduced to vision, yet a vision that is severely limited.[6]

Here, at the end of *The Sound and the Fury,* we see the effect of something Faulkner went on to show was central to the experience of characters (and potentially of his readers) in the thirties: the loss of a sense of immediacy and contact with the world such that Benjy had demonstrated. The visual but flattened image of the church in Dilsey's section stands out against Benjy's synesthetic locutions and his simple but moving association of his sister with trees. It also stands out, interestingly, against language in the passage that describes the "windy sunlight of space and April" and the sound-bearing, palpable "midmorning filled with bells." In such moments, Faulkner contrasts the impression of openness, space, and a concretized sound with a series of depthless, abstract, and two-dimensional images. It is as if, at the novel's end and at the very moment Faulkner also intimates the reifying, "flattening" effects of vision—effects he went on to catalogue throughout the novels that followed—he reminds readers of the material fullness and sensory richness of the premodern, nonconsumer cultural world.

With these remarks, I do not mean to imply simply that with *The Sound and the Fury* or the first section we find a purer, "premodernist" Faulkner. Yet in important ways, *The Sound and the Fury* both does and does not include what I describe as some of the most specifically modernist aspects of Faulkner's later texts. As he attested, this novel gave Faulkner a sense for what he could do with his writing that he had not yet experienced and, following which, he was not to experience again. After writing *The Sound and the Fury*, Faulkner said, "I believed that I knew then why I had not recaptured that first ecstasy, and that I should never again recapture it" ("Introduction" to *The Sound and the Fury*, 227). Faulkner's treatment of Benjy, his immediate, powerful connection to a range of sense perceptions as well as to his emotional life and natural world, differs radically from the combination of modernist literary practices and popular cultural influences that mark the thirties works and characters' experiences in them. In creating Benjy, Faulkner gives us a character who is truly arrested in his development. In his possession of certain qualities that were lacking in most of Faulkner's later characters, however (and arguably in many of his readers), as well as in his longings for an irrecoverable past, Benjy suggests something important about Faulkner's historicizing of the senses. By way of contrast, we might think of Wilbourne's deadened state at the end of "Wild Palms," or the potential extension of that mind-set in a broad cultural melancholy in the modern period. With Faulkner's preoccupation with vision and its various manifestations in the thirties, he repeatedly shows both a cause and an effect of modern social and cultural experience.

Carolyn Porter stresses a similar role for vision in her reading of *Absalom, Absalom!* Porter's specifically materialist, approach to Faulkner and to American literary history is compelling, and it offers terms that suggest another way to see Benjy's place in Faulkner's modernism. In addition to describing the "transcendent," encompassing quality of Sutpen's design, Porter seeks to redress earlier readings of Sutpen that see him as an example of a uniquely southern economics. She points out that throughout the novel Sutpen demonstrates habits of abstraction and calculation that Marxist cultural theory attributes more generally to Western capitalism. His design, in Mr. Compson's words, works by a "code of logic" and resembles a "formula and recipe of fact and deduction . . . [a] balanced sum and product" (*Absalom, Absalom!* 227). Commensurate with that calculating approach to his world is Sutpen's predominating perceptive mode, vision. We have noted the way in which to Quentin, Sutpen and his story appear as a series of moving images similar to those of film. By extension, Sutpen's cold, inscrutable stare, his eyes "at once visionary and alert" (26), and his far-reaching gaze down the "undivulged light rays" (216) align Sutpen himself with a calculating and detached act of looking.[7]

These qualities that characterize Sutpen—vision, rationalization, and calculation—distinguish him thoroughly from Benjy. They also mark for Faulkner, as for others, a particularly modern consciousness and experience. As Jameson puts it, "The very activity of sense perception has nowhere to go in a world in which science deals with ideal quantities, and comes to have little enough exchange value in a money economy dominated by considerations of calculation, measurement, profit, and the like. This unused surplus capacity of sense perception can only organize itself into a new and semi-autonomous activity, one which produces its own specific objects, new objects that are themselves the result of a process of abstraction" (*Political Unconscious*, 229). It is precisely Sutpen's calculation and "production of new objects" in other people like Rosa or Milly Jones that impoverishes him ethically and effects the "semi-autonomous" emphasis on sight that defines him. As Porter and others have shown, Faulkner's critique of Sutpen's design is part of an extended examination of the role of a market economy in both southern and American social experience and history.[8] As the sensory mode most readily associated with detachment, analysis, and cognition ("re-cognition" connoting both an act of seeing and of thought), vision comes under scrutiny in Faulkner's treatment of modern American consciousness—in Sutpen, specifically, but more generally as vision was influenced by commercial and technological culture in the early twentieth century.

My study has endeavored to illustrate the ways that Faulkner's critical awareness of the new mass media and its influences animated his most modernist, supposedly "anti"-popular cultural novels. Chief among the effects of those media were the deleterious workings of cinema, that supremely visual and, in the early part of the century, most reifying of forms. The connections of Faulkner's critique of popular culture to his shift in the thirties to an ever stronger emphasis on vision—what Jameson called the "semi-autonomous activity of sight"—were not incidental. They in fact enabled one another. The seeds of this historical shift, however, began much earlier. Jameson shows how, well before Faulkner, novelists were already seeing a connection between visual experience and changes in social and economic reality. He refers to this connection as "the new ideology of the image, on the one hand, and the objective fragmentation of the outside world, or of the objects of perception, on the other" (*Political Unconscious*, 232). Jameson's model for treating this development, significantly, is Conrad, arguably Faulkner's greatest literary influence. Specifically, Jameson pursues this point though Conrad's *The Nigger of the "Narcissus,"* one of Faulkner's favorite novels and which provided one of the epigraphs for this study. For Jameson, Conrad's stylistic emphasis on perception and particularly on vision in this novel marked an awareness of specific effects of capitalism at the end of the nineteenth century. He means his point about a new "surplus capacity" of the senses literally: as a descriptive account of a period of historical transition in which, as he puts it, "the 'rational,' quantifying functions of the mind become privileged in such a way as to take structural precedence over older functions" (228) such as sensory life. With "nowhere to go" in a new world of economic abstraction and exchange-value, the senses take on a life of their own that is both a response to, and a symptom of, the shift to an industrial, instrumental order. This sensory autonomy and its production of "new objects" then appears for Jameson as a way of understanding Conrad's uniquely visual style, above all its production of radically new textual effects: a weird, otherworldly "refracting" of lighting or color in descriptive passages suggestive of "some new planet in the sky" or even "the presence of nonearthly colors in the spectrum" (231). Despite his own vivid and evocative language, Jameson means to offer these statements evenly: "This . . . is my justification in characterizing Conrad's stylistic production as an *aestheticizing strategy:* the term is not meant as a moral or political castigation, but is rather to be taken literally, as the designation of a strategy which for whatever reason seeks to recode or rewrite the world and its own data in terms of perception as a semi-autonomous activity" (230).

Jameson's claims about Conrad's aestheticizing have particular relevance to what I see develop as a similar, if somewhat more castigating, strategy in Faulkner. For Jameson, these effects are measurable in Conrad's "displacing" of the standard nineteenth-century trope of theatricality, his undermining of it through an appropriation of the metaphor of perspective and an emphasis on vision within the language of Conrad's style. The result, he claims, is something decidedly more modern. "Conrad displaces the theatrical metaphor by transforming it into a matter of sense perception, into a virtually filmic experience" (*Political Unconscious,* 232). Before the advent of cinema, Jameson argues, Conrad displaced the standard nineteenth-century trope of theatricality into a textual effect, one that historicizes sensory activity and its influence by capitalist developments and that, to Jameson, resembles film.[9]

Perhaps in Faulkner's reading of Conrad, but more likely in his own experience with movies and the film industry, he increasingly saw evidence of the abstract and reified consciousness Jameson identified. Film epitomized these negative aspects of a modern sensibility and system, based on audiences' detached and, in Faulkner's early experience, silent consumption of images, as well as by the studios' ever more rigorously calculated profit. As such, film and its related effects compelled Faulkner's attention, appearing in the consciousness that he attributed to his characters and informing his depiction of Yoknapatawpha's social world. Historicizing Faulkner's modernism as I have tried to do—showing his critique of vision and popular culture to be part of his complaint against an overly rational and increasingly capitalist society—lends credence, I think, to assessments of Benjy as a vestige of an earlier historical period. If *The Sound and the Fury* and Benjy's chapter mark one precipitating moment in that complaint, I submit that much of what follows in the thirties represents a way of tracing that moment's development. An impulse originating, in this analysis, in Benjy becomes, in the thirties, Faulkner's broader cultural and social critique.

I have been at pains throughout this discussion to show how Faulkner's writing of the thirties, while sharply critical of various effects and forms of popular culture, avoids precisely the kind of transcending and disavowal of its historical moment described by traditional accounts of modernism. Closely involving himself with the modes of representation of cultural forms he disdained such as film and popular fiction, and including them in his "high-art" novels, Faulkner managed both a striking approximation of those popular forms and a trenchant critique of them. As we have seen, he did not always do so easily or with full control of his appropriations of mass culture, as in *Light in August,* or without ambivalence about those uses, as in *Sanctuary.*

In several ways, and in spite of my characterization of the immanent, engaged quality of his criticism, Faulkner strove at points to fortify himself against the more "sordid" realities of the popular cultural world. This act, repeated symbolically at various points in the decade, allows a final, summary reading of Faulkner's "mass cultural" decade. It also offers a way to understand what I have identified as the thirties' other predominant trope. As indicated earlier, Faulkner begins and ends the period of writing I've treated with the image of a man in prison. That jail cell, as I've noted in my chapters, appears inviting to the characters who inhabit it, and even to one who does not. It is appealing to Horace, to Harry, and to the Tall Convict—and above all, it appears, to Faulkner.

At this point it seems reasonable to ask what the basis of that appeal was. One explanation is by way of another reference to Benjy and the privileged place I am lending him in Faulkner's career. In the terms I am pursuing, at the other end of the spectrum from Benjy stands, not Jason Compson, whom Faulkner referred to as Benjy's foil and an agent of pure "evil," nor the visionary Thomas Sutpen, but the ruthlessly calculating, mercantilist-minded, and exploitative Snopeses. Harbingers of the social and economic systems for the new century, the Snopeses signal the rise not only of a new bourgeois class and economic way of life in the South, but of a new and more modern form of "being." As Faulkner knew well, that mode of life made itself felt not only in the twentieth-century South but in a broader American cultural and economic life, including especially the parts of it that most nearly affected him. The Snopeses are not themselves purveyors of mass culture; they are not Hollywood studio executives or short-story magazine editors. (They are certainly not emblems of the New York publishing world that included figures and institutions like Harrison Smith and Random House.) They are, however, examples of the managerial class that, in contexts outside the South—and in the entertainment and cultural industries in which Faulkner also worked—came increasingly to influence and dominate the work of artists and writers.

One episode from the first Snopes novel strikingly illustrates this view. It recalls scenes from an earlier novel—Wilbourne's "peep show" of Charlotte's body and his viewing of it while in prison—as well as Faulkner's sense of the pornographic nature of the film product and the culture industry generally. Lump Snopes's aborted effort in *The Hamlet* to display Ike's sessions with the cow in Mrs. Littlejohn's stable, and eventually to charge "admission" for it, sounds like an urban nickelodeon displaced from the cities to the rural countryside. Complete with a captive, paying audience drawn to illicit acts of voyeurism, it includes as well a managing theater owner or "distributor" in Lump. Just as importantly, however, the scene at Mrs. Littlejohn's also includes Faulkner's characteristically pointed critique of it and, as with his earlier novels, his always immanent method. When he stops the men's activity of watching, Ratliff does so in a manner that, for him, is uncharacteristically angry: he imagines attacking the crowd of onlookers. "When they looked around at [Ratliff], he already held the loose plank, holding it as if he were on the point of striking at them with it" (*The Hamlet*, 913). Ratliff does not attack the men at the stable physically. But his scorn is obvious. Despite his anger, though, when Ratliff speaks to the group, he condemns not only the men involved for watching Ike, and Snopes for aiding them, but the entire apparatus of a managed, profit-turning spectacle of desire. Surprised by his re-nailing the plank through which they'd been looking, one of the men says to Ratliff, " 'I notice you come to have your own look too.' " To which Ratliff replies "sardonically," "not even in outraged righteousness," " 'Sholy . . . I aint cussing you folks. I'm cussing all of us' " (913). In a manner that might describe Faulkner's cultural critique of the thirties, one that included his recognition of his own position in the culture industry and in the modern culture of which he was a part, Ratliff includes himself—"all of us"—in his damning.

The Hamlet, though, also includes a powerful alternative to the Snopeses and what they represent as well as to Ratliff's (and Faulkner's) "cussing." For outside of that scope lies a character and an experience that offers a striking rejoinder not only to the Snopes episodes and narrative that frame it but to Faulkner's broader focus on mass culture and vision as well. The passage earlier in the book describing Ike waiting for the cow in the creek bottom is notable for its attention to a range of potent sensory stimulation, effects that resemble those we noted with Benjy. Because of what these effects say rhetorically about sense perception in the context of *The Hamlet*'s rapidly commercializing world, and because they manifest themselves in some of the most vivid and rapturous prose Faulkner wrote, I quote the passage at length:

Then he would hear her, coming down the creekside in the midst. It would not be after one hour, two hours, three; the dawn would be empty, the moment and she would not be, then he would hear her and he would lie drenched in the wet grass, serene and one and indivisible in joy, listening to her approach. He would smell her; the whole mist reeked with her; the small malleate hands of mist which drew along his prone drenched flanks palped her pearled barrel too and shaped them both somewhere in immediate time, already married. He would not move. He would lie amid the waking instant of earth's teeming life, the motionless fronds of water-heavy grasses stooping into the mist before his face in black, fixed curves, along each parabola of which the marching drops held in minute magnification the dawn's rosy miniatures, smelling and even tasting the rich, slow, warm barn-reek, milk-reek, the flowing immemorial female, hearing the slow planting and plopping suck of each deliberate cloven mud-spreading hoof, invisible still in the mist loud with its hymeneal choristers. (883)

Perhaps the most important detail of this remarkable passage is the fact that in the midst of a truly teeming array of other sense perceptions, the cow remains "invisible." Sight plays little part of Ike's anticipatory ecstasy, though every other sensory activity does as the empty dawn fills with his myriad impressions. Smell figures perhaps above all. The sense of smell provides, not the first indication Ike has of the cow's arrival, but the fullest and most powerful. The cow's scent pervades the entire scene ("the whole mist reeked with her"), and references to Ike smelling her predominate, in which Ike's olfactory experience mixes with his sense of taste: he "smell[s] and even tast[es] the rich, slow, warm barn-reek, milk-reek." Touch figures importantly as well, as Ike feels the caressing "hands" of the mist "shap[ing]" both him and the cow. Hearing works forcefully, as it provides Ike with his first sign of the cow's approach, then furnishes the onomatopoetic "plopping" of the hooves in the mud as well as, finally, the euphonious, mist-filtered "hymeneal choristers." The outcome of all this fullness of immediate sense perception, figuratively, is one we have seen Faulkner champion before—marriage, and in a moment in another novel in which he also stressed the primacy of a sense besides seeing: the "marriage of speaking and hearing" experienced by Quentin and Shreve in *Absalom, Absalom!* Like the uniquely close relationship Quentin and Shreve forge by listening (and not only by looking detachedly at pictures), Ike and the cow, as the passage above stipulates, are also, significantly, "already married."

This emphasis on sensory perception, including as it does Ike's innocent, pure love and the scene's pastoral setting, serves as a stunning rebuke of the

values represented by nearly all the other characters in the book. Flem's ruth-
less calculations, Lump's amoral pursuit of Houston's money—all transpire in
the developing mercantilist culture of Frenchman's Bend. The significance of
this aspect of the book, of course, relies on the fact that, although published in
1940, with it Faulkner describes events from an earlier historical period. *The
Hamlet* dwells on a rural scene that was in transition to modernity. Against
that rising urban and commercial milieu, Ike's depth of feeling and dazzling
sense of affect seem all the more unique. His affection also contrasts sharply
with the debased scenarios of romantic and erotic activity that surround it:
Flem's arranged marriage to Eula Varner, for instance, or Labove's assault on
her. As with Benjy, I would argue, this quality of feeling expresses Faulkner's
protest over the mercantilist commercial society that surrounded both him
and his characters in their respective contexts. And also like Benjy, it furnishes
Faulkner some of the most arresting moments of his writing. Like Benjy's
portion of *The Sound and the Fury,* Ike's experiences with the cow and Faulkner's manner of depicting them evoke a tenderness and poetic sense that their
world did not support, a world Faulkner described throughout his writing in
the period of the thirties.

Flem's exploitation of the Varners or of Frenchmen's Bend, like Lump's of
Ike, rely on a calculation and rationalization that, although it defined the
encroaching world of the Snopeses, does not obtain in the experience of characters like Ike and Benjy. The appearance of the passage of Ike and the cow in
The Hamlet thus allows Faulkner and his readers an alternative to social and
economic developments of modernity that, as Jameson and others have suggested, threatened to further and further delimit sense perception, and with it
the capacity for human contact and feeling. Connecting Ike back to Benjy
helps mark even more definitively the places in which those losses are expressed in Faulkner's writing, in both his fiction of the thirties and in the
novels that followed, and in which that loss manifests itself in an increasing,
tendentious emphasis on vision. Characters like Ike and Benjy and the protest
Faulkner registers through their fully engaged sensorium appear in this light as
extensions of the larger critique Faulkner leveled at consumer society throughout the thirties and his focus on sight.

If Snopesism may be said to resemble the exploitations of a market economy and of the culture industry, it may also contribute to an understanding of
Faulkner's jail cell metaphor. As I have described it here, Faulkner's "writing
decade" of the 1930s began and ended with a parallel image: a prison cell
occupied by a solitary, isolated, but not altogether frustrated man. That the

decade I describe as most revealing of Faulkner's relationship to popular culture should begin and end with these images of imprisonment is provocative. As I argued at the close of the last chapter, the jail cell offers an apt metaphor for the position of both the producer of popular art and its consumer. Wilbourne both records and "films" images of Charlotte's body, then views them onanistically in Parchman Prison. The imprisoned black man in the Jefferson jail cell in *Sanctuary*, however, offers slightly different possibilities for interpretation. Earlier, we noted Horace's wistful perspective on the jailed murderer: safe from the petty judgments of the townspeople and the frustrations of the trial, removed from the difficulties of his marriage, the jail appears to offer Horace a longed-for sanctuary. We might say that jail cells for Faulkner, as for Horace, offer a sanctuary from the encroaching world of Snopes and Snopesism in the form he understood it most painfully: the world of commercially packaged, mass-market culture and writing.[10]

In addition to the scenes of the condemned Negro murderer in *Sanctuary* and, of course, Parchman Prison, jail cells or their approximation also appear in *Light in August* and *Absalom, Absalom!* In the latter case, they also provide a space in which to pursue acts of imaginative—even modernist—creation. Joe Christmas, of course, spends the early part of his life in the prison-like orphanage. In *Absalom*, Quentin is held captive, first in Rosa's parlor. Then, for a much longer period with Shreve, he is captive both within his and Shreve's "tomb like" common room and to the sustained activity of producing the Sutpen narrative. Faulkner's most celebrated scenario of narrative invention and of characters' acts of "telling," similar to his own creative acts with his novels through the thirties, occurs within a figurative prison. We might say, then, that both the textual "space" and experience of writing—and the spaces that experience produced, such as the Compson household, Sutpen's Hundred, and both literal and figurative prisons like Parchman and Quentin's dorm room—offered Faulkner similar attractions. All these spaces are defined by their separation from what Faulkner obviously saw as a chaotic, depleted modernity. I suggest that jail cells were interesting to Faulkner throughout the thirties because they offered what he—like Horace, like Joe Christmas, like Quentin, Wilbourne, and the Tall Convict—all sought: respite and protection from an alien, hostile world.[11]

The jailed Negro's lament in *Sanctuary* is a curious one, but it is also suggestive for what I am saying about Faulkner's position throughout the thirties. "Aint no place fer you in heavum!" he sings, with his face to the window.

"Say, Aint no place fer you in hell!" In writing *The Sound and the Fury* earlier, Faulkner had, by his own account, discovered something of his writerly "heaven"—that "ecstasy" of writing for himself and without regard for publishers. His momentary heaven of writing this way allowed the formal daring that led him to both a sense of himself as a writer and a recognition of the incredible suppleness of the novel form. That position and pleasure, however, increasingly felt compromised as Faulkner sought to capitalize on the reading market. His short story submissions and screenwriting work, we can recognize, were not satisfying to a writer who in the same period produced such enormously ambitious novels of social and historical questioning as *Light in August* and *Absalom, Absalom!* Throughout those works and others of the period, then, are manifest the frustrations Faulkner felt due to his position competing—not only with the producers of an increasingly dominant mass culture, but with himself and his own position beholden to the culture industry.

After modernism's initial flourish in the twenties—the early masterworks such as *Ulysses, The Waste Land,* and *The Sound and the Fury*—and after the market crash of 1929, occurred a shift in both the perceived efficacy of modernist writing and the position of literary artists. Increasingly, authors like Faulkner (and Nathanael West and Scott Fitzgerald) saw the need, and were given the opportunity, to engage the kinds of audience that in prior moments of personal fulfillment or "ecstasy" had not figured in their experience of writing. Throughout this period Faulkner still, however, sought to produce fiction that operated differently from popular fare, as well as from the proletarian and social realist movements of the thirties. The result of these efforts is perceptible in those examples of his high-art novels of the decade, novels that were extremely demanding formally and aesthetically—purposefully high-modernist—yet at the same time aware and inclusive of the reality that existed outside Faulkner's secluded (modernist) jail cell.

Nowhere is the split between Faulkner's two writing "spaces" and the kind of text it afforded more visible than at the precise midpoint of the thirties. Bracketed on either side by the long period in which he wrote *Absalom, Absalom!, Pylon* offers a strange, fascinating illustration of issues that informed Faulkner's writing of the decade. Considered a minor and less successful novel than his other books of the period, while at the same time a more serious literary effort than the more overtly pandering *The Unvanquished* (1938), *Pylon* offers a synecdoche of Faulkner's approach to his writing in the thirties, a quality we can detect through a glance at the novel's ending. At the book's close, we find the reporter's two aborted versions of his air show story. The first of them is hopelessly romantic; the other "savagely," to use Faulkner's term, ironic. It is significant, I think, that Faulkner is precise about the readers for both stories. Particularly with the first version, he shows the ambitious young copyboy first restoring the article, then reading it avidly and, at its end, evincing a desire to finish writing it himself. Somewhat mockingly, Faulkner refers to him as "a bright lad, about to graduate from high school; he had not only ambitions but dreams too" (323). Apparently those include literary ambitions, because in addition to hoping Hagood will let him finish writing the story, the copyboy sees it as "not only news but the beginning of literature" (323).

Although Faulkner is hard on the copyboy, I suspect he recognized in him some of his own youthful literary ambitions and more romantic leanings. Immediately following his thrill at the prospect of being able to finish the piece, the copyboy encounters Hagood and, in the same moment, reads the very different version of the story that the reporter felt constrained to provide his editor. Scathingly bitter about the "precision pilots" who missed Shumann's body by three-quarters of a mile, replete with "news" and information that the reporter finds unseemly (such as the amount of the plane's horsepower), and brutally frank about the "abandoning" of the search effort, the reporter offers, not literature or even really news copy. Rather, he offers what Faulkner, in his "Introduction" to *The Sound and the Fury,* described as the modernist writer's predicament: "a savage indictment of the contemporary scene" (229). That indictment, I contend, grew out of Faulkner's enormous frustration—but stubborn will—about writing in his period. The contemporary scene for Faulkner included not only an organ of mass readership like the newspaper (or popular forms like pulp fiction or film), but the readers of the 1930s who sought the elevations of "literature." Those very longings, however lofty, Faulkner increasingly saw as naïve. For in this period, as Faulkner learned over and over again, there was no comfortable place for either the producer of literary art fiction, nor, if you possessed ambitions such as his (or the copyboy's), was there comfort in being a practitioner of commercial writing or "hack."

Faulkner's thirties position, then, resembled both a sanctuary and a jail cell. With novels like *Sanctuary,* both the original and the 1931 versions, as well as *Light in August, Absalom, Absalom!* and, perhaps above all, *If I Forget Thee, Jerusalem,* Faulkner demonstrated his deeply conflicted sense of his position as a writer. Aware of the workings of the culture industry, occupying a position, grudgingly but pragmatically, both within those workings and outside them, Faulkner wrote novels that maintained some of the autonomy he enjoyed with his first burst of freedom with *The Sound and the Fury*. Yet importantly, in the books that followed, Faulkner moved beyond the "closed space" of the Compson household and aesthetic formalism. Broadening his treatments of southern history and identity, Faulkner also, throughout the decade, incorporated into his novels the methods and materials of the popular culture he had seen around him growing up, then imbibed while working in the culture industry. In doing so, he allowed "in" to his novels those examples of popular culture he denigrated. The importance of this gesture is that it reveals a vital component of Faulkner's larger project in his mature fiction: addressing the historical transformations of modernity. Over the course of the thirties, Faulkner increasingly saw the limits of a writerly position that allied itself only with the visionary "transcendence" of *The Sound and the Fury* or high modernism. Instead, he adopted a writing practice that included both his modernist ecstasy *and* his recognition of the realities of modern cultural life and writing.

As this discussion demonstrates, Faulkner's tone toward mass art became increasingly bitter as the decade progressed. Much of this was due to its further and further encroachment on American cultural consumption and production, as well as on Faulkner's own literary production. In closing, I submit that this bitterness was directed at figures like Harry Wilbourne or the Tall Convict but also at Faulkner's circumstances. On the one hand, those circumstances included Faulkner's short-story writing and screenplay work in Hollywood. Like his characters, caught in prison cells but exploiting, at least partly, their positions as producers of a certain kind of narrative—visual, entertaining, or even pornographic—Faulkner, in his commercial writing, made the best of a situation in which he felt trapped. On the other hand, and at the same time, he also found productive ways in his art fiction to use his observations about a burgeoning consumer culture. Longing for the lost, perhaps illusory pleasure of complete modernist autonomy, but recognizing the realities of modern cultural production, in his novel writing of the thirties Faulkner reconciled many of the conflicts that defined his writing position. The result, as these several examples demonstrate, are some of the most powerfully modernist and, arguably, the most engaged, historicized novels Faulkner wrote.

Throughout assessments of Faulkner's literary career (including Faulkner's own assessments) are considerations of his historical placing. Faulkner's declaration that with *The Sound and the Fury* he "shut a door between [himself] and all publisher's addresses and book lists" ("Introduction," 227) offers a useful final window onto Faulkner's writing vocation of the thirties. It is precisely the idea of a "timeless" space for Faulkner's writing away from the contingencies of contemporary commercial life and culture, suggested in such comments and advanced by earlier critics, that this essay has questioned. What I hope to have shown is that the more "purely" literary dimensions and deliberate formalism of Faulkner's thirties fiction can be traced to cultural and historical phenomena that existed well beyond Faulkner's novels' aestheticized space. That aesthetic quality is, of course, insistently present in these works, as it is in *The Sound and the Fury*. It is manifest in Rosa Coldfield's densely lyrical speaking voice and Quentin and Shreve's historical vision in *Absalom, Absalom!;* in passages describing Temple Drake's subjectivized sense of time, or poetic descriptions of Clarence Snopes in *Sanctuary;* in the heightened, imagist language surrounding Joe Christmas's death scene; in Faulkner's uncanny, dream-like evocations of the flooded Mississippi River and its metaphor for the film screen in *Jerusalem;* in the generic, stylistic, and narrative experiment of each of the novels I've examined.

What is also in these works, as recent Faulkner and modernist criticism has begun to prove, is not only the presence of specific historical developments and material but the connection of those materials to Faulkner's conception of an otherwise timeless mode of writing. As I've described it, Faulkner's modernism was indeed created by its unique, chaotic inventiveness and beauty and from inside the protected jail cell of Faulkner's acts of writing. It was also, though, created by the ugly or troubling realities outside it.

Notes

AT   Adorno's *Aesthetic Theory*
Blotner 1984   *Faulkner: A Biography* (one-volume edition, 1984)
Blotner 1974   *Faulkner: A Biography* (two-volume edition, 1974)
CS   *Collected Stories*
SL   *Selected Letters*
SO   *Sanctuary: The Original Text*

INTRODUCTION: Adorno's Modernism and the Historicity of Popular Culture

1. Joseph Blotner, *William Faulkner: A Biography* (one-volume edition, 1984), 305. Cited hereafter as Blotner 1984.

2. Several references in Faulkner's fiction to silent and so-called art film, including specific directors, actors, and movies, suggest his sense of the aesthetic or political differences of such cinema from the commercial products of Hollywood. Sergei Eisenstein and Robert Weine, for example, appear in different moments as clear contrasts to the kind of movie associated with figures such as David Selznik or Joan Crawford. The Eisenstein and Weine references (in *If I Forget Thee, Jerusalem* and *Pylon,* respectively) each seek to convey something of silent film's uncanny or otherworldly effects. The "Wild Palms" section of *If I Forget Thee, Jerusalem* refers to an "Eisenstein Dante" as Charlotte and Wilbourne descend into the Utah mine and confront its scene of visual chaos (621). *Pylon* evokes Weine's classic German Expressionist film *The Cabinet of Dr. Caligari.* As the reporter appears for the first time, the narrator describes the way the other characters "were now looking at something which had apparently crept from a doctor's cupboard and, in the snatched garments of an etherized patient in a charity ward, escaped into the living world" (788; see *Annotations to Faulkner's* Pylon, 24–25). References to Hollywood or its leading figures such as Joan Crawford, conversely, evoke cheap, manufactured products like doilies and magazines (*If I Forget Thee, Jerusalem,* 636).

3. Faulkner's different tenures as a contract writer for the studios included extended periods of work at MGM in 1932, at Universal in 1934, at Twentieth Century-Fox in 1935 and 36, and several long-term contracts with Warner Brothers in the mid-1940s (Blotner 1984). In a 1936 letter to his agent, Morton Goldman, Faulkner proposed selling the rights to *Absalom, Absalom!* for $100,000 (*SL,* 96). See John T. Matthews, "Shortened Stories: Faulkner and the Market" for a discussion of Faulkner's extensive efforts at living off of his income from short fiction in the thirties.

4. Greenberg provides several examples of kitsch, including "popular, commercial art and literature with their chromeotypes, magazine covers, illustrations, ads, slick

and pulp fiction, comics, Tin Pan Alley music, tap dancing, Hollywood movies, etc. etc." ("Avant-Garde and Kitsch," 9). As we will see, many of these appear in Faulkner's high-modernist novels of the thirties (for Greenberg, versions of "genuine culture").

5. Another strong advocate for the modernist position of separateness from the realms of both mass culture and mainstream, modern society is Irving Howe. He famously described modernism as a "tacit polemic" that "must be defined in terms of what it is not" (*Decline of the New,* 3). In depicting modernism's "heroic" isolation, Howe declared that "the modern writer can no longer accept the claims of the world. If he tries to acquiesce in the norms of his audience, he finds himself depressed and outraged" (4). Although he writes here about modernism's position against traditional forms of high art, Howe also suggests that the modernist "polemic" was directed at modern consumer culture. "[M]odernist culture soon learns to respect, even to cherish the signs of its division" (4) from mass society. In the same essay, and in a manner similar to Huyssen, Howe asserted that "the modernist impulse was accompanied by . . . a repugnance for the commonplace materials of ordinary life" (17).

6. Since *The Great Divide,* theoretical notions of the split between modernism and mass culture have further been called into question by scholarship that addresses their mutual relationship, particularly in the period I will be discussing. Critics like Ann Douglas (*Terrible Honesty*); Rita Barnard (*The Great Depression and the Culture of Abundance*); and Michel North (*Reading 1922*) have described modernism and popular art as closely intertwined by the 1920s and, particularly, the 30s. See especially Barnard's introduction, "Literature and Mass Culture in the Thirties." In it Barnard cites three major reasons for the 1930s as a pivotal decade for breaking down the cultural divide between "high" and "mass" arts: the rise of proletarian literature; the increasing commodification and popularization of high art; and the fact that "the dichotomy between literature and mass culture [was] also negated and undermined by . . . writers who incorporated the language of mass culture into the body of their 'literary' work" (7). Though in a less direct way than Barnard demonstrates with West and Fearing, Faulkner's "incorporation" of the language of mass culture contributes to his work's breakdown of the great divide. Maria DiBattista offers a particularly helpful idea for approaching modernism in her "Introduction" to the collection *High and Low Moderns,* one that, as we will see has particular relevance to Faulkner. "[H]igh moderns, even those who openly espoused the novel as an art form," she says, "nevertheless regarded low cultural phenomena and entertainments unique to their times—the popular press, cinema, music hall, and the 'art' of advertising—as an inalienable part of modern life, hence unavoidable subject matter whose forms as well as content might be assimilated or reworked, playfully imitated or seriously criticized" (4–5).

7. Recently, in response to new understandings of globalization and the production of culture (both modernist and popular) outside of Europe and the United States, Huyssen has suggested other ways of considering modernism. Detailing cultural studies' tendencies to over-value popular culture, and seeking as well to recast his own "great divide" between modernism and postmodernism (the ways that postmodern studies see high- and mass-cultural postmodern texts readily incorporate one another), Huyssen encourages a new attention to medium, to the complexity of interaction between high literary modernism and visual and technical forms of culture. ("High/Low in an Expanded Field," 371).

8. I offer a necessarily truncated assessment of the modernism/mass culture debate

at the outset of my discussion because doing so provides a conceptual frame for my specific readings of Faulkner's novels. The theoretical stance that I offer here through figures like Adorno, Huyssen, or Jameson, although I do not refer to it extensively in the chapters themselves, informs my approach to passages and strategies throughout Faulkner's fiction. My introductory remarks are meant to establish a ground in a contested and still-emerging debate about ways of conceiving the actual historical relationship between mass culture and modernism.

9. Faulkner famously remarked about conceiving *Sanctuary:* "I took a little time out, and speculated what a person in Mississippi would believe to be current trends, chose what I thought was the most horrific tale I could imagine, and wrote it in about three weeks" ("Preface" to the Modern Library's 1932 edition of *Sanctuary,* reprinted in the Library of America's *William Faulkner: Novels, 1930–1936,* 1029–30; subsequent references to the "Preface" are to this edition). Many of Faulkner's public comments about *Sanctuary* deprecate it as a work that was "basely" conceived. Although the novel does indeed include sensational or lurid elements, it is less clear that Faulkner's motives for writing it were as bluntly mercenary as his comments in the "Preface" and elsewhere suggest. As my chapter on *Sanctuary* demonstrates, the novel's preface and its compositional history make clear that Faulkner's involvement with this novel was, in fact, more complicated than that. Ultimately, I argue that it is the book's revisions for publication in 1931 more than its original conception (as Faulkner here implies) that reveal some of the most deliberately commercial practices in the novel, and in Faulkner's writing.

10. I use this term at several points in my discussion of *Light in August* to refer to actions or institutions of forced enclosure or incarceration. It is a common terminology in D. A. Miller's Foucauldian study, *The Novel and the Police,* from which I draw some of the lines of my argument in my second chapter.

11. Two earlier studies of Faulkner take up the function of vision in his novels: Michel Gresset's *Fascination* and Hugh Ruppersburg's *Voice and Eye in Faulkner's Fiction.* Though their treatments of Faulkner's optical methods differ from mine, most notably in my attention to Faulkner's critical treatment of vision and its connection to mass cultural forms like cinema, Gresset and Ruppersburg's work attests to the central role played by sight in Faulkner's writing. Carolyn Porter's *Seeing and Being* also pays crucial attention to the reifying effects of vision in the experience of Faulkner's characters.

12. Due to several factors, the 1930s saw the continued perfecting of a studio production system that began in the 1910s. The rapid success of silent film through the teens and sound film in the late twenties before the Depression had already contributed to the consolidating of both economic and cultural capital in Hollywood. American domination of the world market for film had began earlier in the century with the wide distribution of films overseas; production became even more centralized in the twenties and thirties with the departure of many European directors and technicians for the United States. All of these developments contributed in the period to the continued growth of film's audience, which after the teens moved beyond its base in working-class, immigrant nickelodeons to national and international distribution. In the 1930s the further standardization of story material and production methods, the solidifying of genres, and the use of recognizable, "bankable" actors and stars all advanced the development of the industry and allowed the major studios (Paramount, MGM, Twen-

tieth Century Fox, Warner Brothers, and RKO) to capitalize on the expansion of the film market and to establish the classical Hollywood paradigm. Part of this process had to do with the notable increase in production in the 1930s. In response to the Depression and due to a decrease in demand, studios paradoxically produced more movies in the 1930s in order to offer double features (and lure back viewers), ushering in the production of the "B" movie. All of these developments contributed to the studios' factory-like approach, which in their peak years produced literally thousands of pictures. See James Monaco, *How to Read a Film*, 208–9; John Hill and Pamela Church Gibson, eds., *The Oxford Guide to Film Studies*, 246–7; Susan Hayward, *Key Concepts in Cinema Studies*, 356.

13. The most relevant work on this aspect of Hollywood cinema were the essays Adorno wrote or collaborated on with Max Horkheimer in *Dialectic of Enlightenment*. In particular "The Culture Industry: Enlightenment as Mass Deception," offered as a response to Adorno's observations of Hollywood in the 1940s, was written in the roughly same period as Faulkner's modernist novels. It mounts Adorno's most rigorous attack on the standardized and reifying products of Hollywood.

14. Bruce Kawin suggests that due to Faulkner's linking of Eisenstein to Dante in *If I Forget Thee, Jerusalem*, "the sense of the reference is to a serious artist" ("The Montage Element in Faulkner's Fiction," 116).

15. Faulkner's brother Murry indicates that they were captivated by the new form of entertainment and that they went together to the Opera House, where films were first shown in Oxford, as often as they could (*The Falkners of Mississippi*, 49–51).

16. Faulkner worked extensively on the production, scouting locations, helping to cast Oxford residents as extras, and revising the script during the movie's shooting. He later wrote of the film's director, Clarence Brown, with whom he collaborated, that he was "one of the best to work with I ever knew" (Blotner 1984, 502).

17. Faulkner received a gift of the source of Griffith's film, Thomas Dixon's novel *The Clansman*, from his first grade teacher (Blotner 1984, 20). He also saw a theatrical version of the novel when it was performed in Oxford in 1908 (Blotner 1984, 33). Kawin makes the claim that Faulkner saw *Birth* (*Faulkner and Film*, 70). Though he does not provide direct evidence for his assertion, it is difficult to imagine the circumstances that would have prevented Faulkner from seeing the most notorious and heralded film of its time.

18. This period was bracketed, at its end, by the release of another wildly popular (and highly romanticized) vision of the South: David O. Selznik's *Gone With the Wind* (1939). Selznik's extravaganza displaced *Birth* as the most popular film of all time.

19. Although Faulkner's novels were critically successful and regarded very seriously, his more ambitious literary projects of the decade failed to reach a wide readership. Other than *Sanctuary* (1931) and *The Unvanquished* (1938), Faulkner's novels of the thirties sold extremely poorly. MGM bought the rights for the later novel in 1938, giving Faulkner a much-needed financial lift.

20. Faulkner's perspective and language here have much in common with another well-known attack on Hollywood, Nathanael West's *The Day of the Locust* (1939). West's negative social criticism, similar to Faulkner's, is manifest both in his protagonist's vision of "The Burning of Los Angeles" (Tod Hackett's unfinished painting) and in his narrator's account of southern Californian architecture: "The edges of the trees burned with a pale violet light and their centers gradually turned from deep purple to black . . .

But not even the soft wash of dusk could help the houses. Only dynamite would be of any use against the Mexican ranch houses, Samoan huts, Mediterranean villas, Egyptian and Japanese temples, Swiss chalets, Tudor cottages, and every possible combination of these styles that lined the slopes of the canyon" (61). Tod's longing to destroy the scene before him echoes West's invocation of the apocalyptic destructiveness of the seven deadly plagues in his title. It also resembles Faulkner's description of Los Angeles in "Golden Land," his own short-story version of the Hollywood novel. Faulkner's *Pylon*, the novel to which "Golden Land" is most closely connected chronologically, shares with West's *Miss Lonelyhearts* (1933) a critique of another mass-market organ: the newspaper.

21. Faulkner's correspondence from the 1930s is laced with references to his frustration over his work in Hollywood and, specifically, to the demands on him financially and in terms of the labor that the studios extracted. Writing to Ben Wasson in 1932, he expressed consternation about his contract with MGM for *Turnabout*. Using a sharecropper analogy, he wrote, "Today I received a letter from Joyce & Selznik asking for their ten percent of this TURN ABOUT weekly pay. Do I owe it to them? and is there any danger of them coming down here [to Mississippi] and taking a tithe of my pigs and chickens and cotton?" (*SL*, 66). In 1937 he complained to his wife in a letter from Beverly Hills about the time demanded of him by another Hollywood contract: "Nothing has happened yet. As far as I know, I will be through at studio Aug 15 and will start home sometime during that week, though according to my contract they can give me an assignment and hold me overtime until I finish it" (*SL*, 101).

22. Several critics and theorists suggest the onset of the increasing role of visuality in modern social, cultural, and political experience. Miles Orvell, in his cultural history *The Real Thing*, traces changes in both lifestyle and epistemology wrought by the advent of photography and the cultural role in modernity of simulacra. Due to photography's widespread popularity and its broad dissemination through the late nineteenth century, the act of looking at reproduced images of objects or events (such as history) increasingly came to substitute for those objects' or events' "reality." See also Alan Trachtenberg, *Reading American Photographs*, for a similar account of images of history, particularly Matthew Brady's early Civil War photographs. Several Frankfurt School thinkers describe circumstances of urban modernity that, ironically, appear in Faulkner's Yoknapatawpha. In "The Metropolis and Mental Life," Georg Simmel argued early in the century for the increased amount of sensory, and particularly visual, experience as a defining category of modern experience. See as well Siegfried Kracauer's essay "Photography" for an account of the way visual imagery distances history. Walter Benjamin's theory of modernity, finally, is especially apt to a consideration of the ways in which sensory experience and its role in social and cultural life can be materially altered by historical and technological changes. As he puts it, "During long periods of history, the mode of human sense perception changes with humanity's entire mode of existence. The manner in which human sense perception is organized, the medium in which it is accomplished, is determined not only by nature but by historical circumstances as well" ("The Work of Art in the Age of Mechanical Reproduction," 222). More recent accounts of these changes include Ben Singer, "Modernity, Hyperstimulus, and the Rise of Popular Sensationalism"; Susan Sontag, "The Image-World"; and the essays in Fredric Jameson's *Signatures of the Visible*.

23. Miranda Burgess argues that the southern romance and its "twentieth-century

manifestation," the narrative cinema, was based on the white male need to position the plantation heroine as the bearer of the desiring looks of white landowners and of black slaves ("Watching Jefferson Watching," 96–99).

24. Several film histories trace the predominance of racial stereotypes in early cinema. Among them are Peter Noble's extensive cultural history, *The Negro in Films;* Donald Bogle's *Toms, Coons, Mammies, Mulattoes, and Blacks;* and James R. Nesteby's *Black Images in American Films.* Michael Rogin, in his essay " 'The Sword Became a Flashing Vision': D. W. Griffith's *Birth of a Nation"* argues for a direct connection between Griffith's film and *Light in August* through both works' use of castration and the threat of black male sexuality.

25. See Hayden White, "The Modernist Event."

26. Bruce Kawin *Faulkner and Film,* 87.

27. Like the other novels I treat, particularly *Sanctuary, Pylon* mixes references to popular sensationalism with invocations and strategies of high-art, literary modernism. The overtness of *Pylon's* references to figures like Eliot, though (its chapters with titles like "Lovesong of J. A. Prufrock"), operates to produce a very different kind of modernist approach than we see in the other novels of the decade. *Light in August, Absalom, Absalom!* and *If I Forget Thee, Jerusalem,* that is, do not perform parodies of earlier modernist texts. In the case of the second half of the decade particularly, and in something of a chronological paradox, Faulkner's novels remain deliberately "high"-modernist works that respond to mass culture in ways different from those in *Pylon* and that have not been demonstrated by earlier criticism.

28. There are, of course, limits to this characterization. *Pylon* makes clear demands on readers and does so in an unfamiliar, "manufactured" language that, as Michael Zeitlin has shown, reveals its deep embeddedness in a modern and alienating urban experience ("Faulkner's *Pylon:* The City in The Age of Mechanical Reproduction"). In its weird, stylized prose, *Pylon* is in many ways a unique modern novel, both within Faulkner's ouvre and otherwise. It does not, however, extend that experimentation into its narrative structure, instead offering events that, with few exceptions follow chronologically. Importantly as well, *Pylon* is often regarded as one of Faulkner's "minor" works. Though the reasons for this designation vary, I suspect they have to do in part with precisely what is uncanny or odd about *Pylon* as Faulkner's only real city novel, as well as with its seemingly uncomplicated storyline.

29. As John T. Matthews puts it, "By then treating the narrative through a single focalization (the reporter), *Pylon* seeks to reduce effort, subject, and effect" ("The Autograph of Violence in Faulkner's *Pylon,*" 247). Though Matthews goes on to qualify this characterization, *Pylon* remains, with *The Unvanquished,* one of Faulkner's less fully ambitious projects of the decade.

30. The phrase is Siegfried Kracauer's. Kracauer makes this assessment of German historical films in his psycho-social study of German cinema and the rise of fascism, *From Caligari to Hitler* (52). He makes a similar case for the destructive cultural work that film performed in the Weimar period and that, he claimed, contributed to the rise of the Third Reich and to Hitler's campaign of historical erasure.

31. Fredric Jameson's critique of 1970s historical cinema centers on the use of nostalgia in contributing to the reification—and consumption—of history: "In nostalgia film, the image—the surface sheen of a period fashion reality—is consumed, having been transformed into a visual commodity" ("On Magical Realism in Film," 130).

32. In an instructive passage from the book, the narrator refers to "Hollywood which is no longer in Hollywood but is stippled by a billion feet of burning colored gas across the face of the American earth" (636).

33. My use of Jameson's theory of commodities in general, and of the commodity aspect of film in particular, follows from Marx's thinking in statements such as the following: "A commodity is therefore a mysterious thing, simply because in it the social character of men's labour appears to them as an objective character stamped upon the product of that labour" (*Capital*, 1:320). In the same passage Marx offers another useful statement that informs Jameson's assessment of film and commodities: "There is a definite social relation between men, that assumes, in their eyes, the fantastic form of a relation between things. In order, therefore, to find an analogy, we must have recourse to the mist-enveloped regions of the religious world" (1:321). It is this "misty," quasi-religious quality of film viewing that, for Jameson, contributes to its capacity for ready commodification and reification.

34. See Adorno's assessment of the coercive effects of film throughout his writing, in particular "The Culture Industry: Enlightenment as Mass Deception." See also Siegfried Kracauer's more specific attention to the visual properties of the film image in *Theory of Film:* "[F]ilm images affect primarily the spectator's senses, engaging him physiologically before he is in a position to respond intellectually," (158 and *passim*), as well as his essays in *The Mass Ornament*.

35. Jameson offers a far more sustained analysis of vision's "historical coming into being," as well as the appearance of that phenomenon as it is mediated by literature, in *The Political Unconscious*. His model for describing these is Conrad and the novel that has furnished one of my epigraphs, *The Nigger of the "Narcissus."* I will return to Jameson's discussion of these issues and this text as a way to extend my discussion of Faulkner's thirties fiction in my "Conclusion."

36. Adorno quoted in a March 18, 1936 letter to Walter Benjamin (*Aesthetics and Politics*, 123).

37. In discussions of Faulkner's early film treatments, such as *Absolution* and *The College Widow*, Kawin shows Faulkner taking up themes that informed his early novels (like *Sartoris* and *Sanctuary*) while applying them to market-friendly genres and settings such as romance stories and the First World War (*Faulkner and Film*, 71–74).

38. "The Montage Element of Faulkner's Fiction," 112–13, 123.

39. Like Kawin, Douglas Baldwin offers a more theoretical consideration of Faulkner's relation to film in his essay "Putting Images into Words: Elements of the 'Cinematic' in William Faulkner's Prose." Critics like Baldwin and I are indebted to Kawin's early work on Faulkner and film.

40. This aspect of the film image informs as well Kracauer's assessment of the links of cinema to dreaming. See *Theory of Film:* "The moviegoer watches the images on the screen in a dream-like state" (303); "To the extent that films are mass entertainment, they are bound to cater to the alleged desires and daydreams of the public at large" (163); and *passim*.

41. Choosing to write in a way that he thought was compromised, that is, but that he believed was necessary in order to sell books, Faulkner experienced a frustration with *Sanctuary* that extended to himself as a practitioner of the consumer culture he disdained. It is this scorn, I suggest, that returns at the end of the thirties in Harry Wilbourne (a potential surrogate for himself as a hack writer). For a similar take on

Faulkner's sense of guilt over these forms of writing, see Vincent Allan King, "The Wages of Pulp: The Use and Abuse of Fiction in William Faulkner's *The Wild Palms* [*If I Forget Thee, Jerusalem*]."

42. I may clarify my perspective here by way of a similar account of Faulkner's, like other writers', unwitting but instructive reproduction of "the circulation of social energy." The term is Stephen Greenblatt's, which I encountered in Philip Weinstein's discussion of Faulkner and Toni Morrison in his chapter of the same name from *What Else But Love? The Ordeal of Race in Faulkner and Morrison.* Using Greenblatt's example of Shakespeare's *Othello,* Weinstein declares that "whatever else Shakespeare saw in his source materials (Cinthio's 1566 Venetian story), he saw a clash of race and gender . . . that illuminated the conflicts of his own culture. His play maximally dramatizes these conflicts, it is in the business less of resolving or correcting them than of getting us to register them" (165). The value of any representation of social conflict, Weinstein argues, is that writers' "achievement is inseparable from their own raced and gendered positioning and from their (always contestable) grasp upon the ferment of their times" (165). Faulkner's treatment of Joe Christmas, I claim, is clearly an expression of Faulkner's "contestable grasp" on historical ferment. If it reproduces some of the same negative effects of racial bias that it questions, this is not a measure of Faulkner's "failure" to control completely his texts' reception or effects. As Weinstein puts it, "Value resides in a text's ability to seize upon (to find imaginative form for) the subjective engagement of individuals with their larger culture's most significant certainties and doubts. That the seeing enacted in such texts is [socially and racially] positioned . . . keeps it from being innocent, making it simultaneously right, wrong, and precious" (165–66).

CHAPTER ONE: "Some Quality of Delicate Paradox"

1. Melinda McLeod Rouselle traces these allusions in her *Annotations to William Faulkner's* Sanctuary. Beginning with the title, she suggests references to *Measure for Measure* and Frazer's *The Golden Bough* (1, 3). She also claims Conrad's *Nigger of the "Narcissus"* as a possible source for Faulkner's description of Popeye as possessed of "that vicious depthless quality of stamped tin" (181). Reading Horace as a Prufrockian figure is commonplace in commentary on the novel. Edwin Arnold and Dawn Trouard, for instance, cite Prufrock as a source for Horace's timidity (*Reading Faulkner's Sanctuary*, 28). See also Noel Polk, "Afterword" to *Sanctuary: The Original Text,* 299.

2. Gangster films proliferated in the period before *Sanctuary* and were an immensely popular genre. Its origins were in silent films such as *The Girl and the Gangster* and *The Making of Crooks,* both from 1914, and D. W. Griffith's *The Musketeers of Pig Alley* (1912). The 1927 release *Underworld* was the first movie to offer midnight screenings to accommodate viewers. Moreover, the year before *Sanctuary's* publication saw the beginning of the well-known gangster cycle *Little Caesar* (1930), followed by *The Public Enemy* in 1931 and by *Scarface* in 1932.

3. Polk, "Afterword."

4. Faulkner made these remarks in his "Preface" to the Modern Library's 1932 printing of the novel; they have been reprinted in the Library of America text, pp. 1029–30. Much has been made of the ambivalent quality of Faulkner's remarks about his original version of *Sanctuary* in the "Preface" and elsewhere. In particular, critics have

doubted Faulkner's sincerity in denigrating the unpublished novel as inferior to the 1931 version, especially as regards its pecuniary motives and sensationalism. See Gerald Langford (*Faulkner's Revisions of* Sanctuary) and Philip Cohen ("'A Cheap Idea . . . Deliberately Conceived to Make Money': The Biographical Context of William Faulkner's Introduction to *Sanctuary*").

5. This change is owed to considerations by Linton Massey ("Notes on the Unrevised Galleys of William Faulkner's *Sanctuary*") and Langford of the two texts (including Langford's "Introduction"), involving the corrected galley proofs, manuscript, and carbon typescripts. Since 1981 critics have more widely used Noel Polk's editorship and publication of *Sanctuary: The Original Text* as well as Polk's comparisons of the book's two versions. See Polk ("Afterword" and "The Space Between *Sanctuary*") and also Kevin Railey (*Natural Aristocracy*) for accounts of the ways that the earlier edition of *Sanctuary* prompts serious (re)consideration of the novel and its place in a crucial period of Faulkner's writing.

6. Polk suggests that this opening initiates both the novel's sustained motif of images of enclosure and its suggestions of Horace's emotional entrapment in his strained marriage ("Afterword," 301). In either reading, the scene offers an example of the earlier version's (modernist) perspectivism and its emphasis on Horace's interior life.

7. In his "Preface," Faulkner claimed he wrote *Sanctuary* in three weeks and with a deliberate eye toward mass-market tastes. Referring to the original process of conceiving the novel, he called it both "horrific" and "cheap," and he made a direct overture to readers to buy it: "I made a fair job and I hope you will buy it and tell your friends and I hope they will buy it too" ("Preface," 1030). However, in its resemblance to what must be seen as meaningful work for Faulkner in *Flags in the Dust* and *The Sound and the Fury*, as well as its treatment of Horace's troubled family relationships, his experiences with southern social reality, and an acute nostalgia, *Sanctuary* is not so readily dismissible as Faulkner himself asserts. Philip Cohen, in his thoughtful consideration of the "Preface," argues that comments like these suggest Faulkner's defensive response to contemporary critics who praised *Sanctuary* but who had failed to recognize the quality and innovation of *The Sound and the Fury* and *As I Lay Dying* ("A Cheap Idea," 54–55). That Faulkner maintained this attitude toward the novel throughout his life is evident in public comments such as that he wrote *Sanctuary* because he "liked the sound of dough rising" (Blotner 1984, 233), or that he "didn't like the book" (Meriwether and Millgate, *Lion in the Garden*, 55). Yet on at least one occasion, Faulkner also gave a strong clue to the disingenuousness of such commentary. Responding to a question at Mary Washington College about whether he would like to "repudiate" *Sanctuary*, Faulkner gave his standard answer: that it was "basely conceived." In the same response, however, he goes on to describe the other ways (besides writing) he had made money earlier in his life: "[W]hen I was footloose I could do things . . . I could run a bootlegging boat, I was a commercial airplane pilot" (*Faulkner in the University*, 90). Although *Sanctuary* does include patently commercial elements, the obvious falseness of Faulkner's remarks about piloting or running liquor suggests a similar deviousness to his reference here to *Sanctuary*'s "baseness."

8. On this point I disagree with the critical reading of this opening scene offered by Fredric Jameson, who sees this moment in the novel as exemplary of what he calls "the high modernist demiurge": "The opening of *Sanctuary* is in this sense canonical: its characters emerging before us in some strange 'always-already' familiarity as though

we were supposed to know who Temple and Popeye and the Virginia gentleman already were—yet here the familiarity is Faulkner's own, and not yet the reader's. He is it who has chosen to withhold the facts of the matter, and the (not terribly complicated) explanation for this prematurely climactic and coincidental confluence of his two narrative strands" (*Signatures of the Visible,* 132). My point is that the reader's familiarity with Popeye and the type he resembles was precisely what Faulkner counted on as he approached the novel. The "explanation" for what Jameson seems to consider a too-early discharge of the novel's narrative energy lies in both Faulkner's complicated understanding of consumer culture, and his recognition of readers' potential for a similarly sophisticated recognition of its function or effect.

9. Huyssen's book, and especially the chapter "Mass Culture as Woman: Modernism's Other," described what he saw as a longstanding tradition of thought about modernism, particularly in the Frankfurt School. Huyssen at points offers a more comprehensive version of modernism and its relation to mass culture than he is often credited for, and one that he has recently revisited ("High/Low in an Expanded Field"). See also Irving Howe's assertion that the modernist artist "must confront the one challenge for which he has not been prepared: the challenge of success" (*The Decline of the New,* 16).

10. Faulkner had several reasons in 1930 to return to a novel that he thought might sell. Polk avers that "it may be that pecuniary motives were larger in [Faulkner's] mind when he revised [*Sanctuary*] than when he originally conceived and wrote it: in the months following the submission of the original manuscript to the publishers he got married and bought a house, so his decision to revise might have been an attempt to salvage a work already at hand which might make him some much-needed cash" ("Afterword," 295–96).

11. Both the original hardcover and later paperback editions of the novel became best-sellers. Each sold more than two million copies, and the book's success led to Faulkner's original contract in Hollywood as well as, ultimately, a film version of *Sanctuary,* released as *The Story of Temple Drake* [Paramount, 1933]). *Sanctuary* generated enough attention on its release that when Faulkner's original publishers of the novel encountered financial difficulty in the fall of 1931, the year of the book's release, Faulkner was considered a prime prospect for literary agents (Blotner 1984, 283).

12. As James Naremore puts it, "The Op recounts everything in deadpan fashion, as if he were making raw reports under pressure" ("Dashiell Hammett and the Poetics of Hard-Boiled Fiction,"57). He even possesses a mechanistic or inhuman detachment that for Naremore evokes the principle and apparatus of modern observation: "[E]ven though [Hammett] tells everything from the Op's point of view, he has been selective about how much subjectivity he allows us to see. The Op is a sort of *camera obscura*" (59). The Op and Popeye, that is to say, share qualities that are unique to the crime genre as a modern, mass form of writing, one that has its correlative in aspects of characterization.

13. John T. Matthews offers a similar perspective on the "mechanical" composition of *As I Lay Dying* in the context of his discussion of that novel's critique of commodification: "That *As I Lay Dying* is produced by the very processes it critiques may be seen in traces of reification in Faulkner's own comments about the novel. He referred to this novel as his tour de force and said that he could write it . . . exceptionally fast. . . . Composed with the hum of the University of Mississippi's power station in the background . . . *As I Lay Dying* takes on the sheen of a highly technical, even machine-

made object" ("*As I Lay Dying* in the Machine Age," 90). Faulkner's references to his act of writing *Sanctuary,* as well as passages in it describing artificial "electrical" lighting, suggest it as a novel that, perhaps even more than *As I Lay Dying,* acquires this technical or metallic "sheen."

14. George Grella offers several useful reflections on the gangster genre, including a reading of Burnett's novel that establishes a connection between Popeye and Rico and sees their abstract quality as part of their authors' critique of modernity. "[I]t seems quite likely that William Faulkner had read *Little Caesar* before he wrote *Sanctuary;* he is the only literary author I know of who used the gangster archetype (and his gangster, Popeye, has a lot in common with Rico) to suggest the breakdown of traditional order and the evil tendencies of anarchic modernism. Faulkner's Popeye is an obviously symbolic, and indeed allegorical character; in his own way Burnett's Cesare Bandello seems no less symbolic" ("The Gangster Novel: The Urban Pastoral," 194).

15. Grella refers to the "grotesque" mix of comedy and solemnity that makes "the gangster funeral a stock scene" (192).

16. The well-known comic strip "Popeye" was already in print when Faulkner published *Sanctuary,* and it may well have contributed to Faulkner's characterizations in the novel. See Rouselle, *Annotations to William Faulkner's* Sanctuary, 4. Popeye was also likely named after a Memphis gangster who attained notoriety in the twenties, Neal "Popeye" Pumphrey. Faulkner heard of him through a woman he met in a Memphis nightclub (see Blotner 1984, 176, and Arnold and Trouard, *Reading Faulkner: Sanctuary,* 5).

17. Like the other gangster novels I discuss here, *Louis Beretti* enjoyed wide popularity. It eventually sold over a million copies, and it appears on a list of the best selling titles for the period (Alice Payne Hackett, *70 Years of Best Sellers*).

18. Richard Godden describes this element of another subgenre, the prison novel, that is suggestive for my reading of *Sanctuary.* Referring to Horace McCoy's *They Shoot Horses, Don't They?* as well as James Cain's *The Postman Always Rings Twice,* he refers to the way in which the novels' use of first-person, confessional narration characterized much pulp, which, Godden asserts, "absorbed its public through empathy" (*Fictions of Labor,* 201). In his descriptions of Popeye at the novel's opening, Faulkner stresses his impenetrability or shallowness as a way of signaling to readers, I think, a resistance to the pulp habit of drawing readers into a character or story through empathy or identification. It is this which may have contributed to Faulkner's notorious answer to an interviewer's question about the novel. Asked about which character in *Sanctuary* he identified with, Faulkner evasively responded, "The cob."

19. It also reads like a stereotypical case study. Popeye's "bio" opens with "His mother was the daughter of a boarding house keeper. His father had been a professional strike breaker hired by the street railway company to break a strike in 1900" (388); it ends with Popeye as a child being sent "to a home for incorrigible children" after maiming a kitten and the statement "His mother was an invalid" (393).

20. At the same time, and embedded in Faulkner's language, is the split in his approaches to Temple and to the novel generally. Presenting Temple as an object of visual consumption and therefore rendered in a manner that makes her above all easy to "see," Faulkner also obscures Temple's image by a figurative use of language: the description of her "long legs blonde with running." In addition, and in a manner that also figures significantly in Temple's subsequent appearances, she is depicted *moving.*

Both of these aspects undermine Temple's static, visualized object-status. Faulkner's use of figuration in descriptions of Temple will recur, demonstrating Faulkner's modernist or literary strategy, but they function in a manner distinct from her appearance earlier in the book as an eroticized spectacle.

21. This last scene in particular draws attention to itself and to its thematizing of the act of voyeurism, compounding the scopophilic act. Faulkner does so by "refracting" it: Minnie's report of seeing Clarence Snopes spying on Popeye's act of watching Temple and Red (324).

22. It may well have been these qualities that prompted Edith Wharton, in an early reaction to the novel, to comment that Temple "is like a cinema doll" (noted by Ilene Goldman-Price; unpublished letter to Edward Sheldon, Edith Wharton Collection, Yale Collection of American Literature, Beinecke Rare Book and Manuscript Library). Feminist film theory has long treated this staple of cinema. As Laura Mulvey says in her seminal essay "Visual Pleasure and Narrative Cinema," "In their traditional exhibitionist role, women are simultaneously looked at and displayed, with their appearance coded for strong visual and erotic impact so that they can be said to connote *to be looked-at-ness*" (750). Even in her "Afterthoughts" to this essay, Mulvey describes the role of women in classical film genres connoting a narrative function as the object of male desire similar to that of Temple's position at Goodwin's. "This neat *narrative* function restates the propensity for 'woman' to signify 'the erotic' already familiar from *visual* representation" ("Afterthoughts on 'Visual Pleasure and Narrative Cinema,'" 127).

23. I mean this as the negative aspect of the experience Jameson describes as "a commodity rush, [in which] our 'representations' of things tend[s] to arouse an enthusiasm and a mood swing not necessarily inspired by the things themselves" (*Postmodernism*, x).

24. Tommy's reactions to watching Temple's door resemble Vardaman Bundren's account of his own painful experience of window shopping in *As I Lay Dying*. Looking into the store window in Jefferson at the electric train he hopes to buy, he gives plaintive voice to the longings of consumers: "It was right behind the window, red on the track, the track shining round and round. It made my heart hurt" (142).

25. Faulkner articulates this idea expressly in the original version of the novel when Horace proclaims, "[S]ay what you want to, but there's a corruption even about looking upon evil" (*SO*, 72).

26. Discussing Faulkner's treatment of Temple's rape and her experiences at Goodwin's, Homer B. Pettey refers to the way Faulkner involves readers in activity similar to that of Popeye's and the other men. "Faulkner develops Temple's peril among the bootleggers in such a way that she becomes the object of perversion. He purposefully includes a urination scene to expose the sordid, voyeuristic world of Temple's entrapment. . . . The anonymous figure observing Temple could be any man, but it is also the reader. . . . The reader's predicament is that he cannot stand back and observe . . . objectively, but must also fix his gaze upon Temple. Thus, the text is fetishized and its reading sexualized by the reader" ("Reading and Raping in *Sanctuary*," 72).

27. As Edwin Arnold and Dawn Trouard suggest of this scene, "the tell-tale cigarette smoke has led Temple, and the reader, to believe that Popeye is standing in the kitchen door. Faulkner, however, has fooled us: Popeye has been watching from around the

corner of the house, not the kitchen, and the smoke has come from Ruby's cigarette" (*Reading Faulkner:* Sanctuary, 52–53).

28. Drawn from the original text, the chapters at Goodwin's retain their uncanny or disorienting feel from the original edition. They may also be said to offer what portion of the earlier version Faulkner valued in their resemblance to the nonrealist qualities of *The Sound and the Fury* and *As I Lay Dying.* Cohen argues that Faulkner resented contemporary critics' higher valuation of *Sanctuary* for its relative "accessibility" ("A Cheap Idea," 58). My purpose in highlighting the novel's obscure moments here is to suggest their difference from other sections of *Sanctuary* that present Temple in more conventional fashion.

29. Such aggressive "blending" of its discursive elements also resembles what for Richard Godden occurs in *If I Forget Thee, Jerusalem:* "Striking against the inert blocks of 'Wild Palms,' 'Old Man' attempts through a violent intensity . . . to smash open the forms of reification" (*Fictions of Labor,* 221). Though *Sanctuary* does not break its narrative modes into discrete or alternating sections as does *Jerusalem,* it nevertheless offers readers a working through of two very different representational and literary strategies. As with the later novel, this contrast enacts a productive discord, pointing up and "smashing" reified models and forms.

30. Here I happily acknowledge the influence of my student in a tutorial at Harvard College, Jonathan Sherman, who used a similar term and treatment to describe the generic "emergence" and self-critique of an anomalous film noir, Joseph Mankiewicz's 1950 *No Way Out* in his undergraduate thesis, " 'We're Gonna Be Ready Tonight: Civil Rights and The Race Politics of Post-War Film Noir" (Harvard College, February 2003).

31. In the absence of a camera or other recording device, Horace makes use of Temple's faltering recollection of her treatment by Popeye. Tom Gunning argues for the importance of recording technology to the development of both modern policing and the detective novel, suggesting that the "indexical" nature of photography allowed the police to shift investigations of crimes such as rape away from criminals to a focus on the victim. As he puts it in his essay "Tracing the Individual Body: Photography, Detectives, and Early Cinema," "when photographs are approached as evidence, the issue rests less on a simulacrum of perception than on the act of recording, the retaining of the indexical trace. The body as the repository of evidence shifts . . . to that of the victim which holds evidence of the violence done to it" (37). Horace, though neither a photographer nor a forensics specialist, nevertheless encounters Temple at Miss Reba's in bed and half-dressed, a circumstance that underscores the sense of her exposure— her body as well as her story—as he arrives seeking information. As such, his investigation approximates something of what Gunning refers to as the use of the body in modern detection as a "repository of evidence."

32. Blotner refers to *Sanctuary*'s split "identity," if in a slightly different fashion than I describe it here. He suggests that with the novel, Faulkner "may have considered something like a three-horse parlay: a spectacular mystery-detective-gangster story, a commercially successful novel, and a work of art that would mirror the corruption of society" (Blotner 1984, 234). Blotner's reference to the "corruption of society" that the novel mirrored implies the evil of public figures like Clarence Snopes or the miscarriage of justice at Goodwin's trial. I submit that this "corruption" included something

of what Adorno refers to as "the social dynamic": the circumstances of cultural production that surrounded Faulkner and constrained him to write a book which, in its use of violence and transparent commercialism, troubled him.

33. Even physical sensation is repressed in the modernist aesthetic. Leonard points out the way in which Stephen, in a Foucauldian exercise of self-surveillance and denial, monitors his sensory experience, on guard against any unexpected physical response to his urban environment—a setting that teems with temptations like prostitutes and pornography. "Stephen's aesthetic theory . . . also creates a category of normativeness"(81). See also Howe: "Imperviousness of mind and impatience with flesh were attitudes shared by Yeats and Malraux, Eliot and Brecht. Disgust with urban trivialities and contempt for *l'homme moyen sensual* streak through a great many modernist poems and novels" (*Decline of the New,* 17).

34. See Faulkner's remarks asserting this in the "Preface": "I . . . sent [*Sanctuary*] to Smith . . . who wrote me immediately, 'Good God, I can't publish this. We'd both be in jail" (1030), as well as a nearly identical statement in *Faulkner in the University* (91).

35. Recall Huyssen's suggestion that for modernists, commodification and mass marketability were "the 'wrong' kind of success" (53).

36. Cohen describes Faulkner's ambivalence in the "Preface" as a cover: "The introduction's double-edged tone of contempt directed at Faulkner's readers and at himself represents a complex role-playing. By thumbing his nose at himself as well as at his public, he could soften the disdain he was exhibiting for their taste and perhaps avoid openly offending the audience he depended on for a living" (" 'A Cheap Idea,' " 61). Cohen's reading of Faulkner's role-playing with *Sanctuary* squares with many events from the author's public life, and I agree that Faulkner's remarks about *Sanctuary* were often diversions from his real feelings about it. Nevertheless, there remains a trace of ingenuousness in Faulkner's comments about this novel that suggests at least a measure of scorn for its sources, motives, readers, and—perhaps above all—its role in Faulkner's career as the novel that first earned him recognition.

37. The passage I have in mind involves Jim on board the *Patna,* looking at the exposed throats of the pilgrims: "and in the blurred circles of light . . . appeared a chin upturned, two closed eyelids, a dark hand with silver rings, a meagre limb draped in a torn covering, a head bent back . . . a throat bared and stretched as if offering itself for the knife" (*Lord Jim,* 12).

38. It also makes more explicit Horace's earlier fantasy of violence and execution. When Horace first sees Clarence Snopes, Faulkner writes, "With the corner of his eye [he] . . . remarked the severe trim of hair across the man's vast, soft, white neck. Like with a guillotine, Horace thought" (298–99).

39. Adorno's treatment of the modernist work's formal "embodying" of its historical reality describes well this aspect of *Sanctuary,* and it offers a clearer way to connect it to mass art: "The unresolved antagonisms of reality appear in art in the guise of immanent problems of artistic form. . . . The aesthetic tensions manifesting themselves in works of art express the essence of reality" (*Aesthetic Theory,* 8).

40. This sense of the trial offering an occasion for again "viewing" Temple voyeuristically and erotically is clear in a fantasy of Horace's that appears in the original text: "[Horace] would sub-poena Temple; he thought in a paroxysm of raging pleasure of flinging her into the court-room, of stripping her" (*SO,* 255).

41. It is important to note that these specifically and, I would argue, deliberately realist passages are not in the original text. Along with Faulkner's deletions of many of the flashbacks and interior monologues, these additions reflect Faulkner's desire to make the revision more accessible and, potentially, commercial. In his account of the revision, Langford addresses this aspect of Faulkner's changes to the original edition: "[F]ar from reworking a lurid sex story into a more significant work, Faulkner seems to have had a single practical purpose—to turn a slow-moving psychological study into a streamlined drama ready for the cameras of Hollywood" (Introduction to *Faulkner's Revision of* Sanctuary, 7). Before the cameras, however, Faulkner needed to ensure that his novel would appeal to a mass readership—which of course the published version did. See also Cohen: "Indeed, Faulkner's revisions made the novel more commercially saleable" ("'A Cheap Idea,'" 56).

42. These sections also vary appreciably from their equivalent passages in the original text. In the original version, the scene of Horace at the window with Miss Jenny appears, but it is buried in a flashback and within several lines of dialogue. In a manner typical of the original edition, one that anticipates Darl Bundren (and recalls "Prufrock"), Faulkner approaches this moment through one of Horace's universalizing reflections. He shows Horace "thinking how man's life ravels out into half-measures, like a worn-out sock; how he finishes his days like a refugee on a levee, trying to keep his entrails warm and his feet dry with cast-offs until he becomes aware of himself, then merely furious trying to cover his nakedness; of the sorry pillar he runs to, the sorry post he leaves. . . . He was standing at the window beside Miss Jenny's chair, watching his sister and a man strolling in the garden" (*SO,* 32–33).

43. Goodwin himself is not actually visible as he burns to death. Faulkner does, however, include the screams of the man who presumably lit the fire as well as the image of the "five-gallon coal oil can which exploded with a rocket-like glare while he carried it, running" (384). Several aspects of the lynching passage are suggestive of Faulkner's lurid approach to the scene as well as, significantly, his understanding of the crowd. He indicates that Goodwin had been brutalized, perhaps sexually, before being killed, and shows the crowd's impulse to attack Horace for his role in defending him: "'Do to the lawyer what we did to him. What he did to her [Temple]. Only we never used a cob'" (384). Beyond implying the crowd's violent reaction toward men in positions like Horace's—that is, in opposition to the passionate vicissitudes of collective will—Faulkner makes clear a connection between the lynch mob and commerce, or the market. For the burning takes place in the same location Faulkner had earlier used as the scene for the onlookers at Tommy's body: the town square. "[Horace] could see the blaze, in the center of a vacant lot where on market days wagons were tethered" (384). Commercial activity and mass desire here become linked directly to a manifestation of violence.

44. As Michael Millgate puts it, "The extensive deletions made by Faulkner [in his revision] in no instance included anything that might be described as anything especially violent or 'horrific'" (*The Achievement of William Faulkner,* 115). In the case of the lynching scene and, as we will see, with others, the revision includes sensational and commercial material that Faulkner in fact *added.*

45. As I indicated earlier, in its belatedness and paucity of detail, this description also amounts to Faulkner's undermining of genre. Though it appears to fit into the formula for pulp crime fiction such as *Me, Gangster* or *Louis Beretti,* it also maintains its

distinctness from them by performing an abbreviated or shorthand version of a life story. Like much of the novel, in other words, it both performs and parodies conventions of generic fiction.

CHAPTER TWO: "Get Me a Nigger"

1. Assessments of the novel's emphasis on acts of looking, on the part of both the characters and the readers, occur frequently in the novel's criticism. The most recent and most comprehensive of these is Patricia McKee's in "Playing White Men in *Light in August*" in her book *Producing American Races*. Though she is right to stress the acts of looking by the novel's white characters, I disagree with McKee's assertion that "In *Light in August* . . . it is mostly white men whose meaning is limited to their looks" (124), as my discussion of Christmas's appearance in the following pages will indicate. Irene Gammel refers to the appearance of Christmas at the mill and notes the use in the scene of a "multi-layered interaction of gazes." She also points out the way this trope engages readers' act of looking: "But Faulkner goes even a step further, since he constructs Joe as an object of sight in the reader's mind" (" 'Because He is Watching Me': Spectatorship and Power in Faulkner's *Light in August*, 13). Miranda Burgess's essay "Watching Jefferson Watching" pays particular attention to the novel's structuring of characters' acts of looking at Joe (99–102). See also Claus Peter Neumann, "Knowledge and Control in *Light in August*" (46). Michel Gresset suggests the potentially "castrating" looks of the men when Christmas dies (*Fascination*, 209–10). Though it is common to note the pervasiveness of watching in the novel, Gresset is one of the few to make the connection of that act to forms of violence and punishment.

2. It is worth pointing out that in Faulkner's account of it, the "audience" for the fire is, as it were, pan-regional as well as multiclass. This is because Faulkner understood that Americans of various regions and economic stations were susceptible to the imaginative vision of a murderous and hypersexualized black man—the way, in other words, that early cinema relied on generic images of the South to produce a national stereotype and idea. See Lary May, "Apocalyptic Cinema: D. W. Griffith and the Aesthetics of Reform" for an account of the rise of a multiclass audience for film after its original viewership in urban, working-class immigrants. See Michael Rogin, " 'The Sword Became a Flashing Vision': D. W. Griffith's *The Birth of a Nation*," and Edward Campbell, *The Celluloid South*, on the capacity of early film to connect audiences of different regional backgrounds and interests.

3. Though it originally appeared in 1915 with enormous notoriety and success, *Birth of a Nation* was re-released in 1930 with similar trappings and responses. Its exposure to a second generation of viewers contributes to what I claim is its influence on Faulkner's thirties novels such as *Light in August*, and especially *Absalom, Absalom!* I will return to a full consideration of the massive impact of Griffith's film—both culturally and to Faulkner's consideration of historical cinema—in the following chapter.

4. Burgess's treatment of the "fantasy" of black rape that informed the romance locates its origin in plantation life and culture. Laura L. Bush also traces the myth of the black rapist in southern thought and social practice, though she points out that it functioned in a later historical context—the period in which events in *Light in August* take place—to enforce Jim Crow rules of power and segregation. "Both Joe Christmas and Joanna Burden know all too well this Southern script of a black male rapist who

ravishes a . . . white woman" ("A Very American Power Struggle: The Color of Rape in *Light in August,*" 491).

5. That Griffith deliberately played on this fear was evident in his manipulation of film aesthetics to create what he believed would be a particularly loathsome image in the scene of Silas accosting Elsie. Lillian Gish, the actress who portrays Elsie in the movie, commented on the role her fair coloring played in Griffith's decision to cast her and to film her scene with Lynch in a particular way: "At first I was not cast to play in *The Clansman.* My sister and I had been the last to join the company and we naturally supposed . . . that the main assignments would go to the older members. But one day while we were rehearsing the scene where the colored man picks up the Northern girl gorilla-fashion, my hair, which was very blonde, fell far below my waist and Griffith, seeing the contrast between the two figures, assigned me to play Elsie Stoneman (who was to have been Mae Marsh)" (quoted in Donald Bogle's *Toms, Coons, Mammies, Mulattoes, and Bucks,* 14).

6. Discussion of early film treatments of the mulatto appears in Bogle, *Toms, Coons, Mammies, Mulattoes, and Bucks,* 9.

7. The Klansmen's act of castrating Gus, Rogin points out, had originally been the culmination of a section of Griffith's film (" 'The Sword Became a Flashing Vision,' " 175). Excised in versions of the picture shown to northern audiences and of the film most viewers were eventually to see, the castrating sequence lay at the heart of *Birth's* convictions about black sexual aggression. In "restoring" this act in his own depiction of vigilantism, Faulkner reproduced actual and historical instances of mutilation, as my later discussion of the Joe's death reveals. In doing so, he also points to the white fear of black potency evinced by Griffith's film and other manifestations of white racist hysteria.

8. Certain of these titles and my discussion of them follow Peter Noble's extensive and critical cultural history, *The Negro in Films.* See especially chapters 3 and 4, "The Negro in Silent Films" and "The Coming of the Sound Film."

9. The story of *Fair and Equal* concerns a wager between a northerner and a southerner about racial equality. To prove his liberal position, the northerner invites an African-American man into his home—who promptly attempts to seduce his daughter, then rapes and strangles his maid. Bogle discusses this film and its reception in *Toms, Coons, Mulattoes, Mammies, and Bucks* (24–25). Although it was not reviewed favorably, the film's release nevertheless reveals a set of assumptions about black men which, if more widely believed in the teens, were not entirely discredited by the period in which Faulkner wrote.

It is worth noting that this image of the black buck or rapist, though powerful, was not as pervasive in early film history as the stereotype of the African American as a subservient, even comic lackey or "Uncle Tom." Bogle points to several early film versions of this type. One appeared as a black spy (for the South) during the Civil War in the film *Confederate Spy* (1910). Before he's shot by Northern troops, he expresses his contentment at dying "for massa's sake." In another film that actually uses this utterance as its title, *For Massa's Sake* (1911), a former slave sells his freedom to help offset his master's economic woes. See Bogle, chapter 1, "Black Beginnings: From *Uncle Tom's Cabin* to *Birth of a Nation,*" for a discussion of these and other films, including the original movie "Tom" in Edwin Porter's 1903 film of Stowe's novel. See also Noble on the weak or submissive black man in early film such as the Rastus comedies (28–29).

The seeming opposition of these two film types—black buck and Tom—may in fact be reconcilable. As cultural theory has shown, variant images or stereotypes may well be said to enable or to confirm one another, even, dialectically, to call one another into being. The image of the cowering or subservient "Tom" is the inverse of the aggressive and threatening buck. But the existence of the one in the popular imagination or subconscious "summons" its opposite forth, into material presence—revealing, in the case of the buck, for instance, what the comic type attempts to sooth or cover over. This seems a way to understand the appearance of divergent racial stereotypes in early film.

10. See Jack Temple Kirby's *Media-Made Dixie*, 39–42, for information about Page's politics and writing. He describes Page's "superimposing" of events from South Carolina during Reconstruction onto *Red Rock*'s supposedly historical account of Virginia. In doing so, Page relied on sources such as a Ku Klux Klan report of 1872 and sought to generalize (and falsify) accounts of the South after the Civil War. Kirby suggests as well that Page's correspondence indicated his support for actual incidents of violence toward blacks such as the riots in 1898 in Wilmington, North Carolina (42).

11. Even before Griffith took up *The Clansman* and turned it into what would become the most influential movie in history, it had offered a vision of black violence and sexual threat that easily translated to film. As Eric Sundquist describes the transition from novel to movie, he points to the facilitating role played in the adaptation by the iconic dimension of both the film image and Dixon's literary practice. "When Dixon's novel became *The Birth of a Nation* in 1915, the image of the 'Negro as Beast,' long a stock figure in the South and elsewhere, was visibly fixed as the icon to which almost any justification of Jim Crow could ultimately be referred" (*Faulkner*, 82). In this perspective, Sundquist shares with Burgess ("Watching Jefferson Watching") an awareness of the way southern ideology, whether directed through a racist myth or by the technical apparatus of the cinema, depended on an instrumentalizing of the look.

12. In its first four months, the book went through four printings. The title itself contributed to the novel's notoriety and success, as did the rumor of Van Vechten's "penetration" of Harlem social and cultural life in his preparation for writing it. For a discussion of Van Vechten's role in Harlem literary activity and of *Nigger Heaven*'s popular and critical reception—including responses by figures as varied as Langston Hughes, James Weldon Johnson, and Gertrude Stein—see David Levering Lewis's study *When Harlem Was in Vogue* (184–89).

13. In his discussion of the Harlem novel, Eugene Arden describes the way popular writers contributed to a conception of the Negro from which Faulkner may have drawn his depiction of Christmas. Referring to sensationalist depictions of black male characters in a number of 1920s novels, including *Nigger Heaven*, Claude McKay's *Home to Harlem* (1928), and Wallace Thurman's *The Blacker the Berry* (1929), Arden summarizes, "It is clear that by the end of the 1920s a stereotyped Negro of Harlem had been created, acknowledged, and assumed; his existence seemed confined to drink, sex, gambling, and brooding about racial matters, with an edge of violence always in view ("The Early Harlem Novel," 112).

14. Perkins ("'Ah Just Cant Quit Thinking'") describes precisely the effect I am attributing to Faulkner in several ways with this novel, as with *Sanctuary*. The use of the razor in Joe's characterization, that is, immediately associates him with a range of popular cultural depictions of race. As a result, *Light in August* combines these popular, "low" cultural elements with Faulkner's willfully modernist, "high"-art strategies.

15. See also Martha Banta's fascinating article, "The Razor, the Pistol, and the Ideology of Race Etiquette." In it, she points to the way political discourse and cultural representations functioned in the North, and in particular in the early New York weekly, *Life* (which began in 1893 and is distinguished from Henry Luce's famous national glossy founded in 1936), to produce an ideology of manners that included codes for all forms of social behavior—including violence. Banta's essay has enormous interest for my analysis of *Light in August;* however, its treatment of American military history at the end of the nineteenth and beginning of the twentieth centuries as well as the influx of ethnic immigration in the same period as spurs to northern racist ideology are beyond the purview of my argument here. Her discussion of codes of violence, though, includes Faulkner's "renditions of how one's existential sense of social 'placement' is expressed by the choice of weapons used at those moments when the rules of etiquette governing one party's ideology of race relationships comes into conflict with another's code" (203). Joe's dilemma over whether to use his razor or Joanna's gun reflects, in Banta's analysis, one such "existential" moment in the novel with which Faulkner, no less than Joe, is struggling.

16. Faulkner's account of Joe's wandering echoes the historical fact of the Great Migration and injects a decidedly urban series of place names into his otherwise mythical Yoknapatawpha: "The street ran into Oklahoma and Missouri and as far south as Mexico and back north to Chicago and Detroit and then back south again and at last to Mississippi. It was fifteen years long" (563).

17. Hugh Ruppersburg points to the advent of cover art of this type in the "Spicy" pulp series as well as in *Black Mask* (*Reading Faulkner:* Light in August, 67). See also Tony Goodstone's anthology and its reproductions of those designs, *The Pulps.*

18. My account of this moment of interpellation or "hailing" by an objective, outside source in Joe's magazine draws on Althusser's model for ideology formation ("Ideology and Ideological State Apparatuses"). Though it is not clear what racial categories, if any, exist in the story Joe reads, Joe's subjectivity as well as his perceived social position are heavily mediated by dominant forms of ideology, as the language in this scene and subsequent events in the novel make clear. Whatever he imbibes in the detective stories, their effect seems to place Joe's subject position *outside* mainstream culture and as the perpetrator of a violent crime.

19. Faulkner's invoking of the novel genre in the context of Joe's reading a detective magazine implies at least the possibility of a similar comparison between Joe's reading matter and that of Faulkner's readers: *Light in August.* We may, then, also read the comparison in reverse, taking this reference as a cue to read Faulkner's novel "as if it were a detective magazine"—an approach I suggest in my later discussion of the novel's generic elements.

20. In this respect Joe strikingly resembles other Faulkner characters from the decade—notably the Tall Convict of *If I Forget Thee, Jerusalem.*

21. In ways that differ somewhat from my reading, Burgess describes the resemblance of Joe's identity to Minnie Cooper's in "Dry September." For her, both are cinematically defined by their objectification: "Like Minnie Cooper, Joe occupies the position of the romantic heroine of narrative cinema, contemplating fatalistically his own abandonment to some external and authoritative gaze" ("Watching Jefferson Watching," 104).

22. Narrative cinema, that is, has a tendency to assert its illusory world as real and with a certain insistence of verisimilitude. Because telling Joe's story involves a con-

tinual tracking of him, an authoritative observation, as in this passage, I here conflate the functions of voice and eye. Faulkner's "silencing" of the action and hence of his narrator (who nevertheless speaks), is also suggested in moments that show the other senses abrogated by vision—as we saw in the fire scene. Alfred Kazin describes the novel as "curiously soundless" ("The Stillness of *Light in August*, 527). For a consideration of the overlapping functions of narration and looking in Faulkner's technique, see Hugh Ruppersburg, *Voice and Eye in Faulkner's Fiction* (10, 31–33).

23. In a manner that anticipates my later argument, it is worth pointing out that the dominant gaze that fixes and constructs Joe, in addition to being identified here with popular culture, also follows from his white male author. Though Faulkner's depiction of Joe reflects critically on commercial cultural effects and practices, we will see how Faulkner himself performs a similar manner of differentiating or defining him.

24. My reading of these sections of Joe's story is influenced by Hayden White's discussion of the modernist interrogation of the event. He describes the way in which, in Woolf's *Between the Acts*, Isabella Oliver's action of reading "leaks into" another physical event, "endowing it with a sinister, phantasmagoric aspect" ("The Modernist Event," 29). White goes on to say that when "events flow out of their outlines and flow out of the narrative as well [,] the effect of the representation is to endow *all* events with spectral qualities" (29). For White, that effect links modernist literary practice to film. It is this spectral "spreading" of Faulkner's narration of Joe at key moments that lends another filmic quality to his narration.

25. Philip Weinstein reads this section of Faulkner's novel (and modernist practice generally) as cinematic because of what he regards as its uncanny (what he terms "unlawful") treatments of space. Weinstein discussed Faulkner's spatial descriptions and Joe's movement as examples of modernism's cinematic affinities in "Anxious Knowledge: Modern Subjects in Uncanny Space," plenary address to the meeting of the Modernist Studies Association, Pennsylvania State University, October 8, 1999.

26. It is important to acknowledge here the role in my analysis of this element of suspicion. Since the novel's publication, readers and critics alike have presumed Christmas's role in Joanna's death, a reading that the book certainly encourages and that, given Faulkner's own references to Joe's act of killing her, seems reasonable. At least one critic, however, raises questions about the substance of Joe's guilt. Steven Meats, in an article titled "Who Killed Joanna Burden?" elaborates a theory of Joe's innocence that points to several gaps in readers' knowledge of events surrounding the crime. In particular, Meats looks at Faulkner's elision of the actual murder and the circumstantial quality of the evidence against Joe; he also raises questions about Joe Brown's shaky, self-interested testimony the evening of the fire. Additionally, Meats speculates, somewhat whimsically, about Joe's response to Joanna's aborted firing of the gun and suggests a reaction like instinctive self-defense that would have pre-empted Joe's act of killing her (273–75). Much of the book militates against Meats's analysis, however, including Joe's motive in a kind of despairing hatred and his possession of what appears to be the murder weapon—details that Meats acknowledges (275). Without replaying fully the terms of his analysis, I raise Meats's essay for its use pointing up readers' perhaps overly credulous response to the prospect of Christmas as Joanna's murderer. As we will see, assuming Joe as guilty reveals an uncomfortable fact about the novels' readers: their complicity with the racist dimension of many of the characters' thinking. In the discussion that follows, I demonstrate that much of the text's

power is drawn from these assumptions, a fact that Faulkner's narrative operations put into play.

27. See Martin Kreiswirth, "Plots and Counterplots: The Structure of *Light in August*," (69). In *Faulkner and the Novelistic Imagination*, Robert Dale Parker also comments on Faulkner's use of generic strategies, both the mystery and the detective story, in initiating the murder narrative (88, 90–92).

28. In this respect, the novel emphasizes what Robert Champigny describes as the "ludic" aspect of the mystery genre: "Mystery stories are designed to sharpen the ludic interest. Either from the start or gradually, they delimit the content of the ending while keeping its particulars in the dark. As he reads the text for the first time, the reader is incited to wonder about not just what will happen but also what will have happened" (*What Will Have Happened*, 5). Part of that "wonder" in *Light in August*, I suggest, includes a vague anxiety or even dread that colors the reading of a novel set in the Jim Crow South and that, in its opening chapters, discloses a plot about the murder of a white woman by a character assumed to be black. In a way that anticipates my later account of the ideological and more troubling effects of Faulkner's novel, I should also here suggest that Christmas's story possesses an element peculiar to narrative generally. As Teresa de Lauretis has pointed out, desire inevitably plays a role in readers' or viewers' experience of narrative. Tracing the development in narrative theory away from the pure emphasis in early semiotics on the "logic, grammar, or a formal rhetoric of narrative" toward an understanding of the "structuring and destructuring, even destructive processes at work in textual and semiotic production," de Lauretis points to the agency of desire in our experience of, and constituting by, narrative operations (*Alice Doesn't*, 103–5). That desire, she suggests, possesses connections to aggressive, even sadistic impulses, structures of feeling and cathected desire that I submit also motivate readers' ongoing engagement with Christmas's story.

29. It also carries with it a sense of deathliness that Walter Benjamin, in his essay "The Storyteller," suggests is particularly novelistic. "The nature of a character in a novel," he writes, "cannot be presented any better than is done in [the] statement, which says that the 'meaning' of his life is revealed only in his death. . . . Therefore the reader must, no matter what, know in advance that he will share their experience of death: if need be their figurative death—the end of the novel—but preferably their actual one. How do the characters make him understand that death is already waiting for them . . . ? That is the question that feeds the reader's consuming interest in the events of the novel" (101). If ever a character appeared in a novel who makes readers understand that death is waiting for him, that character is Joe Christmas.

30. Kreiswirth comments on this moment, suggesting that "The question of murder now becomes subordinate to that of race and identity" ("Plots and Counterplots," 73) and, elsewhere, that "the ramifications" of Christmas's supposed mixed race "come to dominate, disturb, and ultimately deform the text" (72). Judith Wittenberg also hints at what I think is involved in Faulkner's attention to and manipulation of the detail of Christmas's race. Referring to Joe Brown's revelation and the sheriff's credulous response, she says, "In almost parodic fashion, race proves more important than murder and hearsay is quickly accepted as fact" ("Race in *Light in August*," 159). Though she does not indicate what, exactly, Faulkner parodies, I suggest that at least one backdrop for the crime story Brown tells are the pop culture stories and images of blacks that, prior to the novel, had entertained or frightened audiences.

31. This is a variation of Meats's argument in "Who Killed Joanna Burden?" in which he indicates that Brown is able to divert the sheriff's suspicion onto Christmas by claiming that Joe is black (272). The most important part of Meats's approach, however, is his point about readers' willingness, like the characters in the novel, to take for granted Christmas's guilt: "[A]ny person, the sheriff or the reader, judging from evidence we are given *in the novel*, should conclude that Joe Christmas's guilt is an assumption and nothing more . . . [T]his assumption . . . proves something which Faulkner may have been trying to point out. 'Man knows so little about his fellows' (*Light in August*, 433), and yet on the basis of this insufficient knowledge all of us—the sheriff, Gavin Stevens, Percy Grimm, the community, the reader—are more than ready to pass judgment" (277). I contend that the reason for this readiness is Christmas's assumed racial identity as well as readers' exposure to popular depictions of racialized images of crime.

32. We might also call this a form of narrative "guilt." Though it engages readers' longing for suspense or drama, the novel's use of sensationalized violence also capitalizes on their underlying attitudes about race. It is this complicity or susceptibility, which emerges alongside the novel's compelling mystery, that Faulkner is interested in exposing.

33. In its manner of depicting Christmas and of manipulating the reader, the novel offers a version of what Peter Brooks calls the "animating component of (narrative) desire." Echoing, while also inverting de Lauretis's claims for the subjectivizing element of narrative, Brooks states: "Narratives portray the motors of desire that drive and consume their plots, and they also lay bare the nature of narration as a form of human desire: the need to tell as a primary human drive that seeks to seduce and to subjugate the listener, to implicate him in the thrust of a desire that can never quite speak its name" (*Reading For The Plot*, 61). Brooks's perspective on narrative desire sees it perform a subjugating of its audience. Considering the role of agency, which Brooks in this statement leaves unconsidered but which in the case of *Light in August* clearly excludes Joe, my own perspective is closer to that of de Lauretis cited earlier. Through its narrative strategies, that is, Faulkner's novel pointedly reveals that narrative desire's "name." In his descriptions of the murder and the townspeople's reaction to it, as well as in his manner of constructing a mystery out of Joe's narrative, Faulkner shows the nature of the desire of the crime story's different audiences—both the townspeople and the novel's readers.

34. Burgess, "Watching Jefferson Watching," 109.

35. If Christmas is perceived (or constructed) as threatening in this scene, that threat nevertheless is diffused or absorbed into the narrative's eventual subduing of him.

36. Using Balzac as a reference point, Miller states, "On the side of perspicacity, Balzac's omniscient narration assumes a fully panoptic view of the world it places under surveillance. Nothing worth knowing escapes its notation" (*The Novel and the Police*, 23). Yet Balzacian omniscience also fabricates its own limits. *Pere Goriot*, Miller points out, opens with an exhaustive list of the physical space of the *maison Vauquer;* when the narration moves to treating the novel's characters, on the other hand, it falters. But this constructed gap in knowledge is more apparent than real. "[T]he 'origin' of narrative [in *Pere Goriot*] in a cognitive gap also indicates to what end narrative will be directed. Substituting a temporal mode of mastery for a spatial one, Balzac's 'drama' will achieve the same full knowledge of character that has already been

acquired of habitat" (26). Faulkner's "drama," like Balzac's, will (and does) furnish the information about Christmas that here, at its outset, it is "missing."

37. As Miller describes it, this is an ideological effect that is peculiar to the novel form. Referring to his own shift in conceiving of omniscience as a policing element of novels (from earlier conceptions of it, for instance Flaubert's, as God-like), Miller writes, "It doesn't matter finally whether we gloss panoptical narration as a kind of providence or as a kind of police. . . . What matters is that the faceless gaze becomes an ideal of the power of regulation" (24). We will see the full implication of Miller's thinking in my discussion of the novel's later efforts to "regulate" or position Joe, as well as the connection of such efforts to the novel's violent ending.

38. James Snead similarly sees the reader's involvement in producing "arbitrary codes of dominance" such as those the text parodies in Kennedy. He says of the novel's manipulation of omniscience: "In *Light in August* Faulkner diverges from Fielding's omniscient narrators or Conrad's and James's unreliable ones by exposing omniscience as unreliability. The unreliability is an active deception. There is no deficiency, of either intelligence or perspicacity: the narrator is actively creating error. Society here turns arbitrary codes of dominance into 'fact.' To make matters worse, the reader helps accomplish the entire process" (*Figures of Division*, 85). It is this apparently "factual" quality to the black man's guilt in this scene (or that of African Americans generally), I suggest, that Faulkner's novel exposes as "arbitrary codes of dominance."

39. The matron's reactions to the dietician's "discovery" of Joe's "blackness" reveals this aspect of the orphanage and its bureaucratic efficiency at dealing with perceived differences among its charges. Without questioning the veracity of the dietician's story, she moves decisively: " 'We must place him. We must place him at once. What applications have we? If you will hand me the file. . . ' " (499).

40. Michel Foucault's account of the workings of the panoptic model includes all of these institutions, each of which figure in Faulkner's description of the building, as well as a reference to the extension of institutional gazing that applies well to Hines: "Heads or deputy-heads of 'families,' monitors and foremen had to live in close proximity to the inmates; their clothes were 'almost as humble' as those of the inmates themselves; they practically never left their side, observing them day and night" (*Discipline and Punish*, 295). In his discussion of Foucault's model of the Panopticon, Martin Jay describes this internalizing of the gaze. "Here [in the institution] the external look becomes an internalized and self-regulating mechanism that extends the old religious preoccupation with the smallest detail that was still immense 'in the eye of God'" (*Downcast Eyes*, 410). Jay's reference to Foucault's originary model in Christian theology and to God's surveilling eye resembles Hines's fanatical invocation to the dietician, his idea that her discovery of Christmas was "a sign and a damnation for bitchery" (493). Though not practical in this discussion, Joe's eventual adoption by McEachern and his rigid disciplining of Joe to learn the Christian catechism and to convert him to a strict Calvinist moral regimen further suggests the relevance to this novel of Foucauldian models of training the subject.

41. The opening of Dickens's novel bears much in common, imagistically, with Faulkner's description of the orphanage: "LONDON. Michaelmas term lately over, and the Lord Chancellor sitting in Lincoln's Inn Hall. Implacable November weather . . . Smoke lowering from chimney-pots, making a soft black drizzle with flakes of soot in it as big as full-grown snow-flakes—gone into mourning, one might imagine, for the

ᴜ....h of the sun" (49). Though for different reasons than I do, Kreiswirth also finds an implicit connection between *Light in August* and *Bleak House*. In a rigorous reader-response analysis, he suggests that the various, unrelated strands of plot in Faulkner's novel, like those in *Bleak House*, produce an impression of "assimilation," or at the least, a longing for it: "*Light in August*... goes only so far in this direction. It pushes the reader toward a system of meaning, but then questions, subverts, and finally, unlike *Bleak House*, deconstructs it, replacing it with another system—only then to repeat the process once again" ("Plots and Counterplots," 70). This "deconstruction" or replacing one "system of meaning" with another, we will see, is the process of appearing to break down the novel's system of surveillance. The system put into its place is the effort to trace, against the grain of the novel's obscurity, the proper textual and social space for its protagonist.

42. My reading of this aspect of *Light in August* has been influenced by D. A. Miller's treatment of Dickens. Of particular interest is Miller's discussion of the fact that in Dickens's novels, institutions such as the orphanage (and the prison, the factory, etc.) serve as gathering places for those subjects for which that other major institution of social organizing—the family—cannot answer.

43. Referring to *Oliver Twist*, Miller cites Mr. Brownlow's cautionary advice to Oliver about his behavior and comportment as the stipulation for remaining in his home. " 'You need not be afraid of my deserting you [to Fagin's gang],' " Mr. Brownlow tells Oliver, " 'unless you give me cause.' " As Miller says of this moment in the novel, "The price of Oliver's deliverance from the carceral (either as the workhouse or as Fagin's gang) would be his absolute submission to the norms, protocols, and regulations of the middle-class family" (*The Novel and the Police*, 59). It is the affinity that both Dickens and Faulkner have for exposing the workings of socially ordering, subtly coercive institutions like the family or the law that Miller's approach to the novel form facilitates.

44. Michael Rogin cites Seymour Stern's record of this portion of the movie. See his " 'The Sword Became a Flashing Vision' " (175).

45. The beliefs that Griffith's film demonstrates were not, regrettably, limited to their representation in popular culture but were in fact quite real in Faulkner's lifetime. L. O. Reddick cites the rise in national statistics for membership in the Ku Klux Klan in the period following *Birth of a Nation* ("Educational Programs for the Improvement of Race Relations," 372). More specifically, Michael Rogin cites examples of the lynching and mutilation of southern blacks for sexual crimes in the first decades of the twentieth century. He points to a bold-print newspaper headline from Alabama from 1934 declaring that a black man was to be "MUTILATED AND SET AFIRE" in "EXTRA-LEGAL VENGEANCE" (" 'The Sword Became a Flashing Vision,' " 175). Faulkner's own experience with lynching was itself painfully, vividly direct. In 1909 he witnessed a crowd's lynching and castrating of a black man, Nelse Patton, for the murder of a white woman in Oxford (Blotner 1984, 32). This experience, I expect, marked Faulkner in ways that manifest themselves in *Light in August*. Thus, the novel critiques actual events of violence that occurred in Faulkner's lifetime as well as cultural phenomena and stereotypical thinking about race that contributed to that violence.

46. Wittenberg's essay "Race in *Light in August*" points to the way in which verbal classificatory systems in the novel such as those practiced by McEachern with the catechism move metonymically to acts of violence in ways that reflect on the text's own

efforts to "pinion" Christmas's elusive identity (152–55). She also claims, as I do, that the novel's mystery and fluidity surrounding Joe's racial identity serves to intensify readers' efforts to fix it: "Despite the invisibility of his imputed blackness, Faulkner's Joe Christmas is also pinioned by this distorted racial frame. . . . But essentially as indeterminate as Christmas may be, both the operations of the Symbolic order into which he is inscribed at an early age and a series of textual strategies serve to define and 'frame' him" (152–53).

47. The term is Carolyn Porter's. See her *Seeing and Being*, 252.

48. Porter sees a kind of deathliness to this silence and the siren that is encompassed by it. Life, in her materialist reading of the novel, is represented by the transmission of concrete bodily effects like hearing (and figured in the text by sounds such as the town's church bells or insects shrilling in the night). The emphasis on vision and soundlessness in Christmas's final scene denies that sense of real, felt vitality. As she puts it: "To transcend the realm of hearing is to die" (*Seeing and Being*, 252).

49. See André Bleikasten, "*Light in August:* The Closed Society and Its Subjects."

CHAPTER THREE: "Some Trashy Myth of Reality's Escape"

1. The critical commentary on Faulkner and film is extensive, and though much of it is biographical, several critics take a more theoretical approach. Bruce Kawin's is the most comprehensive work on Faulkner's relationship both to Hollywood and to what he calls "the film idea," and his arguments about Faulkner, narrative structure, the visual construction of narrative, and montage in "The Montage Element in Faulkner's Fiction" (103–26) address similar concerns as those in the discussion that follows. John T. Matthews points to strategies in Faulkner's short fiction of "dissent" toward the film industry's approach to genres such as the war movie (see "Faulkner and the Culture Industry," 51–74), a claim I will be making about *Absalom, Absalom* and films of history. Miranda Burgess, in her reading of film and *Light in August* argues that in that novel Faulkner "self-consciously evokes the structuring of history by the tropes of romance (and especially by that specifically twentieth-century manifestation of romance, the 'narrative cinema')" ("Watching Jefferson Watching," 99). Alan Spiegal describes the influence of Hollywood on *Sanctuary*, suggesting that, in addition to simulating the gangster genre, the novel emulates or reproduces film's "photographic space" in its own spatial descriptions: "The entire narrative surface of the novel seems to have been composed not just with any camera eye but with a specifically American camera eye" (*Fiction and the Camera Eye*, 156). All of these approaches take a more fruitful approach to Faulkner's cinematic imagination and its implications for understanding his fiction than earlier, more literal readings of Faulkner's relation to film. Joseph Urgo, for example, argues in "*Absalom, Absalom!* The Movie" for a resemblance to Hollywood story meetings in the novel's "collaborative" acts of storytelling. In "Faulkner and the Silent Film," Jeffrey Folks suggests that Faulkner's depiction of silent, "histrionic" gestures on the part of his characters as well as his use of generic elements was a response to his experience watching silent film. See as well the recent issue of the *Faulkner Journal* devoted to this issue, "Faulkner and Film," edited by Edwin T. Arnold (Fall 2000/Spring 2001).

2. The reference in *If I Forget Thee, Jerusalem* appears in the context of a passage describing Charlotte and Wilbourne's trip from Utah on a bus. Wilbourne sees Char-

lotte asleep next to him, "her head tilted back against the machine-made doily, her face in profile against the dark fleeing snow-free countryside and the little lost towns, the neon, the lunch rooms with broad strong Western girls got up out of Hollywood magazines (Hollywood which is no longer in Hollywood but is stippled by a billion feet of colored gas across the face of the American earth) to resemble Joan Crawford" (636). Referring to the mass-produced, cheaply sold doilies on the headrests, Faulkner associates this product with Hollywood's product—in the figure of Joan Crawford, as well as in the Hollywood magazines. Hollywood's cultural imperialism, as well, is implicit in the passage. The other reference, in *Pylon*, is even more damning: "[L]ooking out through the falling snow she saw a kind of cenotaph, penurious and without majesty or dignity, of forlorn and victorious desolation—a bungalow, a tight flimsy mass of stoops and porte-cochères and flat gables and bays not five years old and built in that colored mud-and-chickenwire tradition which California moving picture films have scattered across North America as if the celluloid carried germs" (984).

3. Pointing to the popularity of war films in the 1930s, Matthews observes that one of Faulkner's own war-time stories, "Turnabout," includes references to the movies that imply Faulkner's awareness of the story's "filmability." In response to these references, Matthews suggests that "[Faulkner's] war story was already thinking self-critically about itself as a movie" (65)—a gesture I believe *Absalom* also makes, in an even more sustained and programmatic way ("Faulkner and the Culture Industry").

4. Faulkner's brother Murry indicates that Faulkner saw silent films regularly when growing up in Oxford. According to Murry, he and William went to the movies as often as they could, and typically the fare they took in were popular genre pictures like Westerns (*The Falkners of Mississippi*, 49–50).

5. In this discussion I have used Edward D. C. Campbell's cultural history, *The Celluloid South*. Campbell offers a comprehensive survey of the popular cultural forms and materials that led to the reception, in the first decades of the twentieth century, of film as a medium that extended the national susceptibility to the Old South myth. See especially the chapter "The Growth of Mythology," 10–15. It is also worth recalling in this context the other depictions of loyal or childish (and hence reassuring) slaves from early film history discussed in chapter 2.

6. Griffith's film would have been extremely difficult for anyone from the South to avoid, especially someone like Faulkner with an interest in representations of its history. Its release in 1915 was widely heralded—and reviled—and it was the highest grossing, most well-attended movie of its time and for the next quarter-century. It was also re-released in 1930, at a point much closer to the period in which Faulkner wrote his major novels, including *Absalom, Absalom!* Early in his life, Faulkner saw the theatrical version of a combination of *The Clansman* with Dixon's other pro-South, secessionist work, *The Leopard's Spots* (Blotner 1974, 1:115). Complete with a troop of horses on stage and ads featuring hooded horsemen, the production familiarized Faulkner with both the rhetoric and the imagery that informed Griffith's adaptation.

7. Griffith quoted in Michael Rogin, " 'The Sword Became a Flashing Vision': D. W. Griffith's *The Birth of a Nation,*" 150.

8. One of Griffith's most ardent admirers and an equally influential early filmmaker, the Russian formalist Sergei Eisenstein, was intensely committed to the political as well as aesthetic efficacy of location shooting. Filming his historical epic *The Battleship Potemkin* in Odessa in 1925, Eisenstein reportedly planned one of the most celebrated

sequences in film history—the massacre on the Odessa steps—after being struck by the atmosphere of the scene. In doing so, Eisenstein claimed, he was swept up with the same "spontaneous" fervor that motivated the actual revolutionaries of his story. See James Goodwin, *Eisenstein, Cinema, and History*, 59–60.

9. One of the reasons for the film's impact on audiences had to do with Griffith's scrupulous and detailed reproduction of key battle scenes, elaborate stagings that included actual Civil War–era uniforms, weaponry, and troop formations. Describing his approach to film realism and comparing it to that of theatre, Griffith wrote, "On the stage these so-called 'effects' are imitations at best. In the film play we show the actual occurrence and are not hampered by the size of our stage or the number of people we can crowd into the scene. If our story traverses to the battlefield we show an actual battlefield. If it means that 10,000 people were part of the conflict we engage 10,000 people, rehearse them in minute detail, and when we are ready we show you that scene as realistically as if you were looking down from a hilltop and watching an engagement of contending forces" ("The Future of the Two-Dollar Movie," 100). Of course, this thinking explains and anticipates the financial ruin—and critical scorn—Griffith incurred when he went on to film his historical epic *Intolerance* (1918) with thousands of extras and at a record cost for movies at that time. Nonetheless, it helps explain the remarkable avidity with which early viewers of his films, particularly *Birth of a Nation*, accepted his screen images as "real." Robert A. Armour has written of Griffith, "He knew that his medium had the potential for documentary effects even though he had never heard the word *documentary* applied to film" ("History Written in Jagged Lightning," 15). Thus the film's "alternative" to history appears ironic, predicated as it was on a formal realism that served to undermine its story's historical accuracy and truth.

10. Janet Staiger, "*The Birth of a Nation*: Considering Its Reception," 196.

11. The number of lynchings annually peaked in the 1890s at approximately 154; their occurrence declined in the early decades of the century, but only as a result of the disenfranchisement of blacks and the institutionalizing of racism in the South.

12. In his discussion of the reaction to *Birth of a Nation*, Michael Rogin describes the perspective of white northerners: "The rapid transformations of the North after the Civil War generated compensatory celebrations of the antebellum South. At the same time, the massive influx of immigrants from Southern and eastern Europe . . . created Northern sympathy for Southern efforts to control an indispensable but [supposedly] racially inferior labor force . . . When the Southern race problem became national, the national problem was displaced back onto the South in a way that made the South not a defeated part of the American past but a prophecy of its future" (" 'The Sword Became a Flashing Vision,' " 153–54).

13. United States Immigration Commission Report to the 61st Congress, 3rd Session, *Senate Document, No. 747*; quoted in Oscar Handlin, *Immigration as a Factor in American History*, 53–56.

14. In the first decades of the century, the concentrated ownership of property and means of production had become a source of popular concern and a defining political issue. As Lary May describes this element of responses to the film, "*The Birth of a Nation* touched a sensitive political nerve. In its message, the film called for an alliance of the common folk from the formerly warring sections to overthrow a tyranny based on Northern commercial corruption. This was indeed a relevant theme for the Democratic constituency in 1914" ("Apocalyptic Cinema," 45).

15. In his landmark study of German cinema, Siegfried Kracauer made nearly the same observation about the impact of historical films on the German national consciousness. Silent post–World War I films such as *Passion* (1919) and *Danton* (1921) cast the history of Germany's enemies, specifically France, in a negative light, altering events from the French Revolution in order to galvanize German audiences and distract them from their own more troubled past. "Designed for mass consumption," Kracauer writes of these movies, they "represent[ed] not so much historic periods as personal appetites and [they] . . . seiz[ed] upon history for the sole purpose of removing it thoroughly from the field of vision" (*From Caligari to Hitler,* 53; 52).

16. Peter Noble discusses these aspects of the film and the varied reactions to it in *The Negro in Films,* 51–54.

17. There was other strenuous and vocal resistance to the early filmic depiction of blacks. Significantly, those objections came most often from black viewers who, like Robeson, understood all too well the inconsistencies between Hollywood film and real historical experience. Voicing those objections as well as the concern over the racial violence they feared a movie like *Birth* would incite, the newly formed NAACP in 1915 initiated a national movement to oppose exhibition of the film (see Staiger, "*The Birth of a Nation:* Considering Its Reception," 196–205). In the 1920s a vibrant culture of black cinema supported the careers of artists like Robeson and Oscar Micheaux. Micheaux's work, in particular his 1919 "answer" to *Birth of a Nation, Within Our Gates,* showed a resistance to the general celebration of films like Griffith's. Although it flourished in the black communities, especially in northern cities, the African-American movement was a decidedly alternative cinema; its impact could not have hoped to offer a block to white audiences' consumption of racial stereotypes and historical revision. See Jane Gaines, "Fire and Desire: Race, Melodrama, and Oscar Micheaux."

18. This was a conception that Faulkner specifically rejected in his novel's depiction of slave owning. Sutpen's violent subjugation of his slaves—evident in their manacled arrival in Jefferson (6) and his bloody contests with them in the ring (23)—as well as his "captive" architect offer a more authentic image of the rigorously coercive practices of slave ownership than the pacific vision of slavery offered by film.

19. Douglas Baldwin raises a provocative question about the connection between Faulkner's skepticism about film and his verbal experiment. He points to Faulkner's understanding of film's realist dimensions as capable of corrupting the popular imagination: "Faulkner's fiction repeatedly refers to Hollywood as a corrupt center of commercial film production whose cultural influence was spreading dangerously across the imagination of the continent. . . . The unspoken subtext to this imagery is Faulkner's own awareness of the increased cultural authority Hollywood's products were gaining as . . . 'accurate representations of life'; this occurred just as Faulkner (and other American modernists) were struggling with the very aesthetic and philosophical concept of verbal representation itself" ("Putting Images into Words," 37).

20. The effect on a reader that I am describing stands as an example of the kind of reaction Roland Barthes declares that he has to all writing: "I have a disease: I *see* language. . . . Hearing deviates to scopia: I feel myself to be the visionary and voyeur of language" (*Roland Barthes,* 161).

21. Fredric Jameson's assessment of what Barthes calls the "scriptible" resembles my approach to Rosa. Challenging language's cognitive function, Jameson refers to exam-

ples of writing that insist on language's sensory aspect. "[W]hat is scriptible indeed is the visual or the musical, what corresponds to the two outside senses that tug at language between themselves and dispute its peculiarly unphysical attention, its short circuit of the senses for the mind itself that makes of the mysterious thing reading some superstitious and adult power, which the lowlier arts imagine uncomprehendingly, as animals might dream of the strangeness of human thinking. . . . [T]his is why the more advanced and rationalized activity can also have its dream of the other, and regress to a longing for the more immediately sensory, wishing it could pass altogether over into the visual, or be sublimated into the spiritual body of pure sound" (*Signatures of the Visible*, 2). Like much of *Absalom* in its capacity to enrapture and its linguistic excess, the prose in Rosa's section clearly suggests its "dream of the other," its rejection of the specifically rational function of language for something irrational and sensory and the wish, potentially, to "pass altogether over into the visual."

22. In his description of "hieroglyphic" writing, Adorno offers a provocative account of film viewing that helps explain what I call the "filmic" effect of reading Rosa's voice. "While the images of film and television strive to conjure up those that are buried in the viewer and indeed resemble them, they also, in their manner of flashing up and gliding past, approach the effect of writing: they are grasped but not contemplated. The eye is pulled along by the shot as it is by the printed line and in the gentle jolt of the cut a page is turned" (Adorno, "Prolog zum Fernsehen," quoted and translated in Miriam Hansen, "Mass Culture as Hieroglyphic Writing: Adorno, Derrida, Kracauer," 86). I offer a similar reading of Faulkner's writing with Rosa—though I do so in reverse of Adorno's effort here.

23. A range of film theoretical approaches is useful here. Stephen Heath points up the unique force of the film image, referring to the "moment of sheer jubilation *in* the image (the spectator 'fluid, elastic, expanding')" (*Questions of Cinema*, 87). Kracauer claims that the "psychophysical correspondences" of random material details experienced when watching film place the viewer in a kind of reverie. Of this mesmerizing aspect of film he writes, "It is as if [film images] urged [the viewer] through their sheer presence unthinkingly to assimilate their indeterminate and often amorphous patterns" (*Theory of Film*, 158).

24. Faulkner's awareness of this manner of presenting southern history in popular narrative, both fiction and film, was evident in his statement in an early letter describing his interests in *Absalom:* "I use [Quentin's] bitterness which he has projected on the South in the form of hatred of it and its people to get more out of the story itself than a historical novel would be. To keep the hoop skirts and plug hats out, you might say" (*SL* 79).

25. Using Freud's formulations of loss and recovery from *Mourning and Melancholia*, Moreland suggests that Freud's assessment was "eventually taken much further by Faulkner" (*Faulkner and Modernism*, 28).

26. In describing Rosa's incapacity to move beyond her longing for a "pre-Sutpen" period, Moreland writes, "Thus Rosa in her 'eternal black' seems . . . one more example of a widespread, melancholic nostalgia for an idealized, prewar South" (29).

27. "Introduction" to *The Photographic History of the Civil War*, 16; quoted in Trachtenberg, *Reading American Photographs*, 79.

28. Describing this perspective, Handlin observes, "The war had been a great pag-

eant, in which the feats of the worthy ancestors of the people who looked back on it had never been marred by dishonor or betrayal, and which had led to the glorious end of the Union strengthened" ("The Civil War as Symbol and as Actuality," 136).

29. Trachtenberg's comments appear in the context of his account of the resurgence of interest in Matthew Brady in the thirties, a popularity, he suggests, that was based in a large-scale forgetfulness about the real causes (and effects) of the war (*Reading American Photographs*, 231). That romantic depictions of the Civil War continued to exert a powerful hold on the public imagination through the thirties was evident in the phenomenal success of both Margaret Mitchell's own novel of the South, *Gone With the Wind*, and David O. Selznik's film version of it.

30. Kawin implies a connection between the opening of *Absalom* and silent film through the language Faulkner uses to describe Quentin's (and the reader's) first encounter with Sutpen. He refers to the montage-like effects of Faulkner's use of oxymoron, the "collision" of language that characterizes phrases describing Sutpen and his slaves, such as "quiet thunderclap," "wild and reposed," and "peaceful conquest." As Kawin puts it, "one of the first and most arresting things that happens in *Absalom* is that the tensions of language embattled against itself (in dialectics, in oxymoron . . .) result in the *vanishing* of language and the appearance of the figure of Sutpen as an image in Quentin's mind's eye, an inner theatre which is, significantly, as silent as the films of his period" ("The Montage Element of Faulkner's Fiction," 123).

31. Though not for the magazines, and not merely for a new gown or a new chair, but more likely to meet the mortgage on Rowan Oak, his estate, Faulkner himself sought to capitalize on the market for southern narrative in the thirties. He did so, as well, with an eye on a specifically visual medium, proposing to his agent that he sell the screen rights to *Absalom* (letter to Morton Goldman, September 1936, [*SL* 96]). In this way Faulkner seems to have become the writer Quentin did not.

32. Unlike Rosa, as well as Shreve, Quentin earlier in the book offers an alternative to the romanticizing of southern narrative. This occurs in his endeavor to explain—and to understand—the basis for Sutpen's design in the complicated connection between racial, social, and economic hierarchies in the South when he narrates the story of Sutpen's "fall" into class consciousness, his rejection by Pettibone's servant at the door, and the decisive event of Sutpen's life: "He went to the West Indies" (184–97). Although ultimately his voice is suppressed by Shreve's, in this prior section Quentin offers the novel's clearest resistance to the other narrators' denials of history.

33. Collen E. Donnelly, "Compelled to Believe: Historiography and Truth in *Absalom, Absalom!*, 118; Robert Dale Parker, *Faulkner and the Novelistic Imagination*, 129, 139. This reference to the cinematic nature of this section of chapter 8 is Noel Polk's, and he bases it on his work with Faulkner's manuscripts for *Absalom*. In editing the manuscripts for the Random House "Corrected Text" edition of the novel, the version used by the Library of America, Polk notes that this section of the novel resembles Faulkner's film scripts from the same period: "As in his movie scripts, Faulkner formats this section of the novel by maintaining all of his margins flush left. Faulkner uses this format to suggest that this section is more visual than verbal, that Quentin and Shreve have finally surrendered their individual voices to a cinematic and virtually silent narration" (phone interview, 10 June 2001).

34. Jean Pierre Oudart, "Cinema and Suture," 35–47. Since its appearance, there has been considerable debate surrounding the notion of suture. Recent studies, such as

Richard Allen's *Projecting Illusion,* provide a background and contextualizing for the suture "argument" (see 34–39). Daniel Dayan, for example, points to the shot-reverse shot sequence as only one of several determinations of film narrative ("The Tutor-Code of Classical Cinema," 31), a point on which Heath elaborates (*Questions of Cinema,* 92–93). I have placed the three theorists together here, despite their differences in approach, in order to provide an account of suture as a model that is comprehensive as well as apt to the narrative movement of Faulkner's text.

35. Dayan describes the central and constitutive role played in film by exchanges of characters' glances, a directionality of the gaze that viewers in turn take up in fashioning narrative. The shot in film is "an image designed and organized not merely as an object that is seen, but as the glance of a subject" ("The Tutor-Code of Classical Cinema," 28).

36. In a far more immediate proximity, but no less emphatic in its stress on the activity of looking, the scene between Sutpen and Henry in the tent hinges on the lingering stare shared between a father and his estranged son. Leading up to what might be one of the emotional climaxes of the book, when Sutpen lays eyes on Henry for the first time in four years and "*holds [Henry's] face between his hands, looking at it*" (291), this scene first shows Henry enter the tent, focalizing through his perspective when he salutes the man he does not yet realize is his father. Registering Henry's vague perception in the tent at night of "*a gray sleeve with colonel's braid on it, one bearded cheek, a jutting nose, a shaggy droop of iron-riddled hair*" (290), Faulkner's narration stresses the visual details Henry apprehends and that lend irony to this moment, if not also perhaps the only poignant image of Sutpen in the book. This insistence on characters' meaningful acts of seeing, in fact, pervades the entire italicized section of this chapter, and it includes readers' as well as characters' encounter with visualized scenarios in moments like this, or others that stress the *process* of vision—as when Henry and Bon sit, after Henry returns from meeting Sutpen, contemplating the coming of day in their campsite "*in the making light of dawn*" (293).

37. The popularity and ongoing influence of melodrama in early film history, and thus in the period of the novel's present-tense events, is a commonplace in theoretical and historical commentary. For a discussion of the centrality of melodrama to film in the period of the novel's events, see Guy Barefoot, "*East Lynne* to *Gas Light:* Hollywood, Melodrama, and Twentieth-century Notions of the Victorian," 95–96. For an articulation of the establishing role melodrama played in film theory, as well as in the genre's isolation from considerations of history, see Laura Mulvey, "It Will Be a Magnificent Obsession': The Melodrama's Role in the Development of Contemporary Film Theory," 121–22. The particular appeal to an emotional and romantic response that Shreve makes echoes strongly the stark visuals and equally striking moral oppositions favored by melodrama and early film, and by Griffith throughout his career (see May, "Apocalyptic Cinema," 29, 38). For an insightful discussion of contrastive lighting effects in theatrical and film melodrama and their connection to the genre's reliance on affect, see Martin Meisel, "Scattered Chiaroscuro: Melodrama as a Way of Seeing," 66–67.

CHAPTER FOUR: Screening Readerly Pleasures

1. My approach is a departure from what are themselves conventional readings of the novel's use of genre. "Wild Palms" has often been read as more "challenging" and

tragic, and therefore more modernist—or at least less commercial—than the more "popular," comic story in "Old Man." My own reading depends on specific uses of language within each section—specifically, abstract vs. realist practices—that reverse this alignment, as well as the striking but also different affinities within each section with film.

2. The novel is saturated with such references, and I treat several of them more extensively in the discussion that follows. At the outset, however, it is worth glancing at a few of the names, both real and fictional, of the novel's representatives of the culture industry. The convict's imprisonment follows his reading of "the Diamond Dicks and Jesse Jameses and such" (509), who wrote popular westerns and crime fiction. In the same passage from "Wild Palms" that describes "the lunch rooms with broad strong Western girls got up out of Hollywood magazines," Charlotte will be described as "resembling Joan Crawford" (636), a star of several 1930s vehicles. Early in his journey on the river, the convict registers his fascination with an icon of the silent cinema, Greta Garbo (596). And late in the novel, as Charlotte lies dying, Wilbourne, seeking solace and a way of understanding his experience, seizes on the author of a 1902 novel, *The Virginian*, which by 1939 (the year Faulkner published *Jerusalem*) had already prompted three film versions: "He was trying to remember something out of a book, years ago, of Owen Wister's, the whore in the pink ball dress who drank the laudanum and the cowboys kept taking turns walking her up and down the floor" (689).

3. Although the River itself does not appear in the novel's other section, "Wild Palms," its function as a metaphor for the couple's escape and their continuous movement, or for the images of liquidity and flow that characterize Charlotte, renders it an ongoing suggested presence in their narrative. Wilbourne's associations of Charlotte with water and with an overwhelming fluidity are apparent from their first meeting in New Orleans, as well as in subsequent descriptions that transport the River from "Old Man" to the "Wild Palms" narrative. Talking to her at the French Quarter party in the second section of "Wild Palms," a scene that locates their meeting on the River, "he seemed to be drowning, volition and will, in [her] yellow stare" (520). Later, in Chicago, her "unblinking yellow stare" produced "an envelopment almost like a liquid" (554). Charlotte's "yellow" gaze and its effect is repeatedly described—like the River—as overwhelming; the color of the River in "Old Man," in a manner that extends this homology, is also frequently described as yellow (592, 600, 602, 611).

4. Charles Hannon sees the influence of Twain, particularly, in Faulkner's treatment of the river, reading Faulkner's descriptions of it as an example of a modernist questioning of nineteenth-century realism. My own analysis suggests that Faulkner is engaged in both a modernist undermining of realism and what Hannon calls, using Fredric Jameson's language, a postmodern "infus[ing]" of his novel "with the forms, categories, and content of [the] culture industry" (Jameson, *Postmodernism*, 2; cited in Hannon, 143). My difference from Hannon is in my account of realism as one of the central strategies of "Wild Palms" (as opposed to "Old Man"), as well as at the book's use of popular cultural models in an effort to critique them. Modernist and opaque linguistic strategies appear in "Old Man," that is, as part of Faulkner's effort to frustrate or disrupt the realist approach of "Wild Palms."

5. As Michael Grimwood says of it, "the flood's meaning transcends its physical existence" (*Heart in Conflict*, 121). At first glance, Grimwood's remark looks similar to earlier "first-wave" readings of the novel that seek in it transcendent, universalizing

meanings—such as the River as an emblem for an omnipotent fate or for the continuous flow of time. Grimwood's interest, however, lies elsewhere. Rather than argue for the River's transcendent meaning, he situates the novel in relation to particular 1930s economic developments, such as reactions to the Depression, and to popular cultural practices and materials such as disaster stories and films (118–23). As Grimwood puts it, "[Faulkner] chose in late 1937 to write about a flood because it was then a topical, and proven, subject . . . He chose it, however, not because he assumed it might lead to popular success but because it *had led* to a kind of success. . . . In effect, Faulkner chose a flood as his subject so that he could invert a theme that seemed marketable. He chose to frustrate his audience's expectations, and his adversarial relationship with his readers is part of his subject" (122–23). Though less combatively, I see Faulkner likewise seeking to undermine his readers' expectations in their act of reading about the flood.

6. We have seen the way Faulkner's treatment of Popeye in *Sanctuary* works similarly to thwart readerly identification. My point here is that on at least one level "Wild Palms" works like popular fiction to involve readers with its characters; working against these conventions, "Old Man" limits that capacity for involvement.

7. One reason for this, which Faulkner could have anticipated, might be the ways in which the parody of adventure and heroism in "Old Man" could be misinterpreted—and misappropriated. In a development that proved highly ironic (at least in light of this discussion), the Hallmark corporation in 1997 sponsored a made-for-television movie of the "Old Man" section of the novel. Playing up the story's sentimental potential—and dramatically altering its ending, turning the convict into a romantic hero who at the end of the story goes free and falls in love—the film reveals the way the culture industry can find sentimental material where it wants to and when doing so serves commercial ends. The Hallmark production of "Old Man" is attributable to the tenacity of the culture industry to seize on seemingly melodramatic material without giving attention to the way the material is originally presented (ironically, as parody, etc.), as well as to appropriate the name of a canonical author.

8. Classical theoretical accounts of film viewers' subject-formation, although they anticipate my discussion of the River as a figure for the screen, are helpful here. Laura Mulvey's seminal essay "Visual Pleasure and Narrative Cinema" follows terms for the specular formation of identity that Lacan elaborates in his mirror stage. The subject's recognition of itself in a mirror, which Mulvey elides with the viewer's contemplation of the figure on a screen, provides another model for what I see the convict experience when he "discovers" himself by looking at the River. For as we shall see shortly, when on the River he treats himself and the characters with whom he interacts there as projected or idealized versions of characters he has seen in film. Richard Allen, in *Projecting Illusion,* provides an extensive contextualizing of Mulvey's model of film viewing. Throughout his considerations, he returns to formulations that repeat the aligning of subject, mirror, and screen: "Although this spectator does not perceive her reflection in the screen-mirror (she has already passed through the mirror stage), her gaze is endowed with an omnipotence that is like the gaze of the child before the mirror" (141). It is the convict's "childlike" discovery of himself when gazing at the River that Faulkner's narrator stresses and that later will prompt for him an experience of cinematic, Lacanian mis-recognition.

9. In this respect he resembles Popeye in *Sanctuary,* another character whom Faulkner self-consciously indicates is a construction. Though we ultimately learn more

of the convict's thinking and inner life, like Popeye he owes his existence or identity to popular cultural materials. Like Popeye as well, he never acquires a "full" three-dimensional presence as do other characters in the novel.

10. Recall Murry Falkner's account of his and his brother Bill's fascination with the movies when they first appeared in Oxford in the earliest days of the medium (*The Falkners of Mississippi*, 49–52).

11. The watery, boundaryless world of the flood, in other words, resembles the fluid state of the unconscious, an area of mental life that has often been compared to the manner of articulation in movies. Film's dream-like feel and its approximations of the unconscious have been noted by its earliest observers, and they have as well informed the aesthetics of whole schools of film practice, such as that of the surrealists. Jean-Louis Baudry begins his classic meditation on film perspective, "Ideological Effects of the Basic Cinematographic Apparatus," with a reference to Freud's use of an optical model for the unconscious (25), and the Freudian and post-Freudian understanding of film's resemblance to dreaming and the unconscious appears throughout film theory. See Christian Metz, "Identification, Mirror" and "The Passion for Perceiving," and Siegfried Kracauer, *Theory of Film*. In addition to these examples from film practice and theory, there is Faulkner's reference to "the silver dream" of movies in the short story "Dry September," suggesting his own awareness of the affinity of cinema with the unconscious or dreaming.

12. Mitchell's novel was published the same year as Faulkner's *Absalom, Absalom!* (1936). Faulkner's biographies do not indicate that he had read it, though by the time he wrote *Jerusalem*, he certainly would have heard of *Gone With the Wind*'s own melodramatic excesses as well as the book's enormous sales. It was precisely the success of this type of treatment of the southern past that troubled Faulkner. Film images of a burning plantation had also appeared in the period prior to *Jerusalem*, figuring centrally in the Civil War sequences in *Birth of a Nation*.

13. Significantly, we are told that the convict does not fall under Hollywood's thrall, or even see a movie, until he is incarcerated (607)—a fact that hints at the sources for the convict's fantasies and that potently suggests the connections between a state of imprisonment and the condition of being captive to the Hollywood dream. This connection will return with even greater urgency in the close of the "Wild Palms" section, with Wilbourne in jail.

14. In addition to film melodramas, by the late 1930s this exposure would surely have included images from still photography and documentary film that detailed the plight of rural Americans in "disaster" areas like the Dust Bowl and Faulkner's South. Michael Grimwood suggests that the imagery of disaster in "Old Man" draws from Depression-era staples like the WPA-sponsored work of directors such as Pare Lorentz or photographers like Dorthea Lange (or in Grimwood's account, Faulkner's friend Lyle Saxon in his photographic and eyewitness account of the Great Flood of 1927, *Father Mississippi* [*Heart in Conflict*, 122]). As Grimwood also points out, documentary and melodramatic modes were not incompatible by the late thirties, despite their ostensible differences. Epitomized in films like Lorentz's Farm Securities Administration documentary *The River* and by John Ford's popular release *The Hurricane*, both from 1937, depictions of disasters like flooding evoked audiences' own economic as well as physical hardship during the Depression. Both kinds of depictions, however, presented viewers with experiences of disasters that, however much they might document or

symbolize their own real-life circumstances, motivated Faulkner's critical attention to documentary and melodramatic method. See Grimwood, 119.

15. Here we would do well to recall the filmic and melodramatic properties of Rosa Coldfield's section of *Absalom, Absalom!*, in particular her references to her own reaction to the Sutpen narrative as "*I, self-mesmered fool.*"

16. See Meriwether and Millgate, *Lion in the Garden: Interviews with William Faulkner, 1926–1962*, 132.

17. See Hannon's reading of the doctor's light as an analogue for the film projector: "Thus the terms of film and photo technology dominate the love story of Charlotte and Harry. . . . In the first 'frame' of *If I Forget Thee, Jerusalem* . . . the unnamed doctor descends the dark stairs of his beach cottage with a 'flashlight's beam lancing on before him'" ("Signification, Simulation, and Containment in *If I Forget Thee, Jerusalem*," 143).

18. In several ways "Wild Palms" resembles a subcategory of melodrama whose preoccupation with flight and movement has been effectively exploited by another Hollywood genre: the road movie. For a medium ontologically defined by its affinity for motion, the road movie has consistently demonstrated its lure. Classic pictures such as *It Happened One Night* and the Bob Hope-Bing Crosby road series, including *Road to Utopia;* revisionist or socially critical films such as *Bonnie and Clyde, Badlands, Easy Rider,* or even *Something Wild;* and more recent, highly derivative movies like *True Romance* and *Kalifornia*—all demonstrate the readiness of commercial as well as independent film to make use of the road genre and its tropes of travel and freedom. Travel and "the road" are, of course, longstanding conventions of literature, beginning well before film (and Faulkner) as early as Homer and including the picaresque tradition that Faulkner and other modern and nineteenth-century writers drew on. The difference between "Wild Palms" and these literary models is its resemblance to more contemporary popular cultural sources. Interestingly, the travels that the road movie conventionally depicts express concerns manifested by Wilbourne and Charlotte. Jack Nicholson in *Easy Rider,* for instance, explaining why Dennis Hopper and Peter Fonda are a threat to the southerners they encounter, talks about their characters' "freedom" in ways that could apply to Faulkner's lovers: "Talking about [freedom] and being it, that's different things. I mean it's hard to be free, when you're bought and sold in the marketplace" (quoted in the Introduction to *The Road Movie Book,* ed. Steven Cohan and Ina Rae Hark, 3). Despite their efforts at freeing themselves from bourgeois constraints, Wilbourne and Charlotte continue to find themselves tied to the commercial market. Steven Cohan provides suggestive terms for a consideration of Wilbourne and Charlotte's wandering, in particular their utopic treatment of travel and the American West. He asserts that the road movie functioned "to represent America as a utopic space in which the nation's citizens . . . feel 'at home' on the road by discovering, through their travels, the popular culture they all share" (*Road Movie Book,* 116). This seems to me as reasonable an explanation as any for the fact that, as they travel across the American West aboard a bus, Charlotte appears to Wilbourne to "resemble Joan Crawford, asleep or not he could not tell" (636). There, in Wilbourne's imagination, he finds the utopic fulfillment of his compulsive travel and longing.

19. The term is Richard Godden's. Describing Harry's watching, mistakenly I think, as a memory, Godden nevertheless provides extremely useful terms for understanding Harry's "consuming" of the images of Charlotte and her husband. "Harry ingests his

past, as another commodity for his own consumption, turning his narrative not into archives but into a hybridization of two popular forms—the movie and the pulp novel" (*Fictions of Labor,* 217). While Harry is certainly "consuming" these images, as he would a film sequence or a pulp romance, he is not "remembering" the scene with Charlotte and Rittenmeyer. Rather, he imagines or fantasizes their meeting (he was not there to witness it and thereby recollect it at a later time). Thus, what we see is Harry, the consumer, sitting on the bench fantasizing and producing the scene he would *like* to see. In doing so, Harry shows readers themselves in another of the novel's reflexive moments that I have earlier attributed to the mirror-like appearance of the River. Showing Harry watching the "movie" of Charlotte and her husband, providing this scene with its referent in popular romance, that is, Faulkner reveals to readers their own (accustomed) pleasure in generic, commercial forms

20. Melodrama's roots in the English morality play are helpful as a way to consider Faulkner's treatment of Rittenmeyer, at least as he is seen and represented through Wilbourne. Thomas Elsaesser, in his essay "Tales of Sound and Fury: Observations on the Family Melodrama," provides a comprehensive genealogy of the genre. Originating in the late medieval morality play and other oral and dramatic narratives, melodrama has as its most prominent formal element an emphasis on recognizable surfaces and character types: "The characteristic features . . . in this tradition are not so much the emotional shock-tactics and the blatant playing on the audience's known sympathies and antipathies, but rather the non-psychological conception of the *dramatis personae,* who figure less as autonomous individuals than to transmit the action and link the various locales" (69). Like the figure of Virtue in *Everyman,* or like the scorned husband in film, Rittenmeyer is brought on to the "stage" or "screen" of Wilbourne's imagination to demonstrate simple and undeniable decency. The role in which Rittenmeyer is "cast" has much in common with other standard plots and characters from melodrama, particularly the way he stands in for a set of assumptions about Victorian, bourgeois respectability.

21. This section of the novel also reveals, at its ending, another of Faulkner's unique spatial and perspectival constructions that resemble those of film and that are relevant to understanding Wilbourne. Leaving Audubon Park and traversing New Orleans in a taxi to the train station with Charlotte, Wilbourne is described as viewing his surroundings as they travel past him (as opposed to he himself moving). Leaving the park, "the scaling palm trunks began to flee past" (649). As the cab continues through the streets, we get another account of space seen from Wilbourne's perspective: "the scaling palm trunks fled constantly past" (649). Alan Spiegal, in *Fiction and the Camera Eye,* argues that spatial constructions which reveal a landscape that moves or shifts take on the impressions of filmed footage. This is so, he claims, because the only time that scenery or a landscape appears to us to move is when it is photographed and then projected in film. To Spiegal these descriptions are a hallmark of much modernist, "cinematic" fictional method; he refers to descriptions of this kind as "the refusal of the cinematographic novelist to recognize what he sees in terms of what he knows" (*Fiction and the Camera Eye,* 133). Spiegal might more properly refer to the *characters* in such novels who, like Wilbourne here, "refuse" to see reality in terms other than cinematic. The appearance of such so-called "cinematic" method in this passage suggests Wilbourne's romantic reluctance to "recognize" reality, produced, perhaps, by his viewing of melodrama.

22. From their inception until the efforts of filmmakers and civic leaders to "dignify" film production and exhibition, movies were predominantly an entertainment for urban, immigrant laborers. Lary May indicates that prior to the advent of the feature film and the "photoplay," audiences for the short subjects were almost exclusively working-class and foreign. "Laborers . . . comprised 70 percent of the 1912 audience [for movies]" ("Apocalyptic Cinema," 30). May also traces the cultivation of a new American middle-class audience for the movies. After 1912, "20 percent [of moviegoers] were now clerical workers and 5 percent were respectable bourgeois men and women. Without losing the original audience of immigrants, then . . . filmmakers . . . created a medium that cut across class, sex, and party lines" (30–31).

23. May refers to the way the "earlier one-reel 'shorts,' " unlike the feature film, were condemned by reformers of the cinema because they eschewed narrative and "merely titillated the senses" ("Apocalyptic Cinema," 29). This aspect of the short subject will return in my consideration of Wilbourne's version of film viewing at the novel's end.

24. Like Achilles' shield as it is forged by Hephaestus in Homer's *Iliad*, Charlotte's drawing is an example of ekphrasis; that is, it is a set piece within an oral or verbal narrative that describes a work of visual art. Like Achilles' shield too, it depicts motion in a static, pictorial image. Charlotte's drawing works in a manner similar to that of ekphrasis generally. Like other examples of classical ekphrasis, the drawing provides the occasion to address ideological or political content with which the narrative proper around it is ill at ease. Through its effect on the miners, Charlotte's drawing introduces a political meaning or effect that Faulkner's novel may not have intended. As a work that deals in both its sections with several aspects of production, labor, the marketplace, and wage earning, *If I Forget Thee, Jerusalem* may be considered a proletarian novel (or perhaps a parody of one). Yet its sympathies, as my analysis of this scene will reveal, are not with the side of labor. I am grateful to Jessica Levenstein for pointing out to me the ideological dimensions of classical ekphrasis.

25. Grimwood refers to this scene in his discussion of *Jerusalem*'s class divisions. He asserts that all of the novel's "laborers"—including the Cajun alligator-hunter, the Polish miners, the fisherman whom Harry sees from his prison window, and the Tall Convict and his fellow inmates—"belong to Faulkner's anonymous, 'enduring' class, whereas Harry belongs to the same self-pauperized 'leisure' class that Faulkner ordinarily perceived as his own" (*Heart in Conflict*, 102). Discussing the plight of the convict in "Old Man," Grimwood refers to the way he, like other Faulkner characters of the labor class, are conferred a measure of dignity through their capacity to suffer and endure but are not allowed, importantly, a willing resistance to the economic circumstances that require that suffering: "Faulkner assigned to his 'enduring' classes not revolutionary zeal but a long, patient submission in life" (104). Charlotte's drawing contributes to a "social discontinuity" that Grimwood claims Faulkner "liked," encouraging the miners' willingness to continue their submission to their exploitative treatment by the mining corporation and thus to maintaining their social and economic position.

26. Kawin, "The Montage Element of Faulkner's Fiction," 116.

27. Thomas L. McHaney, in *William Faulkner's The Wild Palms: A Study*, draws attention to Faulkner's revision (127–28).

28. Godden reads Faulkner's use of the prison-cell narration as similar to that of pulp novelists from the 1930s and early 40s such as James Cain and Horace McCoy, who

employed this strategy to represent "the cry of the little man raised against the market's invasion of every aspect of his life" (*Fictions of Labor*, 200). Godden's reading of the closed-room trope as a means to figure the encroachment on the individual by market forces (or his protest against them) differs from my reading of the novel's close. Unlike Godden, I see Wilbourne's imprisonment exemplifying the capitulation of "mass man" to the effects of mass culture on appetite and desire.

29. These include not only Wilbourne's act of "screening" the melodramatic scene he conjures in Audubon Park, but his proclivity for the pulp confessional stories he writes and, presumably, reads.

30. Charles Hannon refers to the cinematic terms Faulkner uses in suggesting Wilbourne's "filming" of Charlotte's death, such as the Kleig lights and the projector. Because Charlotte and Wilbourne pursue a postmodern strategy of simulation in their affair, "her . . . demise is only representable in terms reflective of simulation: [cinematic] projection and illusion" ("Signification, Stimulation, and Containment," 148).

31. As Adorno succinctly puts it, "The culture industry perpetually cheats its consumers of what it perpetually promises. The promissory which . . . it draws on pleasure is endlessly prolonged; the promise, which is actually all the spectacle consists of, is illusory: all it actually promises is that the real point will never be reached, that the diner must be satisfied with the menu" ("The Culture Industry," 139).

CONCLUSION: Modernism, Jail Cells, and the Senses

1. As Sundquist forcefully argues, efforts to read *The Sound and the Fury* in this manner must, of necessity, be retrospective. Sunquest's reasons for declaring this have to do with his study's major theme: the more fully historical treatment of southern racial conflict in Faulkner's later novels, specifically, the emergence into greater clarity and "consciousness" of the issue of miscegenation and its threat (see "The Myth of *The Sound and the Fury*," in *Faulkner: The House Divided*). John T. Matthews, in *The Play of Faulkner's Language*, offers an account of *The Sound and the Fury* (and Faulkner's comments about it) as the occasion for Faulkner's contending with issues of bereavement in and through language. See especially the chapter "How to Approach Language."

2. Railey's analysis shares its emphasis on sensory experience with a number of materialist and historical interpretations of Faulkner, along with a Marxist critique of rationalization and capitalist exchange. Carolyn Porter offered one of the earliest and most compelling of these, in which Sutpen's attempt at a visionary, ahistorical transcendence—his disconnection both to other people and to the "stream of event"— marks him as a particular kind of historical subject and as deeply, inhumanly flawed. Porter points to the experience of hearing, epitomized in shared acts of speaking and listening and as a means of connecting materially to history, as a counter to Sutpen's visionary isolation (*Seeing and Being*; see especially "The Reified Reader"). Richard Godden and Pamela Rhodes Knight, commensurately, see Harry Wilbourne's color-blindness as the mark of his thorough conditioning (or rather, de-conditioning) by the forces of modern economic and cultural experiences: "Harry's color blindness is a symptom of his debilitation as a consumer, accompanying the way he views the world as a two-dimensional spectacle ("Degraded Culture, Devalued Texts," 113, n. 35)." John T. Matthews repeatedly refers to Faulkner's efforts with his thirties fiction to lend his

novels a sense of "embodiedness" and physical presence, one that counters the overly rational systems of commodity fetishism, abstraction, and exchange (see "*As I Lay Dying* in the Machine Age" and "Faulkner and Proletarian Literature").

3. Bruce Kawin asserts, for instance, that the first section of *The Sound and the Fury* relies on a "series of views" ("The Montage Element of Faulkner's Fiction," 118). As my discussion of Benjy's integration of sense perception indicates, this observation is only partly true.

4. Arnold Weinstein commented early on this quality of Faulkner's rendering of Benjy: "What is at stake [in the first section] is the appeal and intelligibility of feeling" (*Vision and Response in Modern Fiction*, 114).

5. I would submit in passing that despite Lukács's repudiation of *Theory of the Novel*, this work and even his later embrace of what he saw as a critical, socialist realism can offer ways of understanding Benjy and his relation to Faulkner's modernism. In his well-known response to Lukács, the essay "Reconciliation Under Duress," Adorno offers terms that are suggestive for both my reading of Benjy as an example of "the great moment" and later developments in Faulkner's critical treatment of vision. "The notion of the 'immanent meaning of life' from *Theory of the Novel* recurs [in Lukács's later work], but it is reduced to the dictum that life in a society building up socialism is in fact full of meaning . . . Hegel's criticism of Kantian formalism . . . is reduced to the simplified assertion that in modern art the emphasis on style, form and technique is grossly exaggerated—even though Lukács must be perfectly well aware that these are the features that distinguish art as knowledge from science. . . . What looks like formalism to him, really means the structuring of the elements of a work in accordance with laws appropriate to them, and is relevant to that 'immanent meaning' for which Lukács yearns" (*Aesthetics and Politics*, 152–53). It is the structuring of the elements of a work "in accordance with laws appropriate to them" in Faulkner's thirties modernism, in particular its formal characteristics and use of vision, that exemplify an art that Adorno says "is the negative knowledge of the actual world" (160). This development follows from Faulkner's earlier treatment of a character like Benjy and his more forceful sensory life.

6. Describing a later manifestation, and in their view a more heavily determined example of the quality I am here discussing, Rhodes and Godden refer to the Tall Convict's experience aboard the skiff in "Old Man": "Once out on the water, the convict is exposed to a systematic derangement that cleanses and abrades his body and senses. The . . . purgation expresses Faulkner's realization that the coefficient of commodity fetishism . . . is a flattening of perception itself" ("Degraded Culture, Devalued Texts," 102).

7. Porter, *Seeing and Being*, 263–64. As she says, "[He] embodies at one and the same time the transcendent seer and the calculating observer" (264).

8. See Porter, "Faulkner's America," in *Seeing and Being*. Kevin Railey is also concerned, in *Natural Aristocracy*, with the question of economic formations in southern history, specifically the debate about the role of market forces vs. a Jeffersonian plantocracy. See "Faulkner's Mississippi: Ideology and Southern History."

9. In addition to his intensely rigorous reading of Conrad's visualized and what he calls aestheticized style in *The Nigger of the "Narcissus,"* Jameson's reasons for his assessment of Conrad follow from a passage in *Lord Jim*. In an effort to explain his position, he quotes Marlow's statement at the beginning of the book about narrating

his story: " 'All this happened in much less time than it takes to tell, since I am trying to interpret for you in slow speech the instantaneous effect of visual perception' " (30). It is worth repeating in this context the striking similarity of Marlow's statement to that of Faulkner's narrator in the opening scene of *Absalom, Absalom!*, which points to Faulkner's own, perhaps more powerfully cinematic strategy in that novel: "It (the talking, the telling) seemed (to him, to Quentin) to partake of that logic- and reason-flouting quality of a dream which the sleeper knows must have occurred, stillborn and complete, in a second, yet the very quality upon which it must depend to move the dreamer (verisimilitude) to credulity . . . depends as completely upon a formal recognition of and acceptance of elapsed and yet-elapsing time as music or a printed tale" (17–18).

10. Karl Zender sees a prevalence of prisons in Faulkner's later writing, notably the Snopes trilogy, and argues that the confined room represents a shift from the more capacious spaces of mansions and plantations he had used in his early career. Zender claims that the Sartoris household in *Flags in the Dust* provided Faulkner "protection from the intrusions—both literal and metaphoric—of the modern world" (*The Crossing of the Ways*, 142). With *Flags*, this protection was largely for Faulkner's characters. Later it is the act of writing *The Sound and the Fury* that furnishes what Zender terms "a seemingly timeless aesthetic space" from which Faulkner depicts the ravages of modernity. I suggest that the prison setting makes its appearance much earlier than Zender claims and that it may be closer in function to the spaces of mansions and may say more about the circumstances of Faulkner's aesthetic creativity than Zender allows.

11. It is worth noting, even at this late stage, the analogy my reading affords between the jail cell as a site of production for both popular culture *and* modernism. As we've seen with the ending of "Wild Palms," Parchman offers the space in which Wilbourne, already a writer of pulp pornography, withdraws to pursue a melancholy, repetitive consumption of the images of Charlotte that he has "made." If Quentin may also be said to occupy a prison-like space in his dorm room, but one in which he engages in a modernist version of narrative invention, then the figure of the jail cell may appear as a final unifying figure for my argument throughout this discussion: that Faulkner's work throughout the thirties shows an inevitable and forceful link between the two modes of modern cultural life, high and low.

Works Cited

Adorno, Theodor W. *Aesthetic Theory*. Translated by C. Lenhardt. Edited by Gretel Adorno and Rolf Tiedemann. London: Routledge and Kegan Paul, 1984.

———. "Cultural Criticism and Society." In *Prisms*, translated by Samuel and Shierry Weber. Cambridge: MIT Press, 1995.

———."The Culture Industry: Enlightenment as Mass Deception." In *Dialectic of Enlightenment*, translated by John Cumming. New York: Continuum, 1988 (1944).

Adorno, Theodor W., and Max Horkheimer. *Dialectic of Enlightenment*. Translated by John Cumming. New York: Continuum, 1988 (1944).

Allen, Richard. *Projecting Illusions: Film Spectatorship and the Impression of Reality.* Cambridge, Mass.: Cambridge University Press, 1995.

Althusser, Louis. "Ideology and Ideological State Apparatuses." In *Lenin and Philosophy and other Essays*, translated by Ben Brewster. New York: Monthly Review Press, 1971.

Arden, Eugene. "The Early Harlem Novel." In *Images of the Negro in American Literature*, ed. Seymour L. Gross and John Edward Hardy. Chicago: University of Chicago Press, 1966.

Armour, Robert A. "History Written in Jagged Lightning: Realistic South vs. Romantic South in *The Birth of a Nation*." *Southern Quarterly* 19, nos. 3–4 (1981): 14–21.

Arnold, Edwin, and Dawn Trouard. *Reading Faulkner:* Sanctuary. Jackson: University Press of Mississippi, 1996.

Baldwin, Douglas. "Putting Images into Words: Elements of the 'Cinematic' in William Faulkner's Prose." *Faulkner Journal* 16 (2000/2001): 35–64.

Banta, Martha. "The Razor, the Pistol, and the Ideology of Race Etiquette." In *Faulkner and Ideology: Faulkner and Yoknapatawpha, 1992*, ed. Donald Kartiganer and Ann J. Abadie. Jackson: University Press of Mississippi, 1995.

Barefoot, Guy. "*East Lynne* to *Gas Light*: Hollywood, Melodrama and Twentieth-century Notions of the Victorian." In *Melodrama: Stage, Picture, Screen*, ed. Jacky Bratton, Jim Cook, and Christine Gledhill. London: British Film Institute, 1994.

Barnard, Rita. *The Great Depression and the Culture of Abundance: Kenneth Fearing, Nathanael West and Mass Culture in the 1930s.* Cambridge: Cambridge University Press, 1995.

Barthes, Roland. *The Pleasure of the Text.* Translated by Richard Miller. New York: Hill and Wang, 1975 (1973).

———. *Roland Barthes by Roland Barthes.* Translated by Richard Howard. New York: Hill and Wang, 1977.

Baudry, Jean-Louis. "Ideological Effects of the Basic Cinematographic Apparatus." In *Apparatus: Cinematographic Apparatus: Selected Writings,* ed. Theresa Hak Kyung Cha. New York: Tanam Press, 1980.

Benjamin, Walter, "The Storyteller." In *Illuminations,* trans. Harry Zohn; ed. Hannah Arendt. New York: Schocken Books, 1968.

———. "The Work of Art in the Age of Mechanical Reproduction." In *Illuminations,* trans. Harry Zohn, ed. Hannah Arendt. New York: Schocken, 1968.

Bleikasten, André. "*Light in August:* The Closed Society and Its Subjects." In *New Essays on Light in August,* ed. Michael Millgate. Cambridge: Cambridge University Press, 1987.

Blotner, Joseph. *Faulkner: A Biography.* Two-volume edition. New York: Random House, 1974.

———. *Faulkner: A Biography.* One-volume edition. New York: Random House, 1984.

Bogle, Donald. *Toms, Coons, Mulattoes, Mammies, and Bucks: An Interpretive History of Blacks in American Film.* New York: Continuum, 1973.

Brooks, Peter. *Reading for the Plot: Design and Intention in Narrative.* Cambridge, Mass.: Harvard University Press, 1992.

Burgess, Miranda J. "Watching Jefferson Watching: *Light in August* and the Aestheticization of Gender." *Faulkner Journal* 7, nos. 1 and 2 (1991 and 1992): 95–114.

Burnett, W. R. *Little Caesar.* New York: Dial Press, 1929.

Bush, Laura L. "A Very American Power Struggle: The Color of Rape in *Light in August.*" *Mississippi Quarterly* 51, no. 3 (1998): 483–500.

Campbell, Edward D. C. *The Celluloid South: Hollywood and the Southern Myth.* Knoxville: University of Tennessee Press, 1981.

Champigny, Robert. *What Will Have Happened: A Philosophical and Technical Essay on Mystery Stories.* Bloomington: Indiana University Press, 1977.

Clarke, Donald Henderson. *Louis Beretti.* New York: Triangle Books, 1929.

Coe, Charles Francis. *Me, Gangster.* New York: Grosset & Dunlap, 1927.

Cohan, Steven, and Ina Rae Hark. *The Road Movie Book.* London: Routledge, 1997.

Cohen, Philip. "'A Cheap Idea . . . Deliberately Conceived to Make Money': The Biographical Context of William Faulkner's Introduction to *Sanctuary.*" *Faulkner Journal* 3, no. 2 (1988): 54–68.

Conrad, Joseph. *Lord Jim.* New York: W.W. Norton, 1968 (1900).

———. *The Nigger of the "Narcissus."* New York: W.W. Norton, 1979 (1898).

Dayan, Daniel. "The Tutor-Code of Classical Cinema." *Film Quarterly* 28, no. 1 (1974): 22–31.

Debord, Guy. *The Society of the Spectacle.* Translated by Donald Nicholson-Smith. New York: Zone Books, 1994.

DiBattista, Maria, and Lucy McDiarmid. *High and Low Moderns: Literature and Culture: 1889–1939.* New York: Oxford University Press, 1996.

Dickens, Charles. *Bleak House.* London: Penguin, 1971 (1852–53).

Donnelly, Collen E. "Compelled to Believe: Historiography and Truth in *Absalom, Absalom!*" *Style* 25, no. 1 (1991): 104–22.

Douglas, Ann. *Terrible Honesty: Mongrel Manhattan in the 1920s.* New York: Farrar, Straus, and Geroux, 1995.

Elsaesser, Thomas. "Tales of Sound and Fury: Observations on the Family Melodrama." In *Imitations of Life: A Reader on Film and Television Melodrama*, ed. Marcia Landey. Detroit, Mich.: Wayne State University Press, 1991.

Falkner, Murry. *The Falkners of Mississippi: A Memoir*. Baton Rouge: Louisiana State University Press, 1967.

Faulkner, William. *Absalom, Absalom! Novels 1936–1940*. New York: Library of America, 1990 (1936).

———. *Collected Stories*. New York: Random House, 1977 (1950).

———. *Faulkner in the University: Class Conferences at the University of Virginia, 1957–1958*. Edited by Joseph Blotner and Frederick L. Gwinn. New York: Random House, 1959.

———. *The Hamlet. Novels 1936–1940*. New York: Library of America, 1990 (1940).

———. *If I Forget Thee, Jerusalem. Novels 1936–1940*. New York: Library of America, 1990.

———. "Introduction" to *The Sound and the Fury*. New York: W.W. Norton & Co., 1994.

———. *Light in August. Novels 1930–1935*. New York: Library of America, 1985 (1932).

———. "Preface" to *Sanctuary. Novels 1930–1935*. New York: Library of America. [The Modern Library, 1932]

———. *Pylon. Novels 1930–1935*. New York: Library of America, 1985 (1935).

———. *Sanctuary. Novels 1930–1935*. New York: Library of America, 1985 (1931).

———. *Sanctuary: The Original Text*. Edited by Noel Polk. New York: Random House, 1981.

———. *Selected Letters of William Faulkner*. Edited by Joseph Blotner. New York: Random House, 1977.

———. *The Sound and the Fury*. New York: W.W. Norton, 1994 (1929).

Fiedler, Leslie A. "The Blackness of Darkness: The Negro and the Development of American Gothic." In *Images of the Negro in American Literature*, ed. Seymour L. Gross and John Edward Hardy. Chicago: University of Chicago Press, 1966.

Folks, Jeffrey. "William Faulkner and the Silent Film." *Southern Quarterly* 19, nos. 3–4 (1981): 171–82.

Foucault, Michel. *Discipline and Punish: The Birth of the Prison*. Translated by Alan Sheridan. New York: Random House, 1977.

Gaines, Jane. "Fire and Desire: Race, Melodrama, and Oscar Micheaux." In *Melodrama, Stage, Picture, Screen*, ed. Jacky Bratton, Jim Cook, and Christine Gledhill. London: British Film Institute, 1994.

Gammel, Irene. " 'Because He Is Watching Me': Spectatorship and Power in Faulkner's *Light in August*." *Faulkner Journal* 5, no. 1 (1989): 11–23.

Godden, Richard. *Fictions of Labor: William Faulkner and the South's Long Revolution*. Cambridge: Cambridge University Press, 1997.

Godden, Richard, and Pamela Rhodes. "Degraded Culture, Devalued Texts." In *Faulkner and Intertextuality*, ed. Michel Gresset and Noel Polk. Jackson: University Press of Mississippi, 1985.

Grant, Madison. *The Passing of the Great Race*. New York: Scribner, 1930.

Goodstone, Tony. *The Pulps: Fifty Years of American Popular Culture*. New York: Chelsen House, 1970.

Goodwin, James. *Eisenstein, Cinema, and History*. Urbana: University of Illinois Press, 1993.

Greenberg, Clement. "Avant-Garde and Kitsch." In *Art and Culture: Critical Essays.* Boston: Beacon Press, 1961.

Grella, George. "The Gangster Novel: The Urban Pastoral." In *Tough Guy Writers of the Thirties,* ed. David Madden. Carbondale: Southern Illinois University Press, 1968.

Gresset, Michel. *Fascination: Faulkner's Fiction, 1919–1936.* Translated by Thomas West. Durham: Duke University Press, 1989.

Griffith, D. W. "The Future of the Two-Dollar Movie." In *Focus on Birth of a Nation,* ed. Fred Silva. Englewood Cliffs, N. J.: Prentice-Hall, 1971.

Grimwood, Michael. *Heart in Conflict: Faulkner's Struggle with Vocation.* Athens: University of Georgia Press, 1987.

Gunning, Tom. "Tracing the Individual Body: Photography, Detectives, and Early Cinema." In *Cinema and the Invention of Modern Life,* ed. Leo Charney and Vanessa R. Schwartz. Berkeley: University of California Press, 1995.

Hammett, Dashiell. *Red Harvest.* New York: Vintage Books, 1972. [1929]

Handlin, Oscar. *The American People in the Twentieth Century.* Cambridge, Mass.: Harvard University Press, 1954.

———. *Immigration as a Factor in American History.* Englewood Cliffs, N.J.: Prentice Hall, 1959.

———. "The Civil War as Symbol and Actuality." *Massachusetts Review* 3, no. 1 (1961): 133–43.

Hannon, Charles. "Signification, Stimulation, and Containment in *If I Forget Thee, Jerusalem.*" *Faulkner Journal* 7, nos. 1 and 2 (1991): 133–50.

Hansen, Miriam Bratu. "Mass Culture as Hieroglyphic Writing: Adorno, Derrida, Kracauer." In *The Actuality of Adorno: Critical Essays on Adorno and the Postmodern,* ed. Max Pensky. Albany: State University of New York Press, 1997.

Hayward, Susan. *Key Concepts in Cinema Studies.* London: Routledge, 1996.

Heath, Stephen. *Questions of Cinema.* Bloomington: Indiana University Press, 1981.

Hill, John, and Pamela Church Gibson. *The Oxford Guide to Film Studies.* Oxford: Oxford University Press, 1998.

Howe, Irving. *Decline of the New.* London: Victor Gollancz, 1971 (1963).

Huyssen, Andreas. *The Great Divide: Modernism, Mass Culture, Postmodernism.* Bloomington: Indiana University Press, 1986.

———. "High/Low in an Expanded Field." *Modernism/Modernity* 9, no. 3 (2002): 363–74.

Jameson, Fredric. *Signatures of the Visible.* New York: Routledge, 1992.

———. *The Political Unconscious: Narrative as a Socially Symbolic Act.* Ithaca, N.Y.: Cornell University Press, 1981.

———. *Postmodernism, or The Cultural Logic of Late Capitalism.* Durham, N.C.: Duke University Press, 1991.

———. "Reification and Utopia in Mass Culture." In *Signatures of the Visible.* New York: Routledge, 1992.

———. "On Magical Realism in Film." In *Signatures of the Visible.* New York: Routledge, 1992.

Jay, Martin. *Downcast Eyes: The Denigration of Vision in Twentieth-Century French Thought.* Berkeley: University of California Press, 1993.

Johnson, Susie Paul. *Annotations to William Faulkner's Pylon.* New York: Garland Publishing, 1989.

Kawin, Bruce. "Faulkner's Film Career." In *Faulkner, Modernism, and Film: Faulkner and Yoknapatawpha 1978*, ed. Evans Harrington and Ann J. Abadie. Jackson: University Press of Mississippi, 1979.

———. "The Montage Element in Faulkner's Fiction." In *Faulkner, Modernism, and Film: Faulkner and Yoknapatawpha 1978*, ed. Evans Harrington and Ann J. Abadie. Jackson: University Press of Mississippi, 1979.

———. *Faulkner and Film*. New York: F. Ungar, 1977.

Kazin, Alfred. "The Stillness of *Light in August.*" *Partisan Review* 24 (fall, 1957).

King, Vincent Allan. "The Wages of Pulp: The Use and Abuse of Fiction in William Faulkner's *The Wild Palms* [*If I Forget Thee, Jerusalem*]." *Mississippi Quarterly* 51 (1998): 503–25.

Kirby, Jack Temple. *Media-Made Dixie: The South in the American Imagination*. Baton Rouge: Louisiana State University Press, 1978.

Kracauer, Siegfried. *From Caligari to Hitler: A Psychological History of the German Film*. Princeton, N.J.: Princeton University Press, 1947.

———. "Photography." In *The Mass Ornament: Weimar Essays*, trans. and ed. Thomas Y. Levin. Cambridge: Harvard University Press, 1995 [1963].

———. *Theory of Film: The Redemption of Physical Reality*. Princeton, N.J.: Princeton University Press, 1990.

Kreiswirth, Martin. "Plots and Counterplots: The Structure of *Light in August.*" In *New Essays on Light in August*, ed. Michael Millgate. Cambridge: Cambridge University Press, 1987.

Lang, Robert. *American Film Melodrama: Griffith, Vidor, Minnelli*. Princeton, N.J.: Princeton University Press, 1989.

Langford, Gerald. *Faulkner's Revisions of* Sanctuary. Austin: University of Texas Press, 1972.

Lauretis, Teresa de. *Alice Doesn't: Feminism, Semiotics, Cinema*. London: Macmillan, 1984.

Leonard, Garry. "The City, Modernism, and Aesthetic Theory in *Portrait of the Artist as a Young Man.*" *Novel* 14 (1995): 79–99.

Lewis, David Levering. *When Harlem Was in Vogue*. New York: Knopf, 1981.

Lukács, Georg. *Theory of the Novel*. Translated by Anna Bostock. Cambridge, Mass.: MIT Press, 1977.

Lymon, Stanley J. "Black Stereotypes as Reflected in Popular Culture, 1880–1920." *American Quarterly* 29, no. 1 (1977): 102–16.

Marx, Karl, *Capital*. In *The Marx-Engels Reader*, 2nd ed. Edited by Robert C. Tucker. New York: W.W. Norton & Co., 1978.

Massey, Linton. "Notes on the Unrevised Galleys of Faulkner's *Sanctuary.*" *Studies in Bibliography* 7 (1956): 195–208.

Matthews, John T. "*As I Lay Dying* in the Machine Age." *boundary 2* 19, no. 1 (1992): 69–94.

———. "The Autograph of Violence in Faulkner's *Pylon.*" In *Southern Literature and Literary Theory*, ed. Jefferson Humphries. Athens: University of Georgia Press, 1990.

———. "Faulkner and the Culture Industry." In *The Cambridge Companion to William Faulkner*, ed. Philip Weinstein. Cambridge: Cambridge University Press, 1995.

———. "Faulkner and Proletarian Literature." In *Faulkner in Cultural Context: Faulkner and Yoknapatawpha, 1995*, ed. Donald M. Kartiganer and Ann J. Abadie. Jackson: University Press of Mississippi, 1997.

———. *The Play of Faulkner's Language.* Ithaca, N.Y.: Cornell University Press, 1982.

———. "Shortened Stories: Faulkner and the Market." In *Faulkner and the Short Story: Faulkner and Yoknapatawpha, 1990,* ed. Evans Harrington and Ann J. Abadie. Jackson: University Press of Mississippi, 1992.

May, Lary. "Apocalyptic Cinema: D. W. Griffith and the Aesthetics of Reform." In *Movies and Mass Culture,* ed. John Belton. New Brunswick, N.J.: Rutgers University Press, 1996.

McHaney, Thomas L. *William Faulkner's The Wild Palms: A Study.* Jackson: University Press of Mississippi, 1975.

McKee, Patricia. *Producing American Races: Henry James, William Faulkner, Toni Morrison.* Durham and London: Duke University Press, 1999.

Meats, Steven. "Who Killed Joanna Burden?" *Mississippi Quarterly* 24, no. 3 (1971): 271–77.

Meisel, Martin. "Scattered Chiaroscuro: Melodrama as a Way of Seeing." In *Melodrama: Stage, Picture, Screen,* ed. Jacky Bratton, Jim Cook, and Christine Gledhill. London: British Film Institute, 1994.

Meriwether, James B., and Michael Millgate. *Lion in the Garden: Interviews with William Faulkner, 1926–1962.* New York: Random House, 1968.

Metz, Christian. "Identification, Mirror" and "The Passion for Perceiving." In *Defining Cinema,* ed. Peter Lehmen. New Brunswick, N.J.: Rutgers University Press, 1997.

Millgate, Michael. *The Achievement of William Faulkner.* New York: Random House, 1963.

Miller, D. A. *The Novel and the Police.* Berkeley: University of California Press, 1988.

Miller, Francis Trevelyan. "Introduction" to *The Photographic History of the Civil War: Thousands of Scenes Photographed, 1861–65.* 10 vols. New York: Review of Reviews, 1911.

Monaco, James. *How to Read a Film.* Oxford: Oxford University Press, 1981.

Moreland, Richard C. *Faulkner and Modernism: Rereading and Rewriting.* Madison: University of Wisconsin Press, 1990.

Mulvey, Laura. " 'It Will Be a Magnificent Obsession': The Melodrama's Role in the Development of Contemporary Film Theory." In *Melodrama: Stage, Picture, Screen,* ed. Jacky Bratton, Jim Cook, and Christine Gledhill. London: British Film Institute, 1994.

———. "Visual Pleasure in Narrative Cinema." In *Film Theory and Criticism,* ed. Gerald Mast, Marshall Cohen, and Leo Braudy. Oxford: Oxford University Press, 1992.

———. "Afterthoughts on 'Visual Pleasure and Narrative Cinema': Inspired by King Vidor's *Duel in the Sun* (1946)." In *Feminist Film Theory: A Reader,* ed. Sue Thornham. Edinburgh: Edinburgh University Press, 1999.

Naremore, James. "Dashiell Hammett and the Poetics of Hard-Boiled Fiction." In *Art in Crime Writing: Essays on Detective Fiction,* ed. Bernard Benstock. New York: St. Martin's Press, 1983.

Nesteby, James R. *Black Images in American Films, 1896–1954: The Interplay Between Civil Rights and Film Culture.* Lanham, Md.: University Press of America, 1982.

Neumann, Claus Peter. "Knowledge and Control in William Faulkner's *Light in August.*" *Arbeiten-aus-Anglistik-und-Amerikanistik* 24, no. 1 (1999).

Noble, Peter. *The Negro in Films.* London: Skelton Robinson, 1948.

North, Michel. *Reading 1922: A Return to the Scene of the Modern.* New York: Oxford University Press, 1999.

Orvell, Miles. *The Real Thing: Imitation and Authenticity in American Culture, 1880–1940.* Chapel Hill: University of North Carolina Press, 1989.

Oudart, Jean Pierre, "Cinema and Suture." *Screen* 18, no. 4 (1977–78): 35–47

Parker, Robert Dale. *Faulkner and the Novelistic Imagination.* Urbana: University of Illinois Press, 1985.

Perkins, Hoke. " 'Ah Just Cant Quit Thinking': Faulkner's Black Razor Murderers." In *Faulkner and Race: Faulkner and Yoknapatawpha 1985,* ed. Doreen Fowler and Ann J. Abadie. Jackson: University Press of Mississippi, 1987.

Pettey, Homer B. "Reading and Raping in *Sanctuary.*" *Faulkner Journal* 3, no. 1 (1987): 71–84.

Polk, Noel. "Afterword" to *Sanctuary: The Original Text.* New York: Random House, 1981.

———. "The Space Between *Sanctuary.*" In *Intertextuality in Faulkner,* ed. Michel Gresset and Noel Polk. Jackson: University Press of Mississippi, 1985.

Porter, Carolyn. *Seeing and Being: The Plight of the Participant Observer in Emerson, James, Adams, and Faulkner.* Middletown, N.Y.: Wesleyan University Press, 1981.

Railey, Kevin. *Natural Aristocracy: History, Ideology, and the Production of William Faulkner.* Tuscaloosa: University of Alabama Press, 1999.

Reddick, L. D. "Educational Programs for the Improvement of Race Relationships: Motion Pictures, Radio, the Press, Libraries." *Journal of Negro Education* 13, no. 3 (1944): 367–89.

Rogin, Michael. " 'The Sword Became a Flashing Vision': D. W. Griffith's *The Birth of a Nation.*" *Representations* 9 (1985): 150–95.

Rouselle, Melinda McLeod. *Annotations to William Faulkner's* Sanctuary. New York: Garland Publishing, 1989.

Ruppersburg, Hugh M. *Reading Faulkner: Light in August.* Jackson: University Press of Mississippi, 1994.

———. *Voice and Eye in Faulkner's Fiction.* Athens: University of Georgia Press, 1983.

Simmel, Georg. "The Metropolis and Mental Life." In *On Individuality and Social Form,* ed. Donald N. Levine. Chicago: University of Chicago Press, 1971.

Singer, Ben. "Modernity, Hyperstimulus, and the Rise of Popular Sensationalism." In *Cinema and the Invention of Modern Life,* ed. Leo Charney and Vanessa R. Schwartz. Berkeley: University of California Press, 1995.

Snead, James A. *Figures of Division: William Faulkner's Major Novels.* New York: Methuen, 1986.

Sontag, Susan. "The Image-World." In *On Photography.* New York: Doubleday, 1973.

Spiegal, Alan. *Fiction and the Camera Eye: Visual Consciousness and Film in the Modern Novel.* Charlottesville: University Press of Virginia, 1976.

Sundquist, Eric. *Faulkner: The House Divided.* Baltimore: Johns Hopkins University Press, 1983.

Staiger, Janet. "*The Birth of a Nation:* Considering Its Reception." In *The Birth of a Nation, D. W. Griffith, Director,* ed. Robert Lang. New Brunswick, N.J.: Rutgers University Press, 1994.

Trachtenberg, Alan. *Reading American Photographs: Images as History—Matthew Brady to Walker Evans.* New York: Hill and Wang, 1989.

Urgo, Joseph. "*Absalom, Absalom!* The Movie." *American Literature* 62, no. 1 (1990): 56–73.

Van Vechten, Carl. *Nigger Heaven.* New York: Knopf, 1926.

Weinstein, Arnold. *Vision and Response in Modern Fiction.* Ithaca, N.Y., and London: Cornell University Press, 1974.

Weinstein, Philip. *What Else But Love? The Ordeal of Race in Faulkner and Morrison.* New York: Columbia University Press, 1996.

West, Nathanael. *Miss Lonelyhearts & The Day of the Locust.* New York: New Directions, 1962. [1933 and 1939]

White, Hayden. "The Modernist Event." In *The Persistence of History,* ed. Vivian Sobchack. New York: Routledge, 1996.

Wittenberg, Judith Bryant. "Race in *Light in August:* Wordsymbols and Obverse Reflections." In *The Cambridge Companion to William Faulkner,* ed. Phillip M. Weinstein. Cambridge: Cambridge University Press, 1995.

Zeitlin, Michael. "Faulkner's Pylon: The City in the Age of Mechanical Reproduction." *Canadian Review of American Studies* 22, no. 2 (fall 1991): 229–40.

Zender, Karl. *The Crossing of the Ways: William Faulkner, the South, and the Modern World.* New Brunswick, N.J.: Rutgers University Press, 1989.

Zuidervaart, Lambert. *Adorno's Aesthetic Theory: The Redemption of Illusion.* Cambridge, Mass.: MIT Press, 1991.

Index

Homer, 215n. 18; *The Iliad*, 217n. 24

Hopper, Dennis, 215n. 18

Horkheimer, Max, *Dialectic of Enlightenment* (1944), 184n. 13

Howe, Irving, 182n. 5, 190n. 10, 194n. 33

Hughes, Langston, 198n. 12

Huyssen, Andreas, 183n. 8; *The Great Divide*, 2–5, 19, 30–32, 182n. 6, 190n. 9; "High/Low in an Expanded Field," 182n. 7, 190n. 9

ideology, 23, 72, 87, 107, 109–10, 127, 142, 170

If I Forget Thee, Jerusalem (1939), 2, 8, 9–10, 17–18, 105, 129–60, 178, 181n. 2, 186n. 27, 199n. 20, 205n. 2. See also "Old Man"; "Wild Palms"

immanence, 5–10, 18–19, 49–54, 62, 65, 106–13, 130–31, 138, 142–43

immigration, 110–11, 207nn. 12&13

interpellation, 70, 76, 78, 199n. 18

irony, 55, 148, 150, 160, 178

It Happened One Night (dir. Frank Capra, 1934), 215n. 18

jail cells, 28, 155, 158–62, 172–73, 175–80, 189n. 6; as figure for consumers' entrapment, 155–56, 159–60; as figure for space: —of Faulkner's modernist writing, 176–177, 179–80; —of mass cultural production, 176, 178–179

James, Henry, 31

Jameson, Fredric, 5, 19, 32; "Magical Realism in Film," 186n. 31; *The Political Unconscious*, 165–66, 169–71, 187n. 35, 219n. 8; *Postmodernism*, 5, 212n. 4; "Reification and Utopia in Mass Culture," 18–19; *Signatures of the Visible*, 18, 185n. 22, 208n. 21; theory of commodities, 187n. 33

Jay, Martin, 203n. 40

Jefferson, Mississippi, as setting in Faulkner's fiction, 12, 28, 68–69, 73, 77, 94–95, 97, 104, 176

Johnson, James Weldon, 198n. 12

Johnson, Susie Paul, 181n. 2

Joyce, James: *Portrait of the Artist as a Young Man* (1916), 51, 194n. 33; *Ulysses* (1922), 11, 47, 177

Kalifornia (dir. Dominic Sena, 1993), 215n. 18

Kawin, Bruce, 21, 106, 184nn. 14&17, 186n. 26, 187nn. 37&39, 205n. 1, 210n. 30, 217n. 26, 219n. 3

Keats, John, 26

Kennedy, Sheriff Watt, 89–91, 100

King, Vincent Allan, 188n. 41

Kirby, Jack Temple, 198n. 10

Kleig lights, 156–57

Knight, Pamela Rhodes, 218n. 2, 219n. 5

Kracauer, Siegfried, 22; *From Caligari to Hitler*, 186n. 30, 208n. 15; "On Photography," 185n. 22; *Theory of Film*, 187nn. 34&40, 209n. 23, 214n. 11

Kreiswirth, Martin, 201nn. 27&30

Ku Klux Klan, 73, 97, 107–8, 110, 198n. 10, 204n. 45

Lacan, Jacques, 10, 213n. 8

Lang, Robert, 139, 141

Lange, Dorthea, 214n. 14

Langford, Gerald, 189n. 5

Lauretis, Teresa de, 201n. 28, 202n. 33

Lawrence, Massachusetts, 152

Leonard, Garry, 51–52, 194n. 33

Levenstein, Jessica, 217n. 24

Light in August (1932), 2, 14–16, 20, 22–24, 68–102, 140, 172, 176–78, 183n. 10, 186n. 24; and mystery genre, 81–85, 90, 96; omniscience in, 86–90; and popular culture, 73–76, 96–97; and racial coding, 99–102; social ordering in, 91–95, 99–100; and the spectacle of black rape, 70–73, 96. See also Christmas, Joe; policing

Little Caesar (dir. Mervyn LeRoy, 1930), 188n. 1

Lorentz, Pare, 17, 214n. 14

Lukács, Georg, *Theory of the Novel* (1920), 166, 219n. 5

Luxembourg Gardens (Paris), 62–64, 66

lynching, 204n. 45, 207n. 12

Mankiewicz, Joseph, 193n. 30

Marx, Karl, 165–66, 187n. 33. See also Frankfurt School; Marxism

Marxism, 4, 18, 154–55, 163, 169. See also Adorno, Theodor W.; capitalist abstraction; Frankfurt School

masochism, 157, 159

vision, 9–10, 14, 17, 29–30, 39–42, 45–47, 60,
66–72, 76–78, 80–81, 86, 91–93, 95–96, 98–
101, 113–15, 117–20, 122, 124–25, 133, 138–44,
146–47, 150–59, 117, 161–65, 167–71, 173–75;
as collective activity, 16, 41, 69–72, 96, 102; as
corollary of capitalist abstraction, 164, 167–
69, 171, 175; perspective, 16, 45, 96, 171, 216n.
21; as rape, 46–47; and reflexivity, 10, 29–30,
53, 146, 216n. 19; as reifying, 18–19, 168, 170–
71; scopophilia, 39; as simulated in reading,
41, 45–46, 49, 114–15, 117–18, 124, 133, 147; as
social discipline, 14, 68–69, 70, 72, 88, 93–96,
99, 161–63; spectacle, 42, 57, 70–75, 96, 113,
121, 155; as state apparatus, 70, 95–96, 100; as
violence, 69; voyeurism, 9, 39–41, 71, 112,
120–21, 156, 173. *See also* Faulkner, William,
novelistic practices; film, spectatorship;
modernity, role of vision in

Wasson, Ben, 185n. 21
Weine, Robert, *The Cabinet of Dr. Calligari*
(1918), 181n. 2
Weinstein, Arnold, 219n. 4
Weinstein, Philip, 188n. 42, 200n. 25
West, Nathanael, 177; *The Day of the Locust*
(1939), 184n. 20, *Miss Lonelyhearts* (1933),
185n. 20
West of Zanzibar (dir. Tod Browning, 1928), 73
Wharton, Edith, 192n. 22

White, Hayden, 200n. 24
whiteness, 69, 101; notions of white innocence,
72
Wilbourne, Harry, 10, 18, 130–31, 145–60, 164–
65, 167, 172, 176, 179, 205n. 2; as consumer of
pornography, 155–59; as film viewer, 145–50,
155–56, 173, 216n. 21; passivity of, 151, 156,
159, 168; as writer of pornography, 146
"Wild Palms," 10, 17, 130, 132, 145–160; adultery
in, 146; critique of melodrama in, 145–50;
and empathy, 145; jail cells in, 155–56, 159–
69, 176; pornography in, 155–59; and proletarian audience for early film, 151–54; as
travel narrative, 142–43
Wilson, Woodrow, 110
Wister, Owen, *The Virginian* (1902), 17,
212n. 2
Wittenberg, Judith, 97, 200n. 24, 201n. 30,
204n. 46
Woolf, Virginia, *Between the Acts* (1941), 200n.
24
Works Progress Administration, 17, 214n. 14
World War I, 110, 187n. 37, 208n. 15

Yoknapatawpha County, 45, 171, 199n. 16

Zeitlin, Michael, 186n. 28
Zender, Karl, 220n. 11
Zuidervaart, Lambert, 3